Presidents & Terminal Logic Behavior

Joseph V. Hughes Jr. and Holly O. Hughes Series on the Presidency and Leadership

A list of all titles in this series is available at the end of the book.

Presidents & Terminal Logic Behavior

Term Limits and Executive Action *in the* United States, Brazil, and Argentina

GENEVIEVE M. KEHOE

Texas A&M University Press
College Station

First edition

Manufactured in the United States of America
This paper meets the requirements of
ANSI/NISO, Z39.48–1992
(Permanence of Paper).
Binding materials have been
chosen for durability.

Library of Congress Cataloging-in-Publication Data

Kehoe, Genevieve M., 1979– author.
Presidents and terminal logic behavior : term limits and executive action in the United States, Brazil, and Argentina / Genevieve M. Kehoe.—First edition.
pages cm – (Joseph V. Hughes Jr. and Holly O. Hughes series on the presidency and leadership)
Includes bibliographical references and index.
ISBN 978-1-62349-126-0 (cloth : alk. paper)—ISBN 978-1-62349-160-4 (e-book)
1. Executive power—United States—History. 2. Executive power—Argentina—History. 3. Executive power—Brazil—History. 4. Presidents—Term of office—United States—History. 5. Presidents—Term of office—Argentina—History. 6. Presidents—Term of office—Brazil—History. 7. Administrative procedure—United States. 8. Administrative procedure—Argentina. 9. Administrative procedure—Brazil. 10. United States—Politics and government—1981–1989. 11. United States—Politics and government—1989- 12. Argentina—Politics and government—1983–2002. 13. Brazil—Politics and government—1985–2002. 14. Brazil—Politics and government—2003– I. Title. II. Series: Joseph V. Hughes, Jr. and Holly O. Hughes series on the presidency and leadership.
JF255.K45 2014
352.23—dc23
2013043270

In honor of my father, Alfred W. Gross Jr.

Contents

Figures

Tables

Acknowledgments

In researching and writing this book, I have benefited immensely from the support and assistance of a number of individuals. I would like to begin by thanking the faculty of the Department of Political Science at the University of South Carolina for their support and encouragement. Their advice, editorial comments, and encouragement have been invaluable. Special thanks are due to Harvey Starr for his emphasis on theory and research design; to Lee D. Walker for adding greatly to my understanding of Latin America and comparative research in general; and to David Darmofal for advice and direction particularly with regard to methodology. Special thanks to Charles Finocchario and William Ascher and to the reviewers of Texas A&M University Press, all of whom took time to read drafts and provided helpful comments. I would also like to thank Mary Lenn Dixon, editor-in-chief of Texas A&M University Press, for guiding me through the publication process. With that being said, any errors in this work are entirely my own.

I would also like to thank my family. I especially want to thank my father for his encouragement in learning and writing and for his example of hard work and commitment. To my mother, for all her help with the children and for showing me that it is possible to have a productive career and still be a wonderful mother. Most of all, I would like to thank my husband, Jonathan, who supported and encouraged me each and every day despite his deployments, my many working days and nights, and all the chaos that comes with raising our small children.

Presidents & Terminal Logic Behavior

CHAPTER 1

Presidents and Executive Term Structure

1.1 INTRODUCTION

Final-term presidents should be more properly termed "soaring eagles" rather than "lame ducks."[1] Significant things are pushed and accomplished, precisely because these presidents are free from reelection constraint and enthused by legacy to pursue bold projects—and they have the power to make it happen. This book addresses what Pallitto and Weaver (2007, 12) call "an enormous scholarly blind spot" in the study of the presidency—institutional analysis. Presidential studies have long favored work focused on the active and self-reflecting agents, the individuals that occupy the executive office at the expense of structural elements that persist over time.[2] These studies, however, ignore that the executive office may have systematic similarities (Edwards, Kessel, and Rockman 1993; Ragsdale and Theis 1997). The study of executive term structure is an institutional one. Term structure imposes an external constraint on the behavior of individuals residing in the executive office. Although some institutional studies of the presidency have tackled the effects of the electoral cycle on presidential behavior, surprisingly, I have found no cross-country, systematic study of executive term limits that is focused exclusively on presidential behavior as affected by the dichotomy between reelection and termination. Mario Serrafero's 1997 book, *Reelección y sucesión presidencial* (Presidential Reelection and Succession), is the only work that comes close.

Certainly there is reason to be concerned about executive power and the degree to which term structure affects the executive branch's ability to command political direction and control the state. Evidence of the growth in executive power abounds.[3] Most telling is O'Connell's (2008) estimates that more lawmaking in the United States is done by the federal administrative state (which includes cabinet departments, the executive office of the president, and independent agencies) than by Congress.[4] This evidence in combination with Grier and Grier's (2000, 243) conclusion that "the combination of concentrated power and a fixed term means that executive decisions have enormous economic importance" should cause serious pause.

Modern US presidents like other presidents around the world are a constant presence in the minds of the public they serve. Even more alarming is the way in which twenty-first-century technology has fundamentally transformed how the public evaluates politicians. We are instantaneously privy to information of both major and minor detail—forever uninterrupted. Fame can be sparked overnight. Long careers of action and achievement are no longer needed to garner the widespread popularity that makes politicians and their campaigns successful. Richard Cohen of the *Washington Post* writes: "We have substituted the camera—fame, celebrity—for both achievement and the studied judgment of colleagues." This, he argues, has propelled "the out-of-nowhere rise" and success of politicians who have no history of legislative achievement and yet have won public support for office at the highest levels. Cohen calls attention to the less-than-a-decade rise of Sarah Palin, John Edwards, and current president Barack Obama.[5]

This book is less about detailing the specific strategies, tactics, and powers of presidents. Certainly these are all important. Classics by Arthur Schlesinger, Richard Neustadt, Stephen Skowronek, and Theodore Lowi are must-reads for students of the US presidency.[6] But here in the pages that follow I ask broader questions about presidents and the term limits within which they operate. Do term limits pressure presidents in a systematic way, making their behavior more predictable? If so, what sort of behavior do they engender? How may this pressure and its consequences contribute to the distribution of power in a presidential democracy?

Term limits can be thought of as a type of institution. They exhibit properties of organization and actuate change in elements such as functions, authority, control, hierarchy, and incentives. Although not necessarily the sole cause of outcomes, term limits constrain and refract politics.[7] Much variability in the political, economic, and social dynamics surrounds the office of the presidency over time. Yet presidents know they are limited to a fixed period of time within which they must act to achieve their goals. Thus, despite the variability, I hypothesize that similar behaviors emerge from this fact.

What this study finds is astonishing. Presidents issue decrees at extraordinary rates at the end of their tenure despite their standing with the public, despite their standing with Congress, despite their country's economic condition, and despite the makeup of their character or their ideological leanings. If the uptick in presidential interaction with the public, where we have what Lowi (1985, 20) describes as "the excessive personification" of government in the presidency, has contributed to the growth in executive power, the two four-year-term structure within which presidents operate has done no less. When presidents are clearly aware of their exact end in tenure, they succumb to what I call in this research terminal logic behavior, or TLB. With rare exception, presidents in their final months are afire with ambition and purpose and act accordingly.

The lame duck hypothesis is a strange phenomenon in presidential studies. Although research has found that actors in the political process change their behavior in anticipation of an administration's end, as we will see in chapter 2, there is little evidence indicating that presidents' power is actually weakened as a result. This study indicates that term limits may indeed have the opposite effect. They act like a pressure cooker, causing presidents to act unilaterally and decisively on policy as their time in office nears its end. This is not necessarily a bad thing, for it can move presidents to produce what may be effective and good policy. Yet, like using a pressure cooker, the risk of harm is great. Indeed, without proper checks in place such term pressures heighten the risk of abuse. I link not only decrees of foreign affairs and the environment to the cyclical model of presidents' time in tenure but also decrees of emergency power. Above all else, finding a systematic pattern of use in emergency power undermines any assumption that the concept of emergency is what it once may have been—a concern for the security of the state. This gives us more reason to believe that the prince is far from "tamed," particularly at this current moment in history, when the line between foreign and domestic affairs has become blurred. In this book I carefully peel back the layers to reveal why, particularly in the last few decades, term limits have become an agent of force, compelling presidents across administrations and across nations to "unilateral action, energy, commitment, decisiveness"—to what Lowi (1991, 238–39) describes as the "fast track" of presidential activity.[8] I explore what this might mean for the future of presidential democracy if this pressure is left unacknowledged and underappreciated.

1.2 BECOMING TERMINAL: PRESIDENTS OPERATING IN DUAL FRAMES

One of the principal causes of democratic breakdown, according to authors like Diamond (2000), is the abuse of executive power. Although a number of substantive differences exist between the two basic democratic forms, parliamentary and presidential systems, one key difference stands out.[9] Chief executives serve at the pleasure of parliament, whereas presidents serve out their predetermined term. In a parliamentary system the executive depends on the confidence of Congress in order to carry on its duties. The elected Congress has the power to choose and remove the executive. Similarly, the executive has the ability to dissolve Congress and call for elections. In presidential systems, members of the executive serve for a fixed term and are not subject to a confidence vote by Congress. Essentially, the presence of executive term cycles is what makes a democratic system presidential and not parliamentary.[10]

Linz (1990) finds that, since World War II, thirteen out of thirty-nine breakdowns have occurred in parliamentary democracies, while presidential democracies have experienced ten breakdowns out of thirteen.[11] Przeworski et al. (2000, 129) report that between 1950 and 1990 "the probability that a presidential democracy will die during any particular year is 0.0477, and the probability that a parliamentary democracy will die is 0.0138." By Robert Dahl's (2002) count, only twenty-two countries have been "steadily democratic" since 1950, and only two of those have been run by presidents.[12] Furthermore, Blondel (1987, 161) finds that executive heads in parliamentary systems endure longer than the world average, where for elected presidents the fixed term is "on average shorter and typically is shorter—sometimes much shorter—than the term allowed by the constitution." In the United States, presidents, who could serve eight years, average only five. Latin American presidents, who are typically elected to terms of four to six years and in many cases cannot seek reelection, average only about three years in office due to coups and forced resignations.[13] Such findings focus attention on executive term limits and their potentially problematic effects.[14]

Many accept as hard truth that a restricted number of terms for presidents protects democracy by preventing one person from having too much authority for too long a time. Mexico, for instance, despite the dominance of a one-party system, has been classified by some scholars as a democracy precisely because of the absolute ban on executive reelection (Blondel 1987). Term limits are perceived as a key institutional feature of democratic government. Yet, if the executive term is structured in a particular way, it may be disruptive to the continuity of policy. If presidents are permitted to serve in more than one term, yet are restricted to a set number of consecutive terms, they are forced to operate in two distinct frames of reference for choice and desire. When reelection is possible, "survival" defines their frame of reference, and when it is not, "terminal logic" defines that frame. I argue that these dual frames cause presidents to be inconsistent in their valuation of time, which causes inconsistency in the ranking of their objectives and, in turn, inconsistency in the decisions they make throughout the course of their tenure. This idea of inconsistency as a consequence of term structure is supported if behavioral patterns of presidents can be identified and then linked to the term *cycle* itself.

The hypotheses presented here build upon Linz's (1978, 1988, 1990, 1994) seminal work on presidentialism and its potential problematic effects. He argues that this fixed term not only of presidents but also of the legislature creates institutional rigidity.[15] Confining politicians to four years, eight years, or whatever the case may be causes an unnatural break in the political process. Linz (1994, 8) explains further: "The political process therefore becomes broken into discontinuous, rigidly determined periods without the possibility of continuous readjustments as political, social, and economic events might require. The duration of the mandate of a president becomes an essential political factor to which all actors in the political process have to adjust, and this has many important consequences."

On the one hand, political dealing and pandering sometimes engulfs reelectable or *nonterminal* presidents. I argue that presidents considerably discount far-future rewards in light of their short-term self-interest of being reelected. Term limits in light of reelection create a situation in which presidents are forced to seek immediate, albeit transitory, approval of the public, discounting their experience and causing them to veer away from what they may perceive as better long-term policies. When presidents are clearly aware of their exact end in tenure, on the other hand, they are consumed by concerns about legacy and succumb to

TLB. They value far-future rewards more so than when they face the pressures of reelection.

Hirschman (1963, 235–38) is one of the first to identify what this "terminal logic" behavior brought on by fixed term limits may look like. He describes the behavior as *la rage de vouloir conclure,* "the mania for wanting to conclude."[16] Presidents, conscious of their legacy and limited time as leaders, possess a fear of discontinuity in their policies. This leads to a sense of urgency in completing their work. Others, like Indyk and Sicherman (2008), call it the "second-term syndrome." This behavior, Hirschman (1963, 238) claims, reveals itself in "the endlessly repeated calls for a full, integrated, definitive and rapid solution of the difficulties that are being encountered." Although Hirschman attributes this behavior to leaders of underdeveloped states and "latecomer societies," it can be applied to leaders in presidential systems generally. To this effect, I expect that change in the imperative for action from one of "survival" to that of "terminal logic" will cause a unique behavioral pattern to emerge—a rapid and otherwise unexplainable increase in policy activity.

Two points about TLB are important to remember. First, we can expect TLB to be most prevalent among presidents who govern societies that champion extreme individualism *and* where much power is reserved for the executive.[17] The personalization of political leadership in these presidential systems is great, strongly reinforcing the sense that legacy is important. Of course, presidents, in general, have two roles, which in other nations are filled by separate individuals. Rimmerman (1993, 125) explains:

> In the American political system, presidents perform two roles that in other countries are often filled by separate individuals. As head of the nation, the president is required to play a unifying role of the kind played by the monarchs of Britain, Norway, and the Netherlands or presidents of France, Germany, and Austria . . . In addition, presidents serve as political leaders, "a post held in these other nations by the prime minister or chancellor."

In occupying both roles presidents come to be the custodian of the national interest. With the focus on the individual and because presidents have their power mandated by the populace, they possess "a feeling of independent power" (Linz

1990, 11). Here presidents are acutely aware that the public identifies them, this *one* person as the symbolic head of the state, and holds them accountable for the state's progress or decay.[18] They will seek bold change, given that they have the unilateral power to make it happen.

Second, we can expect TLB to be more prevalent today than half a century ago. We must consider presidents acting in *political time.* Skowronek (1993), in his seminal work, *The Politics Presidents Make,* describes a break in institutional order in 1972, which witnessed the dawning of mass communication technologies and when presidential politics moved from pluralist to plebiscitary—from complex bargaining between competing interests to direct political relations with the public. In this current age of plebiscitary politics, presidents—*more than at any other time in history*—shoulder a deep responsibility for governmental success or failure.

Of course, TLB is not a wholly novel idea. For instance, as President Barack Obama sought to win his second term, his opponents and supporters alike predicted that once a win was secured and he was free from reelection constraints, the "real" Barack Obama would step up and "deliver on far-reaching left-wing dreams" (Fahrenthold and Wallsten 2012). This is why NRA chief executive Wayne LaPierre predicts that Obama will "destroy the Second Amendment," why environmentalists predict real movement on climate change, and why conservatives predict a government spending spree of cataclysmic proportions. Obama himself believes "more flexibility" comes to a second-and-last-term president. Huddled, elbows on knees in what he mistakenly mistook as a private moment with Russian president Dmitry Medvedev, Obama declared, "On all these issues, but particularly missile defense, this can be solved, but it's important for him [Putin] to give me space . . . This is my last election. After my election, I have more flexibility."[19] Yet up until now evidence has been largely anecdotal. This book offers a systematic analysis of data collected across presidents and across nations that shows that presidents do indeed become more aggressive in making policy as they see their time in tenure coming to an end.

1.3 RESEARCH DESIGN AND METHODOLOGICAL OVERVIEW

Fixed tenure is, as Blondel (1987, 159) says, "a clear constraint on presidential horizons." This book investigates the psychological consequences that necessarily proceed from such a constraint and how they *actually* affect presidential action. Intertemporal choice is the study of the relative value people assign to two or more payoffs at different points in time (Loewenstein and Elster 1992). It is true, as Loewenstein and Thaler (1989, 191) suggest, that "the policy implications of this line of research are both interesting and treacherous." Regardless of whether one is a president, all individuals discount things at different rates. Although research shows that people commonly consider future events relative to a reference time-point (Loewenstein 1988; Shelley 1993), it is impossible to select the proper rate of time discount that each president attributes to various policies at different points in time. I do not attempt to apply or even specify a specific utility model accounting for intertemporal choice in this research on presidential behavior. Intertemporal choice is useful insofar as it helps develop the assumed premises from which the theory of TLB is derived. The descriptive theory of intertemporal choice offers a constructive way in which to argue theoretically how time pressures and what we may call "interfering tasks" restrict the cognitive resources of presidents, thereby creating discontinuity in the decision-making process.

In order to discern whether a policy continuity problem exists as a result of a term-limit structure, I look to the behavior of individual presidents, specifically their issuance of decrees[20] over the course of their tenure with respect to certain policy domains. From this, I infer insights into how presidents behave as a function of time in office and discern the consequent effects on policy continuity. Ultimately, it is my hope (and it certainly is not a short-measured one) that this book provides evidence that will help determine what executive term structure best serves presidential democracies in the protection and promotion of liberty, stability, and economic success.

As an aside, this book does not seek to differentiate between personality types. This book does not map and match presidents to different character typologies as Barber (1992) and others have done. Each president has a particular motivational structure, and in many instances no two presidents will likely make the same choice on similar issues not only because of the uniqueness in time and political environment in which they each find themselves but also because of their individual uniqueness. Each likely has different conceptions of social causality, human nature, and the like. What this book does intend to do, however, is to attribute change in policy behavior to change in presidents' organizational motivation structure caused by term limits. Once reelection constraints are removed, this structure is reformulated and new priorities emerge. Presidential priorities are no different from basic human needs as described by Maslow (1943; 1954/1987, 82–83). All organisms are dominated first by physiological needs, that is, those needs basic to survival. Then, once these are met, "at once other (and higher) needs emerge and these, rather than physiological hungers, dominate the organism." When the office of the presidency is no longer in question, nonexistential priorities such as esteem and self-actualization come to dominate the motivation structure of presidents.

This book largely revolves around the study of US presidents, specifically those serving a set time period of four years and who have the possibility of reelection to only one subsequent four-year term. Studying this form of tenure is constructive not only because it represents the term characteristics of the US head of state, which is undoubtedly one of the most powerful leadership positions in the world, but also because it allows for a nuanced and sophisticated study of the effect of fixed term constraints both in the space of reelection politics and beyond. Moreover, many other governments, both at the national and subnational levels, maintain a similar form of tenure for their executive officeholder. Of the roughly 87 countries that have presidents who are term limited (as stipulated by their constitution), 19 serve within the bounds of two four-year terms,[21] and 56 serve within a closely analogous structure of two five-year terms.[22] At the subnational level, 23 of America's 50 states ascribe to the two four-year-term design for their respective governors—as do some governors of Brazil's states. Findings here could have implications that reach far beyond US borders.

Two chapters of this study are devoted to a cross-national comparative analysis of presidents in their use of decrees. A comparative case study broadens in scope the application of the TLB theory, testing its overall validity. Do the behavioral effects caused by term limits apply to presidents of other countries? In conjunction with the presidents of the United States, I examine presidents of Argentina and Brazil. These countries share similar characteristics in their political institutions and in their executive term structure. They represent three of the four federal presidential democratic republics in the Americas.[23] Furthermore, presidents of all three countries have the ability to issue decrees, written statements of instruction that effectively become law without previous deliberation by Congress. Thus these countries, more precisely, the presidents they produce, are appropriate test cases, given the theoretical structure on which this study is built.

Without a doubt, this analysis of presidential behavior comes with its difficulties. First of all, the most challenging task of this study is how to empirically justify these theoretical presumptions of presidential behavior (namely, terminal logic behavior) over time and across presidents serving different states. Presidential studies in general are often criticized for lacking in quantitatively based evidence.[24] Although quantitative data on chief executives may be difficult to come by, new resources have sprung up, making more room for this type of methodology in presidential studies.[25] The American Presidency Project, for example, makes more than one hundred thousand documents on the United States presidency readily available online.[26] This is not to say that quantitative analysis is always appropriate. Presidential scholars, in particular, wrangle over taking full account of political contexts, pressures, and ambitions, so much so that some argue that "the study of this political institution's operation is not straightforwardly susceptible to quantification" (Bowles 1999, 3). Even Skowronek (1993, 4), author of the aforementioned work on the institutional history of the presidency and its generalized effects on presidential behavior, concedes that "[I]t is easy to get lost in presidential history. Each story presents itself as baldly idiosyncratic and therefore defiant of any quest for generalization."

Of course, the large-N approach has its theoretical and methodological costs, as does the case study approach. Nonetheless, these approaches can complement one another. Statistically testing the counts of decrees over a set period according to various indicators separates the systematic from the nonsystematic components. Leverage and generalizability are gained when data are systematized and evaluations are quantified. What is more, evidence is reproducible. Yet in exchange, for what this large-N approach gains in leverage and generalizability, it trades away in nuance, context, and complexity.

This book is unusual in that it is part US and part comparative political science. Although comparison may have been the norm in earlier times "before the [US] Presidency became central to both domestic and world affairs" (Benjamin 1985, 71), it is no longer.[27] For this reason, it is important to be clear about its methodology up front. I first present a quantitative analysis of US presidents' use of three instruments of direct action: executive orders, presidential proclamations, and the lesser-known presidential memoranda. The period under review extends from January 1977 to January 2009. Here event count models test and evaluate empirical relationships between variables.

Why begin with 1977? Surely TLB was a factor in earlier presidencies as well. Kenneth Mayer (1999, 457) shows in his analysis of executive orders from 1937 to 1995 that "end-of-term effects are dramatic" for presidents—particularly those who left office to a successor from the opposition party.[28] In fact, except for the intervention coefficient marking the beginning and end of World War II, this is the largest effect in his model.

The year 1977 makes sense as the starting point for the US analysis for a number of reasons. First and perhaps most important, Congress passed the National Emergencies Act (NEA) in 1976 and the International Emergency Economic Powers Act (IEEPA) in 1977. Starting in 1977, we can analyze presidents' use of emergency power—executive orders, memoranda, and proclamations issued pursuant to either the NEA or the IEEPA. Second, this study considers only presidents who served under the two-term-limit rule as codified by law. For the United States, this would mean a start after the Twenty-Second Amendment, which was passed in 1951. Only Dwight Eisenhower (1953–1961) and Lyndon Johnson (1963–1969) would be added to the analysis under this condition. Gerald Ford (1974–1977) never finished a full term. Richard Nixon (1969–1974) resigned sixteen months into his second term, and John Kennedy (1961–1963) was assassinated. Finally, this study is focused on the age of plebiscitary politics as noted earlier. Skowronek (1993) puts the break in the presidency's institutional order where presidential politics move from pluralist to plebiscitary at 1972. In order to broaden the timeline of the US analysis, one would have to account for the norm versus law distinction.[29] One would also have to account for the ways in which the presidency has changed over time—in the scope of power and in the tools used to wield its force. Both of these points exceed the scope of the study at hand.

These case study analyses of Brazilian and Argentinean presidents capture what the large-N US analysis does not. They show how TLB holds from case to case and how differences are primarily due to contextual particularities, highlighting the relevance and generality of TLB's processes. Here this study adopts a particular type of methodological logic, what Skocpol and Somers (1980) call "the parallel demonstration of theory" approach in comparative history. Does the TLB theory hold from case to case, and what are the implications for it in specific settings? This approach is concerned less with the validation of TLB and more with illustrating how it works on the ground in other contexts such as domestic policy and government administration.

A number of issues make these cases more amenable to the case study method than to statistical and formal methods. First and foremost, the rules governing decree use changed in the tenure of each of the presidents under study, and evidence indicates that all three of these reforms changed the way decrees could be issued (in content or in procedure) and as a consequence affected presidents' rate of decree issuance. There is also the problem of changing reelection dynamics. Two of the three presidents who completed full terms within the 1989–2010 time frame spent considerable time and political capital to obtain a constitutional amendment giving them the right to run for reelection. These presidents were technically "terminal," but during that period both were amassing their efforts with a view to reelection, not to solidifying their legacy. These reforms make it difficult to test count levels of decrees with respect to different points in presidents' tenure using statistical methods such as event count models. Yet if other methods can unveil evidence of TLB across presidents even when those presidents are issuing decrees in different legal landscapes, this tells us that the behavioral tendency of TLB is fairly robust. Chapter 7 discusses this in more detail.

Researchers have for the most part speculated only on fixed-term effects. A review of literature in chapter 2 reveals the extent of this gap in research. This study seeks to move beyond this pattern with a new research design and with new evidence.

With this being said, I do not intend for my hypotheses or conclusions to lead to a blanket indictment of bans on reelection. I do believe, however, that if such problematic effects of term limits do exist and exist across presidents and countries, then they can and should be considered in government design. To be sure, determining the most suitable term structure for presidents depends on many things such as the degree of institutionalization of government rules and the party system, relative levels of power among the executive, legislative, and judicial branches, and the checks and balances between them and any history of authoritarianism. Acknowledging the wide variation in institutional histories and traditions of respect for authority and rights, one must concede that two different countries may best be served by two different term structures. For instance, two six-year terms may be good for the executive office of one country, whereas a four-year term with no restrictions on eligibility may be good for another.

Moreover, others may argue that disruption in presidential policy continuity is indeterminable because both the international environment and the country's domestic politics affect presidential policy in such vastly different ways that it defies generalization. In saying this, one questions the simplification that necessarily proceeds from the study of human behavior. Essentially, it is a question of what makes predictions of social science worthy of confidence. I believe that only after a thorough discussion of term limit conceptualization and a proper application of empirical tests to what I set out to explain (based on the premises with which I began my inquiry) will my predictions be ready for any vote of confidence. Great variation does exist, but if the investigation is properly designed, it can be controlled to some degree so that commonalities in the ways term limits determine human behavior can be found. As many scholars protest, country variation should not preclude constitution writers from learning from foreign models and discerning what institutional structure is best for their country—contrary to Hegelian belief.[30]

Finally, others assail the presidential form of government in general.[31] It is often argued that the level of efficacy of a particular politician matters too much and that predetermined terms in general are no good because they either kick out a great president too early or keep a dud too long. Even if theoretically and empirically parliamentary systems appear more attractive for democracy, the fact remains that more than ninety-two countries in the past twenty years have had presidents, and all but five of those countries have had term limits on presidents.[32] This alone validates the need to study and understand the functioning of term limits, their effects on the behavior of politicians, and their effects on state health generally.

Another fact that should focus attention on this subject is that in approximately one-third of those countries, presidents have contravened their term limits either by eliminating term limits altogether or by "staying in office in excess of the tenure the constitution had initially mandated" (Maltz 2007, 128).[33] Whether it is through twists of legal language, constitutional amendments, or an outright suspension of the constitution, presidents have frequently changed the term limit structure either by lengthening the term or stipulating a new number of allowable terms. One need only look at recent events in Latin America. Most recently, Nicaragua's President Daniel Ortega overturned term limits, allowing him to run for a third term in 2011. Venezuela's President Hugo Chávez won a referendum to eliminate term limits. Bolivia's President Evo Morales won a referendum allowing him to run for another five-year term. Columbian President Álvaro Uribe won two congressional amendments extending his tenure possibilities first from one to two terms in 2004 and then from two to three terms in 2009. Ecuador's President Rafael Correa changed the constitution so that he would be allowed to hold office for two more four-year terms.[34] These moves by Latin American presidents cause experts to recall old stereotypes of "the cigar-chomping, camouflage-clad Latin American dictator[s]" (Hawley 2009). Yet this contravening of presidential term limits extends far beyond Latin America to many nations worldwide, particularly those in Africa and Eurasia.[35]

The concern for democracy in term-limit overstep is real and serious. It is critical to burgeoning democracies, teetering between democratic success and failure, that a closer look be taken into how term limit structures work and affect outcomes in more consolidated democracies. It is also critically important for advanced presidential democracies. Executive term structure is intimately linked to critical issues such as the balance of power among the branches of government. Truly, executive term limits are an underappreciated influence on state activity. Change in executive term limit structure either in length of time or in reelection constraints have the potential to change acutely the way state decisions are made—and, consequently, the outcomes of state activity. Dedicated study of executive term limits, an untapped source of influence, has the potential to offer new and surprising insights into state behavior.

1.4 PLAN OF THE BOOK

This book consists of eight chapters. This introductory chapter provides a definitional framework and an overview of research design methodology. Chapter 2 contextualizes the book by briefly charting the history of institutionalism, showing where exactly this research falls within its various internal differentiations. With a broad brush, I present an institutional perspective and the schools of thought that inform my research. I then review past arguments for and against the value of term limits with particular attention to classic arguments made by Alexander Hamilton and James Madison in the *Federalist Papers.*

Chapter 3 discusses the theoretical expectations of and assumptions about terminal presidents—what to expect and why. I construct a theory that addresses how the institution of term limits shapes presidential incentives, creating what Bueno de Mesquita et al. (2003, 9) call "different imperatives of action" over the course of their tenure. I borrow insights from intertemporal choice theory, specifically research on the motivational and cognitive resources involved in the way individuals value rewards over time. I also borrow insights from the work of Friedman and Starr (1997, 105), specifically their adaptation of Maslow's theory of human motivation to an understanding of organizational motivation.

Chapter 4 explains why studying proactive power initiatives, specifically decrees, is fundamental to uncovering TLB. In the case of the United States, the term *decree* encompasses three presidential instruments of direct action: executive orders, presidential proclamations, and presidential memoranda. I focus special attention on memoranda, an instrument neither numbered nor required to be published in the *Federal Register* but yet considered as effective and legally binding as proclamations and orders. A brief section reviews important points as to how Congress and the courts view presidents' use of decrees. The final section of this chapter describes the collection, coding, and counts of US decrees with regard to their type and category.

The analysis of TLB begins with the case of the United States. In chapter 5, I group the three decree types (i.e., executive orders, proclamations, and memoranda) together and examine how presidents shift their use of decrees over time. I test hypotheses linking presidential periods (i.e., transition, regular, and legacy) to presidents' use of decrees in foreign, environmental, and domestic policy areas as well as in the use of national emergency powers.

Chapters 6 and 7 examine the effects of "terminal logic" on presidential behavior in contexts outside the United States. Exploring the use of decrees by Brazilian and Argentinean presidents permits further exploration of the assumptions and conclusions drawn in chapter 5. In the Brazilian context I equate the term *decree* with the presidential instrument *medidas provisórias com força de lei* (MPV), and in the Argentine context the term *decree* is associated with the presidential instrument *decreto de necesidad y urgencia* (DNU). Chapter 6 addresses the country specifics of Argentina and Brazil with regard to the party system, the legislative process, and the role of the courts, all of which influence the interaction between branches of government and, in turn, affect presidential choice in the use of decrees. In particular, I focus on the legal landscape surrounding the use of decrees as shaped by the interpretation of congressional laws and the constitution in each country's courts. This gives us a framework for the subsequent analysis of TLB (chapter 7). Chapter 8 concludes by summarizing the book's findings and discussing their possible implications for future research.

CHAPTER 2

Institutionalism

Presidential Behavior and the Rule of Law

Every word of [the Constitution] decides a question
between power and liberty.
—*James Madison (1792)*

2.1 DEVELOPING A DEFINITIONAL FRAMEWORK

The context of this research has a focus like that of the early institutionalists—on the interaction between the rule of law and political practice.[1] I am interested in the institution of term limits and how it structures presidential behavior. The term *institution* has come to describe many things, and, arguably, it has so much so that its unrestricted inclusivity often detracts from its perceived usefulness in political science.[2] If truth be told, institutionalism or the general study of institutions has a long history and would take volumes to properly expose its conception over time. It can be traced as far back as Aristotle, with his notion of "most perfect forms of government,"[3] and to contract theorists of the seventeenth and eighteenth centuries, like Locke, Hobbes, and Montesquieu.

Early institutionalism (termed old institutionalism), focuses largely on formal, constitutional rules and the centrality of law, and historicism is greatly emphasized. Political thinkers of centuries past recognized the importance of institutions and the need to understand the effects of their design on human behavior. Hobbes, for instance, recognized that humankind needs structure in place to preserve political life. Locke, recognizing more virtue than vice in human nature, saw institutions as a conduit to protecting liberty and property. Montesquieu, in his *Spirit of the Laws* (1748), also related institutional type to behavioral tendency in his connecting of war to regime type.

The mid-1980s experienced a rebirth of institutionalism, a revived social theory that was doggedly less normative and more focused on methodology and theory. James March and Johan Olsen, pioneers of the new institutionalism, emphasized the reciprocity of human agency and structure, perceiving structure as not only an active agent but a reactive one as well. A defining characteristic of new institutionalism is this reciprocated effect and consequence of human agency on structure. With a focus on collective action generally and on this multidirectional relationship between collectivities and the socioeconomic environment within which they operate, the concept of institutions has greatly expanded beyond the formal and statutory. Peters (2005), for instance, describes any approach as "institutional" if it (1) describes a structural feature of society and/or polity, (2) affects individual behavior, and (3) offers some degree of stability in that behavioral interaction over time.

Institutions have been described at the microlevel of individuals and at the macrolevel of societies and international systems.[4] Aside from political science, other academic disciplines such as sociology, psychology, and economics offer their own formulations of what constitutes an institution. Even within the discipline of political science, its various subfields have different notions as to what an institution represents and describes. How, therefore, can such a term be understood and conceptualized in order to pave the way for a more sophisticated understanding of what we are studying? I answer this question by first defining and conceptualizing what is meant by the institution of *term limits* within the context of this study. Term limit is defined as the established law or practice of obligating an elected official to leave office after the official has served a predetermined term. This study focuses exclusively on only one type of tenure and only one type of elected official. The focal point here is those heads of state in presidential systems, who are legally limited to serve a set time period (e.g., of four, five, or six years) and who have the possibility of reelection to only one subsequent term.[5]

Second, I describe the larger framework that informs the construction of my theory and research design. I find that the ideas put forth by Waltz (1954) in his book *Man, the State, and War: A Theoretical Analysis* provide a useful definitional framework. Waltz introduces three images through which international behaviors, particularly those related to war, can be explained. He explains that the locus of cause can be derived from the analysis of human beings, the structure of separate states, and the state system. The focus here is not on the particularities of Waltz's images or their application but on the nature of their connectedness. All three images are linked together through a system of endogenous relationships. Humans are as much defined by a collective society as they are the architects of it. The same is true for an understanding of the state. The behavior of a state is shaped by both the people that make it up and by the international environment within which it exists. The state, in turn, influences the individuals in its domain and the external environment where it behaves. All three images, people, state, and system, are interdependent. Waltz's interpretation of the interdependence of these three images lends a clue to understanding the various levels of analysis where institutions can be found and the importance of seeing institutional cause and effect occurring at all levels. Furthermore, this interpretation allows us to see the implications of this study beyond individuals and how term limits consequently affect the behavior of states.

Finally, it is important to detail the fundamental perspectives I follow in my research. Every researcher begins with an image of politics that is derived from one or more particular schools of thought to which the researcher ascribes. These *schools of thought* organize and direct scientific investigation, acting as a filter so that only central conceptual and theoretical elements are retained. It is necessary at the onset of this study to clearly specify my particular understanding of how the institution of term limits should be conceived, observed, and measured. Although I ultimately use the "what you see is what you get" positivist examination of term limits, I use history (i.e., each country's context, background, and culture) to inform the particular questions that I ask and hypotheses I pursue concerning the consequences of term limits. For instance, these factors help to determine the policy areas I examine for each country.

I also draw from rational choice theory and treat the presidencies of the United States, Argentina, and Brazil all as unitary institutions where presidential policy outcomes are perceived as purposeful acts of a rational, unitary decision maker.[6] I do not consider the internal politics within the executive branch. Rather, I treat the president as an individual with sole control over policy, seeking utility maximization within the bounded rule set of the term limit.[7]

This assumption of rational behavior has its caveats. Herbert Simon (1957, 80–81) notes that:

> Actual behavior falls short, in at least three ways, of objective rationality . . . :
>
> 1. Rationality requires a complete knowledge and anticipation of the consequences that will follow on each choice. In fact, knowledge of consequences is always fragmentary.
>
> 2. Since these consequences lie in the future, imagination must supply the lack of experienced feeling in attaching value to them. But values can be only imperfectly anticipated.
>
> 3. Rationality requires a choice among all possible alternative behaviors. In actual behavior, only a very few of all of these possible alternatives ever come to mind.

Rational choice here does not purport to be based on a full account of reality. Simply, I assume that individual choice is defined by preference and constraint. Rationality is always relative because no individual can make a choice based on complete knowledge of the consequences that follow that choice. Yet, although this relativity brings a certain level of arbitrariness particularly at the theory's conceptual stage, this relativity is necessary in order to acquire theoretical utility (Holt and Richardson 1970, 24). An efficient way to construct theory is to specify and simplify human behavior. Making assumptions about human behavior and the consequent empirical generalizations is a powerful technique because such assumptions are consistent and logically concise and have surprising implications and practical policy applications (Achen and Snidal 1989). More important, the concern here is not what *is* the best course of action at any given point in time but rather how the changing nature of term limit constraints causes change in presidential preferences and what presidents believe to be the best choice given those change in constraints. Chapter 3 is devoted to explaining in detail this change in preference and the behavioral changes I expect as a result. In short, I describe the motivational structure of two types of presidents—*terminal* and *nonterminal*—

and this lays the foundation for my overall theory of presidential behavior, which I term *terminal logic behavior.*

Finally, what follows is a brief note on methods. Kemeny (1959, 96) reminds us that "the key to verification of theories is that you never verify them. Verification is the process of seeing whether something predicted is really so. Since we can only observe particular facts, we must verify particular consequences of a theory, not the general theory itself." My research is designed to uncover an organized system of explanation based on critical tests and limits of validity. I develop rules of interpretation for essential elements (e.g., concepts like "utility") and attempt to put forth a sound argument for what I believe to be its empirical referent. It is important to balance parsimony and determinism and to conduct research through a triangulation of methods.[8] I do not expect empirics to capture all the complexities of the phenomenon under review. Certainly, "an infinity of causal steps" exists between variables, and uncovering the causal link between all of them is impossible (King, Keohane, and Verba 1994).[9] Moreover, in some cases empirically observed data are hard to get to, and supplemental evidence is needed. I choose to supplement my empirical tests with the comparative case study method, which nicely complements the results of empirical design.[10] It is through these methods that I connect the formal structure of term limits to identifiable differences in presidential behavior.

Now I depart from this discussion of methods and examine the two-term tradition, which began with President Washington nearly two and a half centuries ago.

2.2 BEFORE AND AFTER THE TWENTY-SECOND AMENDMENT: NORMS VS. INSTITUTIONS

> Every tradition grows ever more venerable—the more remote is its origin, the more confused that origin is. The reverence due to it increases from generation to generation. The tradition finally becomes holy and inspires awe.
>
> —*Nietzsche ([1878] 1986, 96) [cited in Peabody (2001) in reference to the two-term tradition of US presidents]*

Authors struggle to define a norm separate from concepts such as rule, principle, institution, and regime.[11] Yet, in the case of executive term limits, it is fairly simple.

George Washington chose not to seek reelection to a third term, and for this reason he is credited with setting the regulative norm of a two-term limit for US presidents.[12] The US presidency did not have a two-term limit rule codified as law under the US Constitution until February 27, 1951.[13] The two-term norm had surprising longevity.[14] It remained in force from Washington to 1940, when Franklin Roosevelt sought and won reelection to a third term. This reliance on the two-term norm prior to 1940 necessitates a general discussion of norms and what makes them different from formal law and similar institutions. By Peters's (2005) definition of institution (described earlier in section 2.1), other elements less tangible than formal rules or law (e.g., *norms*) can be defined as institutions. Yet there is a great chasm of difference between abiding by a norm, an informally instituted standard of appropriate behavior, and abiding by a *formal institution* such as an act of law set by a supreme legislative body of a nation (e.g., the US Constitution). As Finnemore and Sikkink (1998, 891) point out, there is a "prescriptive quality of 'oughtness' that sets norms apart from other kinds of rules." As they explain, moral assessment and dimensions of inner subjectivity and evaluation accompany norm-following behavior that need not be present where law has already been set. Moreover, a norm assumes that this behavioral "regularity is combined with an internal attitude involving criticism of oneself or others on the ground that a particular norm is being violated" (Hurrell 2002, 143).

Interestingly, prior to the passing of the Twenty-Second Amendment, members of the US Congress introduced no fewer than 270 resolutions limiting presidential reelection. For them, one could place only so much trust in a norm. Between 1789 and 1890, an average of 1.25 resolutions per session (125 total resolutions) were introduced to Congress. This average grew to 2 resolutions per session (85 total resolutions) between 1890 and 1928 and 3 resolutions per session (60 total resolutions) between 1929 and 1947 (Willis and Willis 1952, 469). Congresspersons (both Democrats and Republicans),[15] and perhaps even the public to some degree, taken that these politicians are meant to serve as proxies for the public interest, believed in the importance of the two-term limitation on presidents and distrusted reliance on the norm. Moreover, the increase in these resolutions signals that either this distrust increased over time or the number of congresspersons in favor of the two-term limit increased over time. Whichever may be the case, these resolutions show Congress's continuous momentum against third-term eligibility and signal a distrustfulness of norm-following behavior.

It is worth noting that "the widespread view of the relationship between Washington and the two-term tradition is misconceived" (Peabody 2001, 439). Contrary to conventional belief, Washington's remarks tell us that he did not see limited presidential tenure as necessary for proper government.[16] Simply put, he wished to retire to his home in Mount Vernon and show the country that it could function without him. Although Washington may not have intended to become the willful founder of the two-term norm, history or, more precisely, the historical narrative that developed through interpretation of his actions over time (erroneous or not), has made it one of his legacies. For instance, in 1875, the House of Representative passed a resolution that stated the following:

> [T]he precedent established by Washington and other presidents of the United States in retiring from the presidential office after their second term has become, by universal concurrence, a part of our republican system of government . . . [and] any departure from this time-honored custom would be unwise, unpatriotic, and fraught with peril to our free institutions ("Moves to Limit the Term," 1947, 15).

Of course, Congress had reason to be leery of presidents bound only by "oughtness" and self-subjectivity. Contrary to Keohane's (1984, 58) argument that rules are more easily changed than norms, codifying this norm in constitutional law ensured that the two-term provision would not be violated (unless by nondemocratic means).[17]

2.3 EXECUTIVE TERM STRUCTURE: AN UNEXPLORED AREA OF INQUIRY

The field of executive term limits is vast and largely unexplored. Most of the work on the subject is speculative and remains unsubstantiated. Why is this the case? One constraint on research is the inherent difficulty of unveiling empirically observed evidence of the nature of term structure effects. This, however, has not inhibited the output of legislative term limit research. Although much work on legislative term limits remains conjectural, empirical "breakthroughs" have occurred. For instance, political scientists have found empirical evidence that suggests that the implementation of legislative term limits has led to increased power of the governor, interest groups, and the state senate; less collegiality and civil discourse; more reliance on staff and bureaucracy; more spending on elections; and, depending on which work you consult, more or less responsiveness to the citizenry (Weissert and Halperin 2007, 516).[18]

The blooming of empirical research on the effects of legislative term limits is recent—only within the last decade or so. Moreover, because legislative term limit reform affects the tenure of many individuals and not just one, arguably its effects are more easily discerned. For instance, according to the National Conference of State Legislatures, more than thirteen hundred legislators have been turned out since 1996 due to term limit reform (Weissert and Halperin 2007, 516). Furthermore, speaking strictly with regard to the United States, term limits of legislators, both at the federal and state levels, are much more apt to change than presidential term limits, which require a change to the US Constitution. Between 1992 and 2000, twenty-one states adopted constitutional or statutory legislative term limits, and in seventeen states more than one hundred measures have been introduced in an attempt to eliminate or amend the term structure (ibid.). The US Constitution has been amended only once with reference to executive term limits.

Another constraint on executive term limit research is certainly the long-standing dominance of the individual-president approach in presidency research, with its focus on presidential differences in personality, leadership, and decision making (see chapter 1). This is not to say that work on the presidency from the institutionalist perspective does not exist. Authors have begun to take on the institutional perspective of the presidency[19] and specifically address the effect of term limits on presidents.[20] For instance, contrary to Neustadt's (1990, 185–209) argument that political leadership (determined by things such as the reputation, persuasiveness, political skills, and self-confidence of the officeholder) plays a significant role in political outcomes, authors like Moe (1993) and Lowi (1985) argue that the modern presidency is so institutionalized that external constraints such as Congress and public expectation matter much more in determining political outcomes than personality or individual character differences.[21]

Both scholarly literature and common sense tell us that these two anticipatable events, reelection and termination, transform the mindsets of presidents and other parties involved in the political process generally. Without doubt, many works focus on the lame duck periods of presidents and how the many actors involved in the political process change their behavior according to the impending endpoint in a presidential administration. Members of the general public react to the presidential term cycle and shift their support accordingly. Mueller (1973) and Stimson (1976) both find that public approval ratings decline as presidential administrations come to their end. Members of Congress may become dissident. As presidential administrations age, some scholars find that presidents lose the ability to bargain, negotiate, and persuade Congress.[22] In Brazil, Amorim Neto (2000) finds that as a president's mandate comes to an end, legislative discipline in roll call votes declines. In the case of the United States, Rudalevige (2002) and Bond and Fleisher (1990) find that the US Senate and House are more reluctant to pass presidents' legislative policy when a presidential administration is in its final stages. Yet, interestingly, President Jimmy Carter (1984) argues that his defeat secured him Republican backing in Congress that he would not have received had he been reelected. Hedtke (2002) challenges this notion, too, arguing that presidents Eisenhower, Reagan, and Clinton all saw their support scores in Congress rise in their final year in office.

Then there are the courts. The US Senate more often rejects presidential Supreme Court nominees (Krutz, Fleisher, and Bond 1998) and usually blocks nominees for the US Court of Appeals (or circuit courts) in the final months of an administration.[23] Helmke (2002) finds that judges themselves may rule differently at the end of presidential terms. In Argentina, where the judiciary operates under the tight control of the executive, she finds "a significant increase in antigovernment decisions occurring at the end of weak dictatorships and weak democratic government" (ibid., 291). Judges rule against the outgoing government's favor when they believe the threat of removal from the incoming administration is high.[24]

Then there are the career executives working in the administration. Pfiffner (1996, 5–6) finds that loyalty wanes among this cadre of veteran party members: "Senior career executives begin to distance themselves from their bosses . . . The bureaucratic machine begins to slip into neutral gear because its present leaders cannot guarantee any commitments beyond January 20." Yet if we measure allegiance by the extent of agency rule making—that is, by cabinet departments, executive agencies, and independent agencies—then perhaps this is less true than Pfiffner suggests. Studies show that an administration's end actually propels unprecedented regulatory activity and that this rapid activity is so extreme that it damages the regulatory process, encouraging shorter review periods and less time for public comment, while increasing agency costs and resources. See work as early as Abbott (1987) and as recent as Morrow (2001), Mendelson (2003), Beerman (2003), Gersen and O'Connell (2008), Brito and de Rugy (2009), de Rugy and Davies (2009), McLaughlin and Ellig (2011), and McLaughlin (2011).[25] Less than a month after President George W. Bush left office, the Subcommittee on Commercial and Administrative Law of the Committee on the Judiciary House of Representatives held a hearing to discuss the flurry of regulatory activity that had occurred between the November 2008 presidential election and inauguration day. In a prepared statement Rep. John Conyers Jr. (congressional representative from Michigan, chairman of the Committee on the Judiciary, and member of the subcommittee) said the following: "Regulations issued during the final weeks of the Bush Administration may have a lasting impact on the environment, on civil liberties at home and abroad, on the wages and working conditions of US workers, on highway safety, and on many other matters of concern to the American people."

Even though the George W. Bush administration may have "[taken] some concerted and constructive steps to introduce order into the end-of-term process," as Representative Trent Franks (congressional representative from Arizona and ranking member of the subcommittee) points out,[26] his administration was still unable to prevent the avalanche of rule making that occurred at the end of his administration.[27]

Not only should we expect the courts, Congress, loyal career executives, federal agencies, and even a nation's citizenry to change their behavior in anticipation of a presidential administration's end, but we should also be prepared for change in the behavior of foreign governments and nonstate actors. For example, Raphaël Ramos (2008), director of analysis for the European Strategic Intelligence and Security Center, claims that in the August 2008 crisis between Russia and Georgia, "Moscow skillfully exploited the context and limited margin of maneuver of a Bush administration on its way out." He warned that Iran and North Korea would likely do the same during the presidential transition. There is also the example of Iran in late 1980 and early 1981. Events and rhetoric suggest that the Iranian government rushed to sign the Algiers Accords before President Reagan's inauguration in part because they believed Reagan would deal much more harshly with its government than President Carter.[28]

States may make bold moves while other states undergo leadership transitions.[29] China's actions serve as a great example. In 2001, a few months after the inauguration of George W. Bush, a People's Republic of China fighter jet closely shadowed a US surveillance aircraft. The two aircraft collided. After an emergency landing, the PRC detained the US crew and likely obtained US classified material aboard their aircraft.[30] Seymour Hersh (2010) reports that, in 2008, only a few weeks after Barack Obama's election, the Chinese "flood[ed] a group of communications links known to be monitored by the NSA (National Security Administration) with a barrage of intercepts." According to Hersh, aides to then vice president Dick Cheney believed that "the barrage was meant as a welcome to President Obama." Then, less than two months after Obama's inauguration, Chinese patrol ships surrounded a US mapping vessel. The Pentagon reported as follows: "On March 8, 2009, five Chinese vessels shadowed and aggressively maneuvered in dangerously close proximity to USNS *Impeccable* in an apparent coordinated effort to harass the US ocean surveillance ship while it was conducting routine operations in international waters."[31] The Chinese vessels came within twenty-five feet of the US ship. Similarly, the Chinese navy targeted a Japanese warship only weeks after Japan's new prime minister, Shinzo Abe, took office. Kuni Miyake, a former Japanese foreign ministry official commented, "This is another test of another new leader."[32]

There is also substantial proof that terrorists see leadership transitions as a time to attack. Terrorists attacked New York City in 1993, shortly after President Clinton first took office; New York City and the Pentagon in 2001, eight months after President George W. Bush took office; Madrid, three days before Spain's 2004 national elections; London in 2005, two months after the British national elections; and Glasgow's airport in 2007, within hours of the appointment of a new British prime minister and cabinet.[33]

The executive term structure matters a lot in politics, and it matters a lot to presidents. What remains to be seen, however, is whether the change in behavior of all of these actors actually causes the power of outgoing presidents to weaken. Both Korzi (2011) and Hedtke (2002), authors of two current works on lame duck presidencies, remain unconvinced. Hedtke systematically analyzes the lame duck effect through "persuasion," "command," and "linkage" variables. He finds no quantitative evidence supporting the lame duck hypothesis. He (ibid., 214) concedes that a qualitative effect may occur, but "for now the lame duck syndrome appears to be more of a political myth than a political reality." Korzi (2011) presents an impressive literature review that details the history of scholarship with regard to the lame duck effect.[34] His conclusion is quite telling: "Most of these scholarly assessments [that favor a lame duck effect] were rooted more in conventional public wisdom on lame duck presidents than in rigorous investigation of the phenomenon." Indeed, there is no scholarly consensus on whether the lame duck effect exists at all.

I leave further discussion of term behavior for chapter 3 and begin a review of the term limit debate—why it matters and what is at stake.

2.4 THE TERM LIMIT DEBATE

The debate over term limits, specifically over the institution of a regular, recurrent pattern of political change that such limitations install is neither new nor clear-cut. Public support for limits on time in office has been strong from classical antiquity well into the present era (Petracca and Jump 1992; Petracca 1992).[35] Petracca (1992) explains that the very idea of "office rotation" came first to the politicians of ancient Rome and Athens and is embedded in classical republican thought. The rotation of fresh, new blood into office is and has been perceived as not only desirable but also essential to the development of the state and the citizenry. It is argued that fairness, impartiality, and justice are all best served when a new mind and a new set of eyes come into leadership. Change allows for a greater chance at ingenuity and invites a renewed vigor for governance. Moreover, one could argue that the citizenry, when forced to vote and evaluate a nonincumbent candidate for office, becomes more engaged in the political process. People are forced to vote on a more meaningful basis of values and campaign promises rather than on name recognition (Petracca and Jump 1992).

Another common point raised is that, even with standardized, recurrent elections, the very possibility of reelection to multiple terms of office invites the emergence of an overly strong president—one who need not be so attentive to the needs of the populace. Cheibub (2007, 167) reminds us that most presidential systems limit executives in their time in office as a protection for the people "to prevent incumbents from exploiting this [incumbency] advantage by requiring them to leave office whether or not voters want them to stay."[36] Stokes's (2001) analysis is quite telling of this incumbency advantage. She finds that Latin American presidents can brazenly break campaign promises and still be reelected to office if state economic performance is strong.

A good point to remember is that "longevity and experience do not correspond perfectly with wisdom and effectiveness" (Mann 1994, 94). Furthermore, capping the number of terms a president is allowed to serve improves the chances of political party alternation of power, and this, arguably, plays an important role in moving regimes out of authoritarianism and into democracy.[37] Making a president ineligible for reelection means a president's party must face opposition and successors of that president's party do not have the same power that incumbents do and fare worse in elections. As a result, this forced rotation gives opposition parties a better chance at power and more incentive to become engaged in the democratic process. Forced rotation in the manner in which it breaks up patronage networks and clientelistic relationships clearly acts as a "causal mechanism for advancing democracy," particularly in authoritarian regimes (Maltz 2007, 135).[38]

There is also something to be said about the nature of the modern state in advanced democracies like the United States. Modernity, marked somewhere around the turn of the twentieth century in the United States, ushered in an era of careerism due to "a heightened respect for professionalism, expertise, and science." This fueled a new reality of supply-side politics, which Will (1994, 19) describes as "hav[ing] government programs, not because groups demanded them, but . . . in order to create groups that will demand their continuation and elaboration." Arguably, careerism in politics brings a certain level of arrogance to officeholders, which may underpin a tendency to ignore the citizenry to pursue self-interests. Both sides could make valid arguments for and against reelection based on its encouragement *or* discouragement, as the case may be, of careerism.

One of the most persuasive arguments against reelection concerns campaign finance. Without proper control over campaign finance, presidents, who are always eligible for election, will likely become political entrepreneurs, attracting capital from campaign contributors and making political choices based on those who have the largest pocketbooks. This is a serious concern for the United States, where politicians are less subject to party discipline and rely more heavily on campaign contributions from interest groups than do politicians from other democracies, like those of Europe (Becker 1990). In addition, the influence of campaign contributions in the United States is only likely to grow following the 2010 Supreme Court case *Citizens United v. Federal Election Commission* (558 US 50), where the court ruled that political spending is protected speech.[39] Essentially, if reelection is always on the table and campaign finance controls are not properly set, the future of a country would move away from the public interest and be put in the hands of players that rule the spending and the giving, which greatly determine reelection power so often.[40] It is reasonable to assume that a cap on allowable terms will discourage this sort of behavior in the long run.

In the short run, however, if reelection is not permitted, we will always be faced with the final term problem. Terminal presidents do not have to worry about reelection, and, therefore, they are less constrained and more likely to overstep their power. Bruyneel (2006) points out that presidents consistently run into scandals during their second term due to "a sense of invulnerability developed after winning reelection." Recall the ethical and legal problems that beleaguered US presidents Reagan, Clinton, and G. W. Bush in their second terms. Yet, on the flipside of this coin, significant things are still accomplished and perhaps even pushed because presidents are free from reelection constraints and enthused by legacy and reputation to pursue bold projects. Recall Eisenhower's second-term efforts to wage peace, Reagan's signing of the Intermediate Nuclear Force Treaty (INF) with the Soviet Union, his Berlin Wall speech, his immigration reform, and his creation of the Department of Veterans Affairs, and Clinton's military actions in Kosovo and Middle East peace efforts (Lizza 2012; Crockett 2008).

Moreover, if campaign finance could be restricted in such a way as to prevent a culture and a cycle of political pandering, then arguably *not* allowing for the possibility of reelection demotes democratic responsiveness and accountability rather than promotes it.[41] This argument is commonly cited by those who oppose legislative term limits.[42] In a letter to the Marquis de Lafayette, dated 1788, George Washington himself said, "I can see no propriety in precluding ourselves from the service of any man, who on some great emergency shall be deemed universally most capable of serving the public" (Corwin 1948, 389). The naked truth is that term limits are a "clear excision from the freedom of choice" (Will 1994), incontrovertibly denying the public and governments of uniquely able leaders honed by experience in office.

Experience is critical to understanding complex issues and discerning what exactly is best for the common good. It is true that time may never bring some presidents this understanding, but it surely cannot be taught or born to without time in office. Certainly, Becker's (1990, 18) argument against congressional term limits can be aptly applied to those of presidents: "Mastering the intricacies of military affairs to weigh the seemingly plausible arguments of brass hats who have spent their adult lives in uniform takes a long time. Members need the background to see through self-serving pleas, whether from environmental activists or chemical industry spokesmen." Of course, even if a president does obtain this acumen for governing and knowing what good policy is *and is not,* it does not mean the president will be able to display it or achieve its effect. Yet this "knowing," so to speak, will give both the president and the country a better chance at success.

I recognize that a steadfast belief in one's "knowing" brings a level of resolve and certitude that can be both dangerous and disastrous. If history has shown us anything, high moral confidence and an unwavering dedication to unilateral solutions have always led to the downfall of empires instead of their triumph. Striking comparisons can be made between Athens at the end of the fifth century BC and the United States in the post-9/11 era. Here I equate "knowing" with wisdom, which by Webster's definition is more than just "knowledge of what is true or right." Wisdom, properly defined, is knowledge met with "just judgment as to action."

Now I turn to the founding of the United States and the political ideology of classical liberalism, which defines the character of its constitution and the design of its executive office.

2.5 CHOICE IN EXECUTIVE TERM STRUCTURE: THE POLITICAL REALITY

The rest of the Americas saw the Great Republic of the North as a great success—economically, politically, and socially—and a country worthy of emulation. Argentina, Brazil, Mexico, and many other countries over the past two centuries have grafted the US Constitution either in part or as a whole onto their governing charters, thereby accepting a particular set of political institutions that defines legitimate political power.[43] Lane (1996, 67) describes this copying of the US model by Latin American countries in the nineteenth century and Third World countries in the twentieth century as a strange phenomenon in which "a kind of spell [was cast] over constitution makers, as the American political system appeared to be so successful in every way."

Keeping this in mind, let us now turn to the classic arguments of James Madison and Alexander Hamilton, two American politicians and political philosophers influential in the founding of the US Constitution. Both Madison and Hamilton had great concern and many misgivings about designing the executive office.

Their colonial experience fed their fear of tyranny. James Madison, in particular, saw term limits as a way to properly install the presidency so that it would not turn into what Virginia's George Mason described as a "fetus of a monarchy" (Kamber 1995, 119). Madison and Hamilton shared a preoccupation with what Will (1994, 19) describes as "the sociology of virtue," but both interpreted it differently. They maintained starkly different views of executive term limits. Madison was fiercely in favor of their installment, whereas Hamilton believed such an institution would be "an excess of refinement."

Madison ([1787] 1920b) writes:

> [I]f it be a fundamental principle of free government that Legislative, Executive and Judiciary powers should be separately exercised; it is equally so that they be independently exercised . . . It is essential then that the appointment of the Executive should either be drawn from some source, or held by some tenure, that will give him a free agency with regard to the Legislature.

Hamilton writes:

> There is an excess of refinement in the idea of disabling the people to continue in office men, who had entitled themselves, in their opinion, to approbation and confidence; the advantages of which are at best speculative and equivocal; and are overbalanced by disadvantages far more certain and decisive. (*Federalist Papers,* no. 72)[44]

Fear of tyranny fed Madison's compulsion for term limits. Without them, he believed the executive would have such a disproportionate share of power as to essentially "destroy all symmetry and beauty of form, and to expose some of the essential parts of the edifice to the danger of being crushed by the disproportionate weight of other parts" (*Federalist Papers,* no. 47). Alexander Hamilton, on the other hand, was clearly opposed to limiting the number of allowable terms in the executive office. He lists a number of reasons. Mainly, he argues that excluding incumbent presidents would deprive the nation and the public of experience and effectively serve as "a constitutional interdiction of stability in the administration" (*Federalist Papers,* no. 72). He explains, "By necessitat[ing] a change of men, in the first office of the nation, it would necessitate a mutability of measures" (ibid.). Hamilton believed that barring incumbents from reelection would lead to "a diminution of the inducements to good behavior" (ibid.). He alludes to the destructive power of a president knowing the endpoint.

The following excerpt is taken from *Federalist Papers,* no. 72:

> Another ill effect of the exclusion would be the temptation to sordid views, to peculation, and in some instances, to usurpation. An avaricious man, who might happen to fill the offices, looking forward to a time when he must at all events yield up the emoluments he enjoyed, would feel a propensity, not easy to be resisted by such a man, to make the best use of the opportunity he enjoyed, while it lasted; and might not scruple to have recourse to the most corrupt expedients to make the harvest as abundant as it was transitory; though the same man probably, with a different prospect before him, might content himself with the regular perquisites of his station, and might even be unwilling to risk the consequences of an abuse of his opportunities. His avarice might be a guard upon his avarice. Add to this, that the same man might be vain or ambitious as well as avaricious. And if he could expect to prolong his honors, by his good conduct, he might hesitate to sacrifice his appetite for them to his appetite for gain. But with the prospect before him of approaching an inevitable annihilation, his avarice would be likely to get the victory over his caution, his vanity or his ambition.
>
> An ambitious man too, when he found himself seated on the summit of his country's honors, when he looked forward to the time at which he must descend from the exalted eminence forever; and reflected that no exertion of merit on his part could save him from the unwelcome reverse: such a man, in such a situation, would be much more violently tempted to embrace a favorable conjuncture for attempting the prolongation of his

> power, at every personal hazard, than if he had the probability of answering the same end by doing his duty.

Strangely, although term limits did exist in the Articles of Confederation, the Founding Fathers deliberately chose to leave term limits out of the Constitution. The original tenure for the executive office (prior to the passing of the Twenty-Second Amendment) was that of a four-year term with no cap on the number of eligible terms.

Constitution making is a delicate process. Designers of constitutions bring different philosophical perspectives of human nature and different levels of knowledge of the workings of political institutions. Some consider history—that of the government under construction or that of others. They look to where a constitution was successful and where it failed. Oftentimes, however, the final draft accepted and promulgated by a nation is more a result of bargaining and concession among groups in power than a result of scrupulous, unbiased thought with regard to the nature of their effect.

Much has been written about delegate voting behavior at the US Constitutional Convention of 1787.[45] Research largely concerns how much constituency interest and personal ideology figured into delegates' voting decisions. Careful examination of voting patterns reveals that "practical politics," or matters of economic interest that ruled day-to-day politics, strongly affected voting behavior. Without doubt, the design of the Constitution did not hinge solely on hallowed principles of balance and power. The design of the executive office was no exception, and it is worth exploring the way in which the original terms of office came to be. Delegates at the US Federal Convention of 1787 were concerned with the interplay of three elements as it concerned the executive office, namely, (1) the mode of appointment, (2) the length of the term, and (3) reeligibility (Warren 1928). Two competing options emerged at the convention. The first option (the Virginia Plan, drafted by James Madison) had the president selected by the national legislature. He was to serve a long term of seven years and would not be eligible for reelection. In the second option, the president would be selected indirectly by the populace through state electors, serve a short term of four years, and would be eligible for reelection. Warren (ibid., 364–65) states that "in almost all the votes a long term with no re-election was favored, if the choice of Executive was to be by the Legislature; and a short term with possibility of re-election, if the choice was to be otherwise than by the Legislature. In other words, the views of most of the delegates as to length of term and as to re-election were dependent on the mode of election." If a president was to be picked by the national legislature, delegates believed a single, long term best because this form of tenure, they believed, prevents the development of collusion between the legislature and the executive. A grave danger would be to put the executive at the mercy of the legislature for reappointment. Selection by an electoral college, on the other hand, essentially put the executive at the mercy of the people. A short term with the possibility of reelection made presidents accountable.[46]

The decision on the method of selecting the president did not come easily. Riker (1984, 2) describes discussions as "protracted—it recurred all summer; confusing—the decision was changed; and multifaceted—it involved consolidation and equality of states as well as separation of powers." In early June the convention decided in no less than two days to accept the first option, the Virginia Plan. These executive issues were revisited again by the delegates between July 16 and July 17 and then again in early September. Familiar arguments on election, term length, and eligibility were put forward. Governor Morris of Pennsylvania, for instance, argued that without eligibility for a second term, the presidency would be in the grips of inexperience. Yet an executive that could serve in long, continuous terms raised concern even among advocates of strongly empowered presidents (Jillson 1988, 116). Others, like Elbridge Thomas Gerry, were against popular election, stating "the people are uninformed, and would be misled by a few designing men" (ibid.). In the end, a short four-year term, eligibility for consecutive terms and electors won out.

When we dig a bit deeper into the detail, it becomes clear that this choice was more than a careful balancing of pros and cons. It was a "by-product of a path-dependent sequence of political compromises" (Robertson 2005, 240). As Jillson and Eubanks (1984) explain, it was "the peripheral states" that had the first "win." They successfully won the initiative to keep the clause "to be chosen by the National Legislature" in the Constitution. The Middle Atlantic states countered this "win" by winning approval to remove the phrase "to be ineligible a second time." The delegates then found themselves left with an unwanted design—an executive chosen by the national legislature for unlimited seven-year terms. As James Madison ([1787] 1920a) pointed out, executive independence is voided the moment it becomes dependent on the legislature. At an impasse it was decided that discussions would move to an ad hoc committee, where an acceptable design could be crafted.

A grand compromise on the mode of presidential election was finally reached. A complicated formula emerged that satisfied states, large and small, and those weary of dependencies between the branches of power. The president would be elected by the Electoral College, where "the number of electors allocated to a state would equal the sum of its House and Senate seats, a formula equivalent to a joint vote of the House and Senate and one that modestly equalized the weight of the states in choosing the president" (Robertson 2005, 239). If the candidate fell short of the needed majority, the House of Representatives would elect the president from those top candidates who received the most electoral votes. It is important to note that there was nothing particularly significant about "four years" that made it the foreseeable period of choice. It, too, was a likely compromise—shorter than the original seven-year term but longer than the term of governor of any of the thirteen states (Benjamin 1985, 81).[47]

The original US term structure was not a product of a single plan but an "unanticipated by-product" resulting from a patchwork of compromises made between competing factions at the Constitutional Convention. Similarly, the executive term structure decided upon in newly independent Mexico not only was a "battle cry of the revolution against the dictatorship of Porfirio Díaz" but also "served the interest of the many competing factions within the new leadership. The chances that all of them could one day take turns in the presidential office would be enhanced by a provision that ensured that any one *caudillo*'s term in office would be his last" (Shugart and Carey 1992, 88).

Unlike Mexico and the United States, Argentina's first democratic constitution was largely the result of one man, Juan Bautista Alberdi, who was the leading intellectual figure of Argentina's 1853 constitution. Miller (1997, 1502) claims that Alberdi's book, *Bases y puntos de partida para la organización politíca de la República Argentina* (Bases and Points of Departure for the Political Organization of the Argentine Republic), published in 1852, is the "most politically influential book in Argentine history." The appendix of the book's second edition included a draft constitution. It was a forward-looking constitution, born of Alberdi's belief that the problems of Argentinean society could be fixed by imposing constitutional principles meant to govern a more prosperous and more stable unified state than presently existed. Miller (ibid., 1511) estimates that "roughly two-thirds of the [1853 constitutional] text used the same approach as Alberdi's draft, and approximately two-thirds originated in the United States' Constitution—often by way of Alberdi."[48] Similarities and differences of the 1853 Argentinean Constitution and the US Constitution are as follows:

> Like the US Constitution, the 1853 text provided for a federal system of government with the power of the federal government divided between a President, a Judiciary, and a bicameral Congress, with a Senate having equal representation for each province and a House of Deputies based proportionately on population. Unlike the US Constitution, there was no separation of Church and State, the Executive enjoyed comparatively stronger powers[49] but sat for only a single consecutive six-year term, and the federal government possessed broader authority vis-à-vis the state and explicit authorization to take over provincial governments in the case of unrest. (ibid.)

What is interesting is that Alberdi studied the US Constitution in depth and often cited arguments found in the *Federalist Papers.* He emulated most of the US Constitution, roughly two-thirds of it, as noted earlier. Yet unlike the United States and Latin American countries like Brazil, he chose a different term structure for the president—a single, consecutive six-year term. Although presidents did have the ability to serve in another nonconsecutive term, this divergence is important. Allowing for one interim term was a way to prevent incumbency, which he believed was conducive to dictatorship, but still allow experienced individuals another chance at the presidency.

2.6 CONCLUSION

This chapter briefly charts the history of institutionalism, showing where this research connects within the institutionalist perspective. I next review past arguments for and against the value of term limits with particular attention to classic arguments made by Alexander Hamilton and James Madison in the *Federalist Papers.* As it turns out, these arguments were not the impetus behind the executive term that eventually won out. The rules for a four-year term, eligibility for consecutive terms, and electors were more a result of bargaining and concession among delegates at the US Federal Convention of 1787 than of scrupulous, unbiased thought with regard to the nature of the rules' effects. Yet because countries like Brazil viewed the United States as a country worthy of emulation, the US executive term structure was adopted into other governing charters. To be sure, even if constitutions represent carefully laid plans, the effects of these plans will not likely reach their stated objective exactly as originally planned.

I now set aside normative arguments surrounding term limits and move to discuss the actual behavior we can expect of presidents as a result of term limits. The next chapter discusses the theoretical expectations of and assumptions about terminal presidents—what to expect and why.

CHAPTER 3

The Motivational Structure of Terminal Presidents

What to Expect and Why

Rolling Stone publisher Jann Wenner arrived in the Oval Office bearing socks. President Obama had admired Wenner's flashy pair on a previous visit, and this gift fit the bill: one pair salmon with pink squares, the other black and pink stripes. "These are nice," the president said. Then he paused. "These may be second-term socks."[1]

3.1 INTRODUCTION

In chapter 2 I review research on how actors in the political process change their behavior in anticipation of the end of a president's tenure and find that a surprising few address this topic when it concerns the president personally. Studies of outgoing presidents often show a strong prescriptive element that instructs them on the "dos and don'ts" of the outgoing administration. Because many scholars view outgoing presidents "as little more than informational resources for incoming administrations," less attention is given to the specific terminal behavior of outgoing presidents (Howell and Mayer 2005, 2–3). Yet we can assume that, just as other actors begin to perceive the president as a "lame duck" and change their behavior accordingly, so, too, must the behavior of presidents change. The trick is to identify how terminal presidents change their behavior and their policies in anticipation of this end. Authors like Howell and Mayer (2005) and Indyk and Sicherman (2008) provide us with a jumping-off point. Howell and Mayer find that the last hundred days of US presidential administrations are accompanied by a "flurry of activity" that has "a lasting impact on his successor's ability to govern." They cite President Clinton as a quintessential example. They describe him as:

> a whirling dervish of a President who appointed judges, signed treaties, gave campaign-style speeches, issued scads of executive orders, rescinded ethics regulations he had penned in his first term, raised political money, gave dozens of interviews, granted 234 pardons and clemencies, fired an enemy from her government job, negotiated his own plea-bargain agreement, cast aspersions on his successor, installed a crony as head of the Democratic Party, and gave an entire series of farewell addresses in which he essentially said he wasn't leaving at all. (Howell and Mayer 2005, citing Cannon 2001, 274)

Similarly, Indyk and Sicherman (2008, 1) explain that "second-term presidents believe they can accomplish things that are, in reality, beyond their grasp." Particularly interesting is their observation that late-term, legacy-driven presidents often suffer from "an adaptive version of the Jerusalem syndrome."[2] They claim that such may even cause a shift in presidential policy with regard to the Israeli-Palestinian arena. They detail the change in President Reagan's policy behavior:

> President Reagan was not fully engaged in the Arab-Israeli conflict during his second term because of the Iran-Contra affair. In the summer of 1988, however, Secretary of State George Schultz pressed for engagement on the peacemaking front. He argued that if Reagan did not act on the issue, his administration would be forever marked by the failure. In the end, Reagan's shift of focus from the presidency to his legacy compelled him to begin work on the conflict, which resulted in Washington's

> recognition of the Palestine Liberation Organization (PLO)—a historical event attributed to Schultz and Reagan. (Indyk and Sicherman 2008, 1)

President George Bush, they observe, began to show signs of the same syndrome in 2008—visiting Jerusalem in February and voicing his renewed hopes for a peace treaty by the end of his term.

In this chapter I develop a theory on the behavior of terminal presidents, a theory that I call terminal logic behavior, or TLB. I discuss its main propositions using insights from intertemporal choice theory and the work of Friedman and Starr (1997, 105) in their adaptation of Maslow's (1943, 1954/1987) theory of human motivation to outline these processes. Intertemporal choice is the study of the relative value individuals assign to costs and benefits foreseen at different points in time. Intertemporal choice is particularly applicable to this study because it focuses on the passage of time as an independent variable acting on the preference of individuals—a key assumption of TLB. Next, I introduce a cyclical model of presidential tenure that helps us to predict the space in which TLB is likely to operate, laying the foundation for the empirical analysis in my subsequent chapters.

3.2 DUAL FRAMES OF REFERENCE

Recall that in chapter 2, note 7, I describe my perspective on institutions and my assumptions based on Allison's Rational Actor Model. I explain how, in the context of this study, I assume policy behavior is the result of purposeful acts of one rational, unitary decision maker—the president. The president is the one most responsible for setting the utility function of perceived goals, options, and estimation of consequences. Viewing choice as an output of one unitary actor allows us to consider mechanisms at the individual level that drive behavior. For instance, I begin with the assumption that there exists "a set of the most basic, universal, and irreducible needs" to which all leaders subscribe regardless of their era, ideology, party affiliation, race or tribe, nation or culture (Friedman and Starr 1997, 105). Such basic needs are described by Maslow (1954/1987, 80–98) as (1) physiological requirements, (2) safety, (3) belongingness and love, (4) esteem, (5) self-actualization, (6) the desire to know and understand, and (7) aesthetic essentials, and their hierarchical nature can be applied to the policy decision making of political elites. Friedman and Starr (1997) point out that Maslow's hierarchy is based on the priority of existential needs over nonexistential ones. Maslow (1954/1987, 82–83, as cited by Friedman and Starr 1997, 105) explains:

> If all the needs are unsatisfied, and the organism is then dominated by the physiological needs, all other needs may become simply nonexistent or be pushed into the background. . . . But what happens to man's desires when there *is* plenty of bread and when his belly is chronically filled? *At once other (and higher) needs emerge* and these, rather than physiological hungers, dominate the organism. And when these in turn are satisfied, again new (and still higher) needs emerge, and so on. This is what we mean by saying that the basic human needs are organized into a hierarchy of relative prepotency.

Once reelection is not possible, term limits in their very restriction of limiting a president to a fixed time period allow for the materialization of raw ambition that goes beyond the existential, the physiological. So it follows that once presidents have secured their tenure in office, they can move on to satisfy those nonexistential needs of esteem and self-actualization. Legacy becomes the motivating mechanism driving the decision process since the security of their presidential position is no longer in question.

Some individuals may sacrifice themselves for higher-level values, calling into question Maslow's hierarchy.[3] Yet presidents are a special class of individuals—leaders of the highest rank. The motivations of leaders are different from those of nonleaders.[4] Among other things, studies find that power leads people to act on the basis of their own preferences and goals and to experience a sense of entitlement (De Cremer and Van Dijk 2005; Guinote 2007; Smith and Trope 2006). Maner and Mead (2010, 483) explain further that "these effects of power could psychologically liberate leaders from the prosocial motives that normally keep them from exploiting others and prioritizing their own power." I argue that leaders first protect the power that defines them as such and address higher-level values only after that power has been protected.

The term *legacy* in this analysis is used in the sense that it is a gift—implying that it is something that is notable and positive. It refers to something bequeathed, a contribution willfully made by the president to the American public to be actuated over time. It describes more than just one's historical eminence. Simonton (1986) reminds us that historical eminence can be reached from two pathways—from positive acts *and* negative ones. In fact, research shows that historical eminence does not necessarily rest on successful performance or virtuous intent. Simonton (1986, 278) finds, for instance, that historical distinction can have a "curvilinear inverted-U relation" in that "eminence is attained by either being famously moral or infamously immoral."[5] From this, two important points arise. First, I assume that presidents believe legacy is a function of how they actually perform in office and that they do not seek eminence in history by simply being "infamously immoral" or the like. Second, there is a great difference between political success judged in real time and political success judged in posterity. I assume that outgoing presidents are less concerned with judgment by the public while in office.[6] A certain level of introspection is required when presidents seek to satisfy nonexistential needs such as esteem and self-actualization. This, in effect, causes them to fix their attention more on how future generations will perceive them and less on how current popularity polls rate them.

In essence, I hypothesize that the mechanisms that drive motivation change course in midtenure from survival to legacy. Survival in the context of presidential tenure is a short-sighted aim. In contrast, legacy (perceived as a conduit for the fulfillment of esteem and self-actualization) is attained only by securing one's positive impact in the context of a more distant future. Because of the immediate need to be reelected, nonterminal presidents heavily weigh the present relative to the future. Conversely, terminal presidents weigh the distant future more heavily. Yet how do we interpret such propositions in the context of presidential behavior?

In general, social scientists have found that individuals exhibit behavior that generally gives precedence to the present relative to the future (Lowenstein and Elster 1992, xiii). Governments too often exhibit much shortsightedness—for example, the lack of money spent on education, necessary road maintenance versus less necessary new construction, or Band-Aid approaches to failing banking systems (Ascher 2009). The intent of this study is not to offer a normative evaluation of optimal and suboptimal time discounting, that is, the proper weighting of the present relative to the future, given a set of options and constraints (resulting in an optimal choice). Certainly the psychology of how individuals relate to future benefits and costs is quite complicated. Psychologists find great variance in discount rates across individuals, even in the behavior of a single individual. Lowenstein and Elster (1992, x) explain as follows:

> For example, when purchasing energy-consuming appliances or insulating their houses, people display extreme temporal myopia, underinvesting in efficiency to a degree that implies discount rates in the hundreds of percents. At the same time, however, many of these people visit the dentist regularly, eat nutritious but bland breakfast foods, and manage to finance comfortable retirements. These behaviors are difficult to reconcile with an economic perspective which assumes that each person has a single discount representing his or her attitude toward the future.
>
> The same apparent inconsistency can be observed at a societal level. We construct shoddy highways, refuse to switch to the metric system, even type on a keyboard that was designed to slow the typist down to a rate that 19th-century typewriters could accommodate. But we also invest in basic research whose payoff is remote and eschew nuclear waste disposal sites because they may cause problems centuries hence. While the mechanisms that drive discounting behavior at the individual and societal levels are different, both domains display great variance in apparent concern for the future.

Indeed, much variance exists in how the present and the future are perceived and how that perception translates into courses of action. The theoretical focus here, however, is not on individual behaviors and choices per se but instead on how preferences become dynamically channeled by a structure instilled by term limits. Said differently, Elster (2009, 189) explains that "a given political or social system can offer individuals the opportunity to choose in certain ways." When reelection is no longer possible, "terminal logic" begins to define a frame of reference for choice and desire. Since presidents in this study serve a set time period of four years and have the possibility of reelection to only one subsequent four-year term, they operate in two distinct frames of choice and desire. Simply put, they operate in one frame where terminal logic constitutes its boundaries and in another where it does not. I hypothesize that this change in the imperative for action causes a sense of urgency in completing one's work—to what Hirschman (1963) calls *la rage de vouloir conclure,* resulting in a rapid and otherwise unexplainable increase in policy activity.

The next section I use the theory I have constructed to predict the space of time in which TLB is likely to operate during a president's tenure. This lays the foundation for the case studies and empirical analysis carried out in subsequent chapters.

3.3 THE CYCLE OF PRESIDENTIAL PERIODS

A president's tenure is marked by a cycle of presidential periods. Presidents begin in a *transition period.* Often called the presidents' honeymoon period, during the transition period, presidents can expect positive press (Grossman and Kumar 1981; Hughes 1995), high public opinion (Brace and Hinckley 1993), and legislative success on Capitol Hill. Moreover, Beckman and Godfrey (2007, 259) find that "substantial, genuine honeymoon effects are possible even if a president wins a close election and faces an oppositional Congress." Presidents' standing and influence are at their highest peak with Congress and the public during their first year.[7]

Presidents then move into what I call a *regular period.* During this period, they act within the normal constraints and dynamics of politics but do so without the protection afforded them during the transition period. Furthermore, they decide, act, and execute without the immediate prospect of termination—but instead with a focus on reelection. As discussed in chapter 2, the Twenty-Second Amendment, formally limiting presidents to two terms, was not enacted until 1951.

History shows that it is rare for presidents to decline a second run for office. Prior to the passing of the Twenty-Second Amendment, nine of twenty-eight eligible presidents did not seek reelection to a second term. Yet, after Congress passed the Twenty-Second Amendment, only one president out of the ten eligible turned down the bid for reelection—President Lyndon Johnson.[8] Only sixteen men in US history have been reelected to two or more terms. Despite these odds against achieving a second term, however, the drive for reelection to a second term, particularly in the present era, is assumed axiomatic.[9] Therefore, I assume

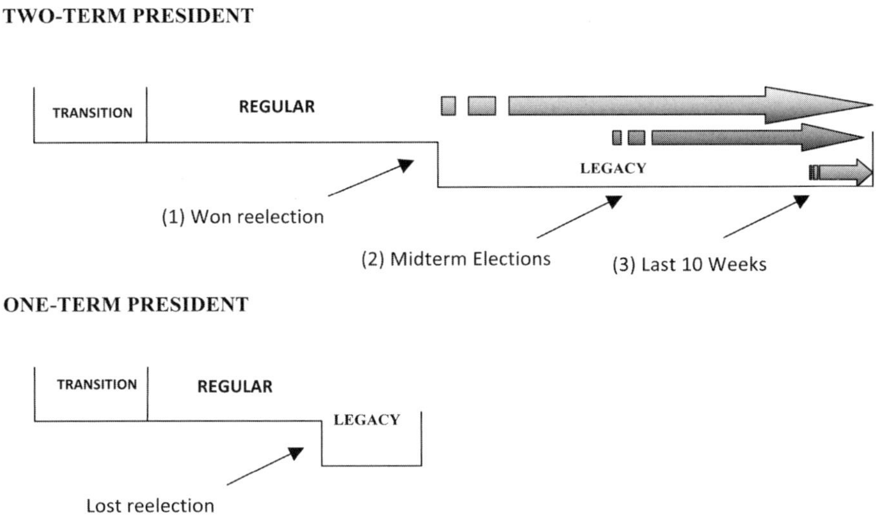

Figure 3.1. *Hypothesized legacy period of one- and two-term presidents.*

the *regular period* is largely dictated by reelection behavior. In contrast, the *legacy period* constitutes the period when presidents are terminal, and TLB begins to acutely affect presidential decision making.

Following the work of others, the *transition period* simply constitutes a president's first full year in office. (Expectations of behavior for this period and others are explained in detail in chapter 4.) For one-term presidents the *legacy period* simply begins the day after they lose the second election—the last ten weeks they are in office. The *regular period* constitutes the period in-between, after the transition year and prior to the loss of the second election.

The *legacy period* for two-term presidents, however, is not as clear-cut and may begin at a number of possible points in tenure. I test three particular such points: (1) the day after winning the second election; (2) the day after congressional midterm elections during presidents' sixth year; and (3) like the first-term presidents, the day after their successor has been named—their final ten weeks in office (see figure 3.1).

At first thought, one would expect TLB to begin to acutely affect a president the moment after winning reelection to a second term. Clearly, it is then that presidents are aware of their endpoint in tenure since they are constitutionally mandated to serve only two terms. Yet in politics much can happen in four years. Spurred on by unforeseeable events and shifting public moods, the political climate can change in an instant. Without a doubt, no matter what presidents do, they will likely never see the kind of support they saw early in their tenure. As Rockman (1984, 116) points out, "The effects of time (in essence, the decomposition of a winning coalition) are both buffered and reinforced by particular events and circumstances, though these are too weak to disturb the main tendency." And recall that loss of support matters because as presidents' partisan base of support begins to erode, they lose much leverage in Congress.[10] In the postwar United States the president's party has always done poorly in the midterm congressional elections (Alesina and Rosenthal 1989, 373), and this usually goes from bad to worse in the successive midterm election (Abramowitz, Cover, and Norpoth 1986; Campbell 1991).[11]

This is not to say that loss of support and terminal logic thinking will cause presidents to disregard politics and their party altogether. Presidents may still care about the success of their party. Although they are aware of their endpoint in tenure, they may not see this point as the *ne plus ultra* of their party. Presidents may work (and some more than others) to preserve and build the momentum of their party—and care enough to do it at the expense of their legacy objectives. Hoddie and Routh (2004) find a clear, systematic pattern to presidential campaigning during midterm congressional elections. Presidents campaign for party candidates who are running in the most competitive races, whether for a Senate or a House seat or a governorship. Hoddie and Routh make no distinction, however, between first- (nonterminal) and second-term (terminal) behavior. Brace and Hinckley (1993, 392–396), on the other hand, do make this distinction in their study of presidents Truman through Reagan. They find "a lessening of effort" by presidents in midterm campaigning when they become terminal. They are less likely to travel domestically during midterm elections, and in general their activities are fewer and "less coherently structured across the term."[12] And although Jacobsen, Kernell, and Lazarus (2004, 176) show that terminal presidents can "indeed use their extraordinary fundraising ability to help their parties win congressional contests they might otherwise lose," they also show that in President Clinton's case, campaigning efforts at his terminal stage were driven less out of devotion to the welfare of the party and more for reasons of payback to loyal followers.

Terminal presidents may not be consumed by the party's collective electoral experience but simply by the game of politics itself. Thus TLB may not begin to acutely affect presidential decision making until after their successor has been chosen—just like one-term presidents. It is then that one's end in tenure is most clearly felt. For one, although the outgoing presidents' preparations for their successor may begin months earlier, the formal transition activities take place in the last ten weeks of their tenure.[13] Presidents-elect put their staff in place, personnel for the White House, and high officials for the fifteen executive branch departments and establish their policy priorities. They are poised to act—and the retiring president knows it. This is a difficult pill for presidents to swallow, especially if their replacement is of the opposing party, which is promising that the new administration will change the way things are done in Washington. The outgoing presidents see that their policies and hard work during their years of service are likely to undergo a major overhaul—and they are not wrong in assuming so, according to Gaddis (1982) and Bunce (1980). Gaddis (1982) finds that presidents shift foreign policy and that shifts in strategy and position are particularly likely if there is a transition from one party to another.[14] In Bunce's 1980 study of the United States, Austria, Canada, Germany, Great Britain, Japan, and Sweden, she finds that succession in the United States and Sweden has the strongest impact on budgetary change. In these two countries, "innovation is quick and durable" (384). In countries such as Japan, on the other hand, Bunce finds that "succession there has little immediate impact" (ibid.). There is a clear pattern of budgetary fluctuations following succession. Bunce (1980, 384–90) puts it quite succinctly: "In the case of budgets, political leaders are not Tweedledum and Tweedledee but different persons with identifiably different policy objectives."

Publically, outgoing presidents offer their support even while signaling their disappointment. President George H. W. Bush in a cabinet meeting told his staff: "It's very important that we not be begrudging during the transition . . . Let us all finish the job with the same class with which we served" (Smith 2008, 18). Especially in the case of presidents who lose reelection to a second term but also true of two-term presidents handing over the presidency to an opposing party, tensions are very much in the air. Turnover tensions can be sensed in some of the press talks given by outgoing administrations following the general election. Remarks from both President Carter and Jake Siewert, President Clinton's press secretary (just two days before Clinton was to relinquish the presidency) reminded the public and the incoming president that they make the decisions until the very last day in office. Siewert's answers to the press are particularly revealing. He hints at the tension and turnover troubles experienced during the Bush-Clinton transition in 1992. And when asked whether the Bush team had inquired about how to overturn an executive order, Siewert explained that that information is "very jealously guarded in our discussions with them."

President Carter's Election Remarks with Reporters on the Results of the 1980 Election, November 5, 1980

THE PRESIDENT: It's important for the world to realize and for the American public to realize that I'll be the President for the next 2½ months. Governor Reagan and I had a very clear discussion of this, as did President Ford and myself 4 years ago. We will keep him informed, but the full constitutional responsibilities and authority, obviously, will be mine.

Q. Mr. President, through meetings next week with Governor Reagan, do you plan to consult with him on approaches to such things as the hostage issue, the Palestinian autonomy talks, so that it can be somewhat of a joint approach?

THE PRESIDENT: Yes. I'm not trying to put any responsibility on him. I will inform him; I think that's the better word than consult.

Press Briefing by Jake Siewert (President Clinton's press secretary), January 18, 2001

Q: On the hard drives, do you leave any sort of institutional memory for the Bush people—

MR. SIEWERT: I'll take a second on that, because we've been in regular contact with the Bush team, everyone from Ms. Jenny, "Tiger" Engebretsen has been consulting with them on how to do the clips, and Christine has been explaining to them how the pool works. And that's a level of cooperation that I think is really unprecedented at this level. We've been working with them across a broad array of issues. John has been in touch with his counterpart, Mr. Card, on a regular basis, and we've been doing everything we can to explain where things are, how they work, and we'll continue to do that. The Bush team's been

> in here virtually every night, at some level or another, to walk around, take a look at the place, see how it works.
>
> I know—I did this job myself, for the Clinton transition in '92. We did not have that opportunity. So we've been doing everything we can to make it easier for them to get settled in, and get to work right away.
>
> Q: Why did you not have an opportunity? Were you refused?
>
> MR. SIEWERT: I don't know. Some people were very helpful, but generally it was a little bit tougher to get information and figure out where things were in '92 than it is today. And the President asked John Podesta to make the arrangement as cooperative as possible, particularly because we had had some trouble in '92, and he didn't want to replicate that.
>
> Q: Did the Bush team ask for any particular guidance on how to overturn a previous administration's executive order?
>
> MR. SIEWERT: No. I mean, that is something that we very jealously guarded in our discussions with them. There were conversations where we told them what we were doing. John, I know, has kept them informed about what we had planned, in terms of worker safety rules, environment rules. They said they would like to take a chance to review those, and we said you can certainly do so, but there is—under no circumstances are we going to change our minds about what we think is important and what is right.
>
> Based on their own ideas, they will have a full chance to review them when they're in the White House and in power. *But we will reserve the right at the time in discussions with them to exercise presidential authority up until the last days.* (emphasis added)[15]

Since the mid-1960s the federal government has set aside funds for the purpose of facilitating the presidential transition process. These federal funds are intended to support the incoming and outgoing administrations by providing temporary office space; payroll, financial, contracting, and administrative services; and communications systems and IT support to both sides. Additionally, the National Archives and Records Administration gives support to the outgoing president in the "establishment and maintenance of their libraries" and "help[s] familiarize key [incoming] Administration officials with information about each department and agency."[16]

Table 3.1 shows the dollar amount of total federal appropriations allocated for the presidential transition, the allocated amount for outgoing administrations and the actual amount of federal funds spent by outgoing presidents.[17] This does not include private funds, which presidents often use in their exit from office. In fact, President Reagan received much criticism for private funds he solicited from the public for his transition.[18] It even prompted Congress to require public disclosure of private contributions and the names of transition personnel under the 1988 Presidential Transitions Effectiveness Act.[19]

In 2004 Congress passed the Intelligence Reform and Terrorism Prevention Act.[20] A subsection of this act stipulates the following:

> Activities under this paragraph shall include the preparation of a detailed classified, compartmented summary by the relevant outgoing executive branch officials of specific operational threats to national security; major military or covert operations; and pending decisions on possible uses of military force. This summary *shall be provided to the President-elect as soon as possible after the date of the general elections* held to determine the electors of President and Vice President under section 1 or 2 of title 3, United States Code. (emphasis added)[21]

This act of 2004 allows the president-elect to join the inner circle of information about military and foreign policy decisions "as soon as possible after the date of the general elections." Later reports issued by the National Academy of Public Administration and the Homeland Security Advisory Council call on federal departments and agencies "to work with the Presidential nominees, their senior staff and the Senate, prior to the election, to establish an expedited process for handling appointments" and "[to] encourage all Presidential nominees to identify members and organize homeland security advisory groups in preparation for the administration transition." A 2008 report states the following:

> It is vital that the Presidential candidates identify transition teams prior to the election. This will allow ample time for the appointees to complete background information forms and financial disclosure documents so that the processing of clearances and review of financial information can be accomplished prior to the election. The executive branch must facilitate the process so that transition team members are ready to fully perform their duties.[22]

The latest federal legislation governing presidential transitions is the Presidential Transition Act of 2010, which was in play for the first time in 2012. This act "encourages, almost mandates, that candidates begin transition plans in earnest starting right after the party conventions at the end of August and early September," extending the transition process to nearly five months before inauguration.[23] In fact, Mitt Romney, who had not yet been formally named the Republican Party's nominee for the 2012 presidential election, had already begun to meet with the General Services Administration (GSA) about "planning for a Romney White House."[24]

Prior to the Eisenhower/Kennedy transition in 1960–1961, the president-elect (not to mention a presidential candidate) was expected to stay away from Washington until inauguration day and have minimal contact with the outgoing administration (Smith 2008, 11). Since then, the contact and involvement of presidents-elect in state affairs has increased exponentially. Figure 3.2 shows the increased level of recorded speeches, press conferences, and remarks by presidents-elect following the general election. Particularly astonishing is President-Elect Barack Obama's level of press describing his administration's plans and actions.[25] Prior to inauguration Obama regularly issued statements, press releases, or remarks ten to twenty times a week. Also note in figure 3.3 how the level of recorded speeches, press conferences, and remarks by outgoing presidents following the general election has increased with each successive president (with the exception of George H. W. Bush) in the last three decades. What all of this tells us is that presidents are not only thinking about their transition out of office during this last ten-week period but also actually watching new leadership happen. For the reasons listed earlier I expect the highest level of TLB activity to occur in their last ten weeks in office—just like that of one-term presidents.

Table 3.1. Federal funds given and spent for presidential transition purposes (1968—2009)

Year	Transition	Total Federal Appropriations (Incoming and Outgoing Administration)	Outgoing Administration Allocation by GSA	Outgoing President Actual Federal Funds Spent	Outgoing President Actual Federal Funds Spent (2008 Real Dollars)*
1968–1969	Johnson–Nixon	900,000	450,000	370,276	2,289,753
1976–1977	Ford–Carter	3,000,000	1,000,000	635,000	2,401,617
1980–1981	Carter–Reagan	3,000,000	1,000,000	672,659	1,756,750
1988–1989	Reagan– George H. W. Bush	5,000,000	1,500,000	697,034	1,267,977
1992–1993	George H. W. Bush–Clinton	5,000,000	1,500,000	907,939	1,392,648
2000–2001	Clinton–George W. Bush	7,100,000	1,830,000	1,505,688	1,881,673
2008–2009	George W. Bush–Obama	8,520,000	2,200,000	NA	NA

Source: Smith (2008).
* Calculations based on Federal Reserve Bank of Minneapolis CPI Calculator.

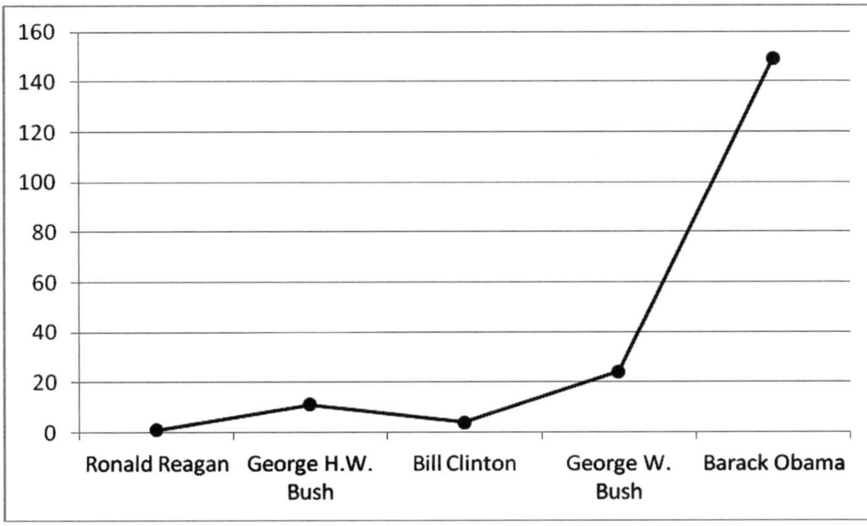

Figure 3.2. *Count of recorded speeches, press conferences, radio addresses, and public remarks as listed in the public papers of the president for outgoing presidents during their last eleven weeks in office.*

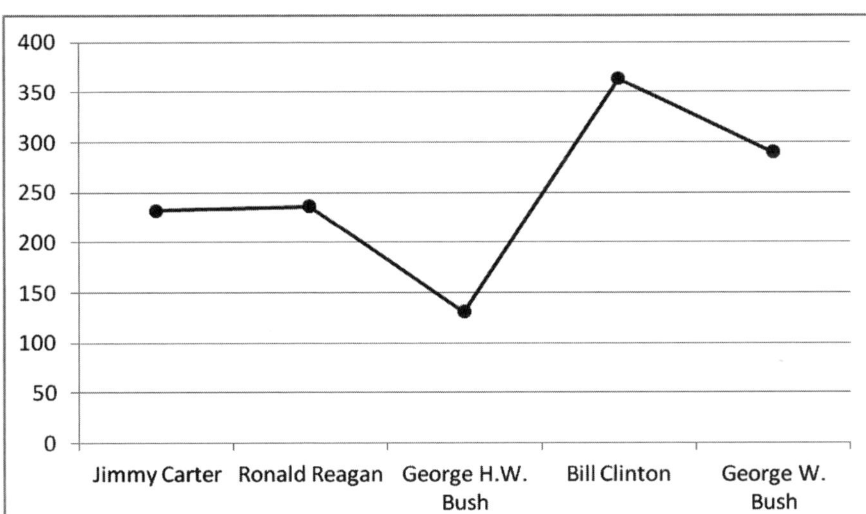

Figure 3.3. *Count of documents listed in public papers for outgoing presidents in their last eleven weeks in office.*

3.4 LEGACY AGENDA OF PRESIDENTS: DOMESTIC POLICY VS. FOREIGN POLICY

In the next four chapters I examine presidential decree use in three countries—the United States, Argentina, and Brazil. I expect these countries to diverge in the policy area in which their presidents seek to fulfill their legacy agenda. For instance, I hypothesize that presidents in the United States seek to fulfill their legacy agenda in foreign affairs. In contrast, I expect the legacy agenda of presidents of Argentina and Brazil to be more directly related to issues in the country and less so to issues surrounding the country's interests in world politics.[26] These expectations are based on the fundamental differences that separate the United States from Argentina and Brazil. The United States is a mature, industrialized nation with established formal market structures. Argentina and Brazil, on the other hand, represent emerging market nations. Brazilian and Argentinean presidents are less in a position to build a legacy out of involvement in affairs abroad. They must fix their sights on domestic arrangements—a place where they are capable of making real, positive change.

The United States stands in stark contrast. Its dominance economically, militarily, and culturally has allowed it to amass a level of power "unseen since the emergence of the modern state system" (Walt 2005, 31). With a few exceptions, promotion of US influence abroad has always been on the agenda of US presidents—so much so that the use of "imperial discourse" to describe the United States has become quite commonplace among academics.[27] There are those like Bender (2006) and Williams (1980) that suggest that there is something about being American and believing in the entrepreneurial spirit and classical republican values that inspires global involvement. Others like Stokes (2005, 218) explain that the United States' neoliberal ideology along with this entrepreneurial spirit spawns a will to pursue a world order conducive to the "generic reproduction of global capitalism." Regardless of whether US presidents view their country as the central protector of transnational capital or the world's bastion of freedom and entrepreneurialism, it is hard to dispute its global involvement and its strategic and ideological predominance in recent history. It is because of this that I assume US presidents, "frequently described as the most powerful person[s] on earth" (O'Loughlin and Grant 1990, 505), view their country as "the city upon the hill" and seek to carve out their legacy in acts of foreign affairs rather than in matters more closely tied to home.

Subsequent chapters support these propositions. In chapter 4 I show that the majority of decrees issued by US presidents concern foreign affairs policy. Likewise, in chapter 7, I show that the majority of decrees issued by Brazilian and Argentinean presidents address issues of domestic policy and government administration.

3.5 CONCLUSION

In this chapter, I develop my theory of terminal logic behavior and how term limits, specifically those that put restrictions on reelection, frame choice and desire in terms of terminal logic. I argue that reelection is characterized by a different frame of reference—one that does not structure choice and desire according to such logic. As a consequence, presidents of the two-term limit structure must operate from dual frames of reference over the course of their tenure, thereby creating discontinuity in their decision-making process. I then divide presidential tenure into distinct periods and formulate my hypotheses as to when TLB is likely to occur. Presidents begin their tenure in a *transition period.* Then they move into the *regular period,* which is largely dictated by reelection behavior. I hypothesize that TLB begins to acutely affect presidential decision making in the third and final period, the *legacy period.* Next, I discuss possible points in time during which TLB activity is most likely to occur in two-term presidencies: (1) the day after winning the second election, (2) the day after congressional midterm elections during presidents' sixth year, and (3) the day after their successor has been named—their final ten weeks in office. I conclude that, as with one-term presidents, the highest level of TLB activity is likely to occur in presidents' last ten weeks in office. Finally, I discuss my expectations concerning the areas in which presidents seek to fulfill their legacy agenda. In the United States, presidents, both Democrat and Republican, are likely to fulfill their legacy agenda in the area of foreign affairs, while Brazilian and Argentinean presidents are likely to do so in domestic politics.

I now move on to the construction of a research design based on the propositions set forth by the theory of terminal logic behavior. What we will find is that my analysis uncovers a repeated pattern of dependence—a true relationship between time and events that helps to define the end behavior of presidents.

CHAPTER 4

Changing the Status Quo

The Decree Power of US Presidents

4.1 INTRODUCTION

Chapter 3 develops a theory of terminal logic behavior (TLB) and seeks to fit its logic into a broader explanation of political behavior. The chapter addresses the overall structure of predetermined terms and the likely effects of this structure has on presidential behavior and other actors in the political process. The structural effects of fixed terms are assumed to be generalizable, a consequence of a fundamental relational structure invariant in all cultures, *not* the actual behavior and organization found in various societies. The elemental components are the same but are perhaps patterned differently due to historical or cultural conditioning. The comparative analysis of chief executives offers a unique avenue of inquiry into understanding and determining not only *whether* TLB exists but, if it does, also in what forms and under what conditions it may manifest itself.

This chapter focuses on presidents' proactive and reactive power generally and on why studying proactive power initiatives, specifically decrees, is fundamental to uncovering TLB. This leads to a discussion of the term *presidential initiative,* how others perceive it and how it is defined here in the context of this study. Then I begin my analysis of TLB with the case of the United States. Here I equate the term *decree* with three presidential instruments of direct action—executive orders, presidential proclamations, and presidential memoranda. I review the characteristics of each instrument and make a compelling case for their inclusion in the analysis over similar instruments such as national security directives (NSD) and presidential signing statements (PSSs). A brief section highlights important points as to how Congress and the courts view presidents' use of decrees. The final sections describe the collection, coding, and counts of decrees with regard to their type and category.

4.2 PROACTIVE POWER AND THE INITIATIVE TO DECREE

Carey and Shugart (1998) explain that presidential legislative power can be grouped into two categories: reactive and proactive. This delineation is based on what each category describes as the "reversionary outcome" or "the state of the world that obtains if the executive does not exercise authority" (ibid., 5). Reactive powers, such as an exercise of the veto, prevent a deviation from the "reversionary outcome" (i.e., the status quo). Conversely, presidential proactive powers change both the status quo and that which Congress would not have done on its own. In order to find evidence of TLB, it is most appropriate to analyze presidents' use of proactive power.

Two examples of proactive power are presidential decrees and agenda setting. According to Carey and Shugart (ibid., 6), if policy decisions are implemented "in lieu of any legislative action" and have the effect of changing the status quo, even temporarily, presidents are exercising their decree authority. Agenda power, by their definition, is less absolute in that it gives Congress more flexibility in choice. Agenda power allows Congress a choice of policy alternatives and/or a time frame during which decisions must be made. A presidential decree offers the most visible form of presidential preference. It is an unambiguous, clearly stated attempt made by presidents to change and formulate policy.

It is important to discuss the term *presidential initiative* and how it relates to proactive power, specifically presidents' use of decrees. Presidential initiative is the readiness of presidents to initiate action *and* the ability to act according to their own judgment. Scholars often join a discussion of initiative with that of authority. Is a decree a result of presidential initiative, or is it more a result of direction given by Congress? Carey and Shugart (1998) claim executive initiative when presidents cite the Constitution as their authority to issue decrees, whereas actions under statute are defined as merely acts of "delegated authority." In this study, evidence of presidential initiative is simply the very issuance of a decree.

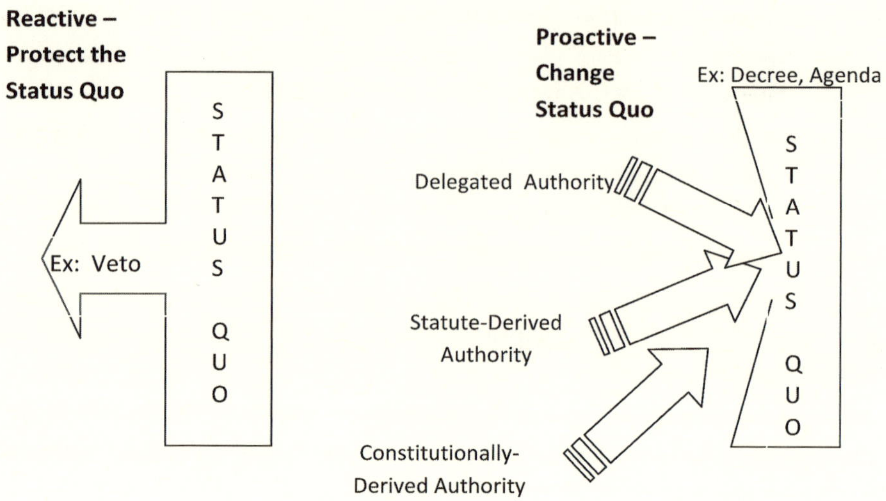

Figure 4.1. *Proactive versus reactive power.*

To be sure, it is not uncommon for presidents' claims of statutory or constitutional warrant to be disputed by assemblies and in the courts. There is much legal debate over presidential decree authority.[1] Figure 4.1 shows the types of authority by which presidents claim their right to issue particular decrees. A president derives authority from one of two places—from the country's constitution or its Congress.[2] Whether a president cites statutory or constitutional authority is not a relevant distinction for this study.[3] It is true that when Congress delegates legislative power, the scope of decree use is discussed beforehand, and limits are often set to the power delegated. However, once Congress delegates power on a certain issue with or without limits, the president is free to implement policy change that has immediate effect.

Furthermore, Carey and Shugart (1998, 12) themselves comment, "Virtually any legislation implies some level of discretion in implementation for the executive."

Statutes are generally quite broad, leaving much room for presidents to decree as they see fit. Look at how presidents use the American Antiques Act of 1906. This statute stipulates:

> That the President of the United States is hereby authorized, in his discretion, to declare by public proclamation historic land-

> marks, historic and prehistoric structures, and other objects of historic or scientific interest that are situated upon the lands owned or controlled by the Government of the United States to be national monuments, and may reserve as a part thereof parcels of land, the limits of which in all cases shall be confined to *the smallest area compatible with proper care and management* of the objects to be protected. (Statute 16 USC. 431–433, § 2; emphasis added)

According to Tseng (2003), presidents have used this act to declare more than one hundred monuments covering in excess of one hundred million acres. President Carter declared seventeen monuments with nearly fifty million acres of land in Alaska. President Clinton declared twenty-one monuments, and President George W. Bush declared three, covering large sections of the Mariana Islands, the Marianas Trench, Pacific remote islands, and Samoan islands. This example illustrates that although statutes may condition presidential action, there is still much room for presidential discretion and initiative. What is important for this study is the manifest exercise of proactive power.

Moreover, proving or disproving warrants of authority is a tricky business. Adjudicating on the constitutionality of specific presidential action is beyond the scope of this study. Although I outline how presidents claim their right to issue decrees within the context of each country under study, I do not differentiate, rank, or disqualify decrees based on the type of authority evoked by presidents. Presidential initiative is assumed with every issuance of a decree.

This is not to say that levels of initiative are assumed to be constant. Presidents act with varying levels of charge, intensity, and independence according to the circumstance of issuance—and it is important to account for those circumstances. Scholars have connected presidents' issuance of decrees to bargaining problems associated with Congress.[4] Some researchers, both in US and comparative politics, argue that presidents in issuing decrees are egregiously usurping power and setting policy. They often point to presidents' lack of legislative support as evidence of such usurpation. Others find that presidents' exercise of decree authority is more altruistic than this description of usurpation assumes. Presidents, they argue, use decree authority in anticipation of the preferences of others.[5] They claim that this is less about purposeful circumvention of the legislative process by presidents and more about congressional acquiescence; assemblies may actually prefer executive issuance of decrees to trying to get legislation passed through traditional channels. Assemblies often face bargaining problems and have difficulty maintaining the coalitions needed to pass legislation. In addition, legislators may deem the executive more competent than the legislative branch in information gathering and have more policy expertise on particular issues (Krehbiel 1992).[6]

Germane to this study are the pattern and the timing of decree use on particular issues. Of course, the timing of particular decrees is not just a function of where a president falls in the cycle of tenure. Depending on the issue, a number of factors may come into play, from Congress, public opinion, and the state of the economy to the changing general dynamic of a country's affairs. Conducting political affairs is a game of strategy in the administration of the state. As discussed in the previous chapter, a politician must first win favor and retain power. Once this condition is met, presidents can more freely act on a personal basis of conduct, and as a consequence, they shift focus. This study is an attempt to uncover when and where this focus shift might occur and whether it translates to an empirically significant change in the level of a president's decree issuance in specific policy areas.

4.3 DECREE POWER IN THE UNITED STATES

Broadly defined, a decree is a written statement of instruction or a declaration issued by the president that effectively becomes law without previous deliberation by Congress.[7] In the United States I equate the term *decree* with three presidential instruments of direct action: executive orders, presidential proclamations, and presidential memoranda.[8] In the United States, presidential decrees are known generally as presidential directives (Olson and Woll 1999, 8). It is worth noting that although the terms *directive* and *decree* can both be defined as authoritative instruction, they carry different connotations. The term *decree* is associated with absolute authority and powers associated with states of emergency or martial law. Although *directive* is a softer term, connoting a more restricted leader, instructing rather than dictating, its meaning is essentially the same—*a specific order by the president directing officials, agencies, citizens, those inside government and out on how to act.* Furthermore, this study is comparative in nature, applying hypotheses across presidents from three separate countries. For this reason I follow Carey and Shugart's (1998) executive policy-making typology described earlier and use the term *decree.*

A number of reasons dictate the choice of specifically defining US presidential decrees as orders, proclamations, and memoranda. First, each decree type is issued by the president directing officials, agencies, citizens, those inside government and out on how to act. They lack unique, mutually exhaustive characteristics. Presidents have never adhered to consistent usage. For instance, the 1957 House Committee on Government Operations set executive orders apart from proclamations by explaining that orders are directed to and regard action by US government officials and agencies, whereas proclamations affect those outside the government. Cooper (2002), however, reveals that this is not always the case. Courts have allowed executive orders to affect the property of citizens and companies. Mayer (2001, 35) adds that executive orders have "shaped the employment practices of government contractors, the travel rights of American citizens, foreign economic policy, private claims against foreign governments, and claims on natural resources on government-owned lands."[9]

Second, presidents from early on in US history have issued at times one type of decree when another might have been expected. For instance, President Abraham Lincoln used proclamations extensively in the early Civil War, and as Gaziano (2001, 9) argues, "there is not much that distinguishes Lincoln's executive orders from his wartime proclamations—apart from the title." In fact, Crowther (2000, 651) states that the Emancipation Proclamation, one of the most famous proclamations issued in US history, is actually two executive orders—one issued on September 22, 1862, which gave freedom to all slaves in the Confederate States of America who had not come under Union control by January 1, 1863, and one issued on January 1, 1863, which named the states to which this rule applied.

Third, the blurring of distinctions among these three types of presidential decrees is in part due to the fact that there is no law, statute, or other authority that delineates in substance one type from another. In fact, the White House currently lumps memoranda in with executive orders and together calls them presidential directives. Gaziano (2001) notes that "apart from tradition, historical usage, and a few words common to each device (such as the title), there are no rules regarding the substance of each directive." In fact, the Code of Federal Regulations maintains the same form and routing requirements for proclamations and executive orders.[10]

Time, however, has molded some general guidelines of practice in how each is used. In the following three sections, I briefly review features of each type. In doing so, it becomes clear how easily one type can blur into another.

Presidential Proclamations

Proclamations are largely ceremonial or rhetorical in nature. Of the 3,860 proclamations issued from Carter to W. Bush (1977 to 2009), 3,432 of them are hortatory—88.9 percent of the total proclamations issued.[11] Although substantive policy proclamations may deserve attention, hortatory declarations should not be easily discarded. Symbolic proclamations allow presidents to "rhetorically and ceremonially address the public" (Rottinghaus and Maier 2007, 342). Proclamations of this type designate holidays and days of observance that honor individuals or groups. Cooper (2002, 136) explains that they "generally cost nothing, require no follow-up, and, perhaps most important, rarely provide a reason for anyone to be upset." Quite simply, they offer presidents a way to recognize their constituents without costing them political capital. Recognizing the utility of hortatory proclamations, President Reagan issued a total of 1,028—his highest count of unique proclamations occurring in the year of his reelection. President Carter also issued his highest count the year in which he sought reelection and lost (figure 4.2). Reagan used hortatory proclamations to make political statements against foreign governments. For instance, he proclaimed Andrei Sakharov Day twice, once in 1983 and once in 1985, to recognize Sakharov, a Soviet nuclear physicist and human rights activist who suffered harassment by the KGB and detainment by Soviet officials until 1986.[12] Many hortatory proclamations cycle over and over each year like those that declare national holidays. Once a unique proclamation has been issued, it is quite common to see it reissued in successive years—even by different presidents from opposing parties.

Proclamations have had substantial impact on politics and in history; consider, for instance, Washington's Proclamation of Neutrality in 1793 and Lincoln's Emancipation Proclamation in 1863. Rottinghaus and Maier (2007, 339) list recent proclamations that have made "substantial impact" on economic and domestic policy—"President Nixon's wage and price freeze in 1971, President Clinton's declaration of federal lands for national monuments under the Antiquities Act of 1906, and President Bush's declaration of the areas affected by Hurricane Katrina as disaster areas."[13] Both presidents Clinton and George W. Bush made these declarations during their final days in office. In fact, President George W. Bush signed Proclamations 8335, 8336, and 8337, designating the monuments mentioned earlier on January 6, 2009, just two weeks before leaving office. By declaring land as monuments, areas are restricted with regard to mining, forest-

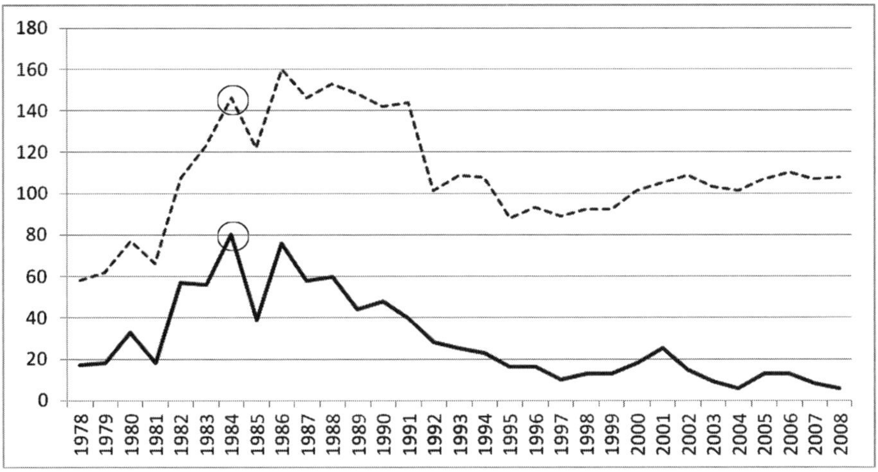

Figure 4.2. *Count of total (dotted line) and unique (solid line) hortatory presidential proclamations by year (1978–2008).*

ing, logging, water usage, grazing, and even off-road vehicle usage. This can result in substantial loss in tax revenue for both the state and federal government (Tseng 2003).

Executive Orders and Presidential Memoranda—Differences of Form

Memoranda and executive orders share striking similarities in substance and effect and even form. Cooper (2002), however, identifies some basic differences in form that set memoranda apart from executive orders. He describes three distinct forms of memoranda: presidential determinations, memoranda of disapproval, and hortatory declarations. Hortatory memoranda are much like hortatory proclamations and styled similarly, calling attention to certain observance periods, perhaps recently declared by proclamation, such as National Heritage Week or Red Cross Month. Presidential determinations "stem from statutes that require the president to make findings concerning the status of a country or some activity in the foreign policy field" (ibid., 86). Oftentimes these findings are needed in order to enact sanctions or proceed with development assistance. Presidential determinations are the only type given a specific number. For instance, Presidential Determination no. 97–36 of September 30, 1997, addresses the Export-Import Bank loan given to China for the Shanghai Metro. At times, however, there are substantial gaps in these numbers, reminding us that a complete list of published memoranda does not mean a complete count of total memoranda.

Memoranda of disapproval are essentially public veto statements. Although some may be seen therefore as a manifestation of presidential reactive power, this study includes them since a clear identification of this memorandum type is not always evident in the title.[14] As I describe in more detail later, solely for reasons of practicality the coding of decrees is based on the title alone.

Although memoranda may be distinguished as a "presidential determination" and "memoranda of disapproval," executive orders have no distinction of type in their title though they are used in "a variety of ways and for a plethora of reasons" (Cooper 2002, 21). Yet executive orders and proclamations are all numbered—where no systematic ordering exists for memoranda.[15] To make matters more confusing, Harold Relyea (2007), in his report to Congress, cites twenty-four types of decrees:[16]

administrative orders
designations of officials
general licenses
letters on tariffs and international trade
national security action memoranda
national security decision directives
national security directives
national security study memoranda
presidential decision directives
presidential findings
presidential review directives
proclamations
certificates
executive orders
interpretations
military orders
national security council papers
national security decision memoranda
national security reviews
presidential announcements
presidential directives
presidential reorganization plans
presidential review memoranda
regulations

His categories, however, are not mutually exhaustive. Relyea (2007, 4) concedes that "some items appeared to overlap other types of presidential directives." He states that in the past forty years, decrees (presidential directives) published in the *Federal Register* "in forms other than those of executive orders, or proclamations, have been denominated as administrative orders" even though they may be in the form of delegations of authority, determinations, directives, findings, letters, memoranda, and orders.

Although Cooper (2002) and Relyea (2007) make little mention of notices, a type of memorandum, decrees of this type are included in this study. Notices are listed both in the *Public Papers* and in the *Federal Register* under the heading "administrative orders." Presidents use notices to declare an emergency or allow for the continuation of one. Presidents Clinton and George W. Bush issued memoranda of this type in record numbers. Chapter 5 addresses the effects and usage of notices in greater detail.

National security directives (NSDs) and presidential signing statements (PSSs), on the other hand, are omitted from this analysis. The former is the general term given to decrees establishing policy through the National Security Council.[17] Although NSDs are very much like executive orders as they have many of the same effects, they are not covered by the Federal Register Act, and many remain classified.[18] Cooper (2002, 145) explains further: "Most administrations to date have refused to notify Congress of the existence of NSDs, to provide copies if they are specifically requested by Congress, or to send witnesses to testify at hearings on the subject."[19] In addition, PSSs are "announcements made by the president, usually prepared by the Justice Department, that go beyond merely lauding passage of a statute to identify provisions of the legislation with which the president has concerns" (ibid., 201). Although PSSs are published and instruct executive officials on how to administer law, presidents mainly use them to identify and reject specific statute provisions of which they do not approve. They are presidential comments on a bill and declarations of what they approve of and what they intend to ignore (Woolley and Peters 2010). Although PSSs can have substantive effects, they are best described as a reactive presidential power; power used to prevent a deviation from the status quo. The focus of this analysis is on presidential initiative to change the status quo—*not* on preventing change from occurring.

Presidential Memoranda: Quiet Power with Great Consequence

It is striking how little attention has been paid to presidents' use of memoranda, especially considering that they generally are accepted as equally effective and legally binding as executive orders and proclamations—even though they have not been put to the test in court in recent times.[20] Memoranda can be revoked like executive orders.[21] They can even be amended or superseded by executive orders themselves.[22] Presidents use memoranda like executive orders and at times seem not to know or see a difference between them. Clinton on more than one occasion declared that he was going to sign an executive order on an issue but signed a memorandum instead. This presidential tool has enormous potential to shape and even create policy—and to do so outside the Administrative Procedures Act.[23] Contrubis (1999, 20) states that "If issued under a valid claim of authority and published, executive orders and presidential memoranda have the force and effect of law and courts are required to take judicial notice of their existence."[24] Phillip Cooper (2001, 2002), in particular, has written extensively about the "use and abuse of memoranda" and how presidents, particularly in recent history, take advantage of their obscurity to "cloud the status and operation of formally promulgated executive orders." Others agree. Todd Gaziano (2001, 12) of the Heritage Foundation contends that "some of them [memoranda] are more important than many executive orders that are published." In his legal memorandum advising President George W. Bush on the "Use and Abuse of Executive Orders and Other Presidential Directives" and which he refers to in his testimony before Congress, Gaziano (ibid.) explains that "a President may use one of the less public types of directives in almost any circumstance in which he could issue a published executive order or presidential proclamation." Gaziano refers to President Clinton's use of a memorandum to issue the initial ruling allowing openly gay individuals to serve in the military (later changed to the weaker "don't ask, don't tell" policy) and the ruling allowing abortions to be performed on military bases overseas.[25]

Memoranda allow presidents to issue controversial decrees under the radar. For this reason, they have become an increasingly valuable tool for presidents. It is no wonder that they have "expanded the use of the memorandum for significant purposes and in ways that make them appear far more like executive orders than anything else in terms of their substantive effect" (Cooper 2002, 127–28). A blurring of formal distinctions, particularly between executive orders and presidential memoranda, has the potential to enhance a president's power. Presidents can use these tools in conjunction with each another as part of what Cooper (ibid., 91) describes as a "policy mix," where "these devices are mutually reinforcing, allowing an administration to have both scope and intensity in a particular area of policymaking." Gaziano (2001, 12) agrees, even stating that "it is unwise to arbitrarily exclude nontraditional directives, such as memoranda, when examining a President's rule by executive decree" (ibid.).

Examples of memoranda creating significant policy abound. President Kennedy established the National Communication System (NCS) by memorandum in 1963 after the Cuban missile crisis (Moteff 2004, 5).[26] In the memorandum of January 22, 1993, President Clinton instructed the secretary of health and human services to remove the moratorium on federal funding of research involving the transplantation of fetal tissue from induced abortions. Moreover, the use of memoranda as executive orders continues under the current Obama administration. For instance, on May 20, 2009, President Obama signed a memorandum on preemption, declaring: "The purpose of this memorandum is to state the general policy of my Administration that preemption of State law by executive departments and agencies should be undertaken only with full consideration of the legitimate prerogatives of the States and with a sufficient legal basis for preemption."[27] According to Jack Park (2009, 3), special assistant to the inspector general for the Corporation for National and Community Service, this memorandum has serious consequences for private businesses: "[W]ith the President's Memorandum in effect, producers and distributors can expect their compliance with any new regulatory requirements to be seen as a 'floor' but not a 'ceiling' if they are sued in state court."

Although presidents are required to cite a basis for their actions for executive orders, in some instances presidents have flouted this requirement for memoranda.[28] President George H. W. Bush used a memorandum to impose a moratorium on rule making. He cited no legal authority for action but instead explained that the promulgation of this memorandum was due, because "Congress has thus far failed to pass most of the Administration's regulatory reform proposals" (Cooper 2001, 138–39). According to the *Washington Post,* in 2007 the administration of President George W. Bush was prepared to seek "as much new policy as it [could] by administrative order [memorandum]," not because of statutory mandate but because the administration faced an uncooperative Congress.[29] As it turns out, he may have learned this trick from his father, who initiated more than one-third *more* rule makings in the final quarter of his term than did either President Clinton or President Reagan (O'Connell 2009, 2).

There is little doubt that presidents use executive orders, memoranda, and proclamations interchangeably and supplement one tool with one or more of the others for purely utilitarian or political aims. If presidents want to place an issue on public stage, they may promulgate a proclamation, a memorandum, or an executive order *or* issue all three types at once to address the issue. Similarly, if it is more preferable for a decree to go under the political radar, a president may issue a memorandum instead of an executive order or do as President Reagan did in January 1985. Reagan issued Executive Order 12498, which in itself seemed only administrative and routine in nature, calling for the publication of planned agency regulations. Yet he issued this order in conjunction with a memorandum that delivered instruction that was consequential *and* controversial. The memorandum gave the Office of Budget and Management broad power to monitor regulatory efforts. This memorandum was not published in the *Federal Register,* the *Weekly Compilation of Presidential Documents,* or the *Public Papers of the President* (Cooper 2001, 138). The Federal Register Act, which Contrubis cites as proof of the claim that memoranda should be published, applies only to executive orders and proclamations.[30]

4.4 EXECUTIVE INITIATIVE VS. DELEGATED AUTHORITY: HOW THE COURT AND CONGRESS HANDLE PRESIDENTIAL DECREES

Despite some general practices that have developed historically, the only consistent distinction of memoranda from executive orders and proclamations is that memoranda are not numbered, nor are they required to be published in the *Federal Register.*[31] Randolph D. Moss, the acting assistant attorney general, advised President Clinton to this effect:

> There is no substantive difference in the legal effectiveness of an executive order and a presidential directive that is not styled as an executive order. We are further of the opinion that a presidential directive would not automatically lapse upon a change of administration; as with an executive order, unless otherwise specified, a presidential directive would remain effective until subsequent presidential action is taken.[32]

The judiciary has held that in order for a decree to have the force of law, presidents must have constitutional or statutory warrant for its issuance. Presidents derive their decree authority from "express or implied statutory authority from Congress" or from Article II of the Constitution, which states that "the executive power shall be vested in a President of the United States," and the president "shall take care that the laws be faithfully executed."[33] Yet, proving that a president does not have warrant to issue a particular decree is difficult, and the burden of proof lies heavily on the plaintiff (Contrubis 1999, 2). Olson and Woll (1999, 8–9) explain that in "the absence of clear constitutional or statutory definitions and the lack of sustained judicial guidance, there remains a wide divergence of opinion about the proper scope, application, and even legal authority of presidential directives." Prior to 1999 there were few instances in which the Supreme Court invalidated a presidential decree.[34] *Youngstown Sheet and Tube v. Sawyer,* 343 US 579 (1952), was a landmark case where the court invalidated President Truman's EO 10340, which called for the seizure of private US steel mills during the onset of the Korean conflict. In *Youngstown Sheet and Tube v. Sawyer,* the court found that President Truman did not have the authority either from Congress or the Constitution to take possession of the property. The court has since relied on the framework set up by Justice Jackson in his concurrent opinion to evaluate the legality of executive orders (Contrubis 1999, 7).[35] Justice Jackson writes (*Youngstown Sheet and Tube v. Sawyer,* 343 US 579 [1952] at 635–38):

> Presidential powers are not fixed but fluctuate, depending upon their disjunction or conjunction with those of Congress. We may well begin by a somewhat oversimplified grouping of practical situations in which a President may doubt, or others may challenge, his powers, and by distinguishing roughly the legal consequences of this factor of relativity.
>
> 1. When the President acts pursuant to an express or implied authorization of Congress, his authority is at its maximum, for it includes all that he possesses in his own right plus all that Congress can delegate. In these circumstances, and in these only, may he be said (for what it may be worth) to personify the federal sovereignty. If his act is held unconstitutional under these circumstances, it usually means that the Federal Government, as an undivided whole, lacks power. A seizure executed by the President pursuant to an Act of Congress would be supported by the strongest of presumptions and the widest latitude of judicial interpretation, and the burden of persuasion would rest heavily upon any who might attack it.
>
> 2. When the President acts in absence of either a congressional grant or denial of authority, he can only rely upon his own independent powers, but there is a zone of twilight in

> which he and Congress may have concurrent authority, or in which its distribution is uncertain. Therefore, congressional inertia, indifference or quiescence may sometimes, at least as a practical matter, enable, if not invite, measures on independent presidential responsibility. In this area, any actual test of power is likely to depend on the imperatives of events and contemporary imponderables rather than on abstract theories of law.
>
> 3. When the President takes measures incompatible with the expressed or implied will of Congress, his power is at its lowest ebb, for then he can rely only upon his own constitutional powers minus any constitutional powers of Congress over the entire matter. Courts can sustain exclusive presidential control in such a case only by disabling the Congress from acting upon the subject. Presidential claim to a power at once so conclusive and preclusive must be scrutinized with caution, for what is at stake is the equilibrium established by our constitutional system.

The court continues to adhere to Justice Jackson's standard of review for executive orders and proclamations (Mayer 2001, 36–40). The *Youngstown* case was the "high-water mark for judicial review of executive usurpation of legislative authority" (Olson and Woll 1999, 18). The court continues to give much deference to the president in matters related to foreign affairs or national security (ibid., 11; Contrubis 1999, 15). Particularly striking is Howell's (2003) finding that of all the executive order challenges heard in federal court from 1945 to 1998, 83 percent of the time those challenges failed. Moreover, the court "has declined to review whether the president has properly invoked his statutory powers—and declined not because of jurisdictional or standing problems, but instead on the basis of its own freestanding reviewability doctrine" (Stack 2009, 1172–73). Congress often requires that certain findings be made before a president can invoke statutory power. This is called "contingency or conditional form of delegations" (ibid., 1174). Yet under the reviewability doctrine the court excludes these findings from judicial review. These findings are formally called "presidential determinations" and recall that presidential determinations are a form of presidential memoranda. The court will not consider whether presidents invoked statutory power according to the proper conditions set by Congress—making their action in these cases virtually immune to scrutiny.[36]

Furthermore, if a directive is instructing a federal agency or department on how to act and what regulations to issue, then it constitutes only "an indirect effect on the public" (Gaziano 2001, 21). Memoranda, orders or proclamations that do not directly affect the public are not subject to judicial review. Gaziano (2001, 21) attests in his legal memorandum that, "In litigation or other administrative challenges to the regulation [of this type] is irrelevant unless the President possesses some constitutional or statutory power that augments the agency's authority."

Clearly these points show that the court is unassertive and reluctant to pass judgment on executive action of this type.[37] This discovery is not new. In fact, Schubert (1953) called attention to this nearly a half century ago. It remains true that unless Congress acts, presidents have broad discretion in the use of decrees. Congress can do a number of things. It can enact a statute that modifies, even nullifies, a presidential decree as it did with EO 12806.[38] Here Congress passed a statute stating that "the provisions of Executive Order 12806 shall not have any legal effect."[39] It can repeal statutory authority retroactively or put in place a "sunset provision," whereby authorization is effective only through a specified date unless reauthorized. Finally, Congress can pass legislation that is in contradiction to the decree issued by the president. Nevertheless, what is most important to remember is that the judiciary essentially determines who has the weight of authority, the president or Congress, by how Congress acts when confronted with presidential action. Congressional acquiescence earns the president great weight in the eyes of the judiciary (Contrubis 1999, 18).[40] Similarly, the 1974 Senate Special Committee on National Emergencies and Delegated Emergency Powers found that little congressional oversight and few provisions restricting presidents' use of statutory power allow presidents the freedom to do as they please. The committee explains as follows:

> [T]he institutional checks designed to protect the guarantees of the Constitution and Bill of Rights are significantly weakened by the growing tendency to give the President grants of extraordinary power without provision for effective congressional oversight, or without any limitation upon the duration for which such awesome powers may be used. (Olson and Woll

> 1999, 29, citing the Senate Special Committee on National Emergencies, *Executive Orders in Times of War,* 8–9)

Scholars agree, finding that Congress has largely been passive to presidents' use of unilateral power.[41] In general, it is fairly safe to assume that because the court and Congress are unassertive and reluctant to challenge decrees, presidents have broad discretion in exercising their use.

4.5 THE COLLECTION AND CODING OF US PRESIDENTIAL DECREES

Two critical components of research design in the evaluation of theory are data collection and coding. Figure 4.3 shows the total counts of executive orders, proclamations, and memoranda in the eight four-year terms in this study. For the time period under study (from January 20, 1977, to January 19, 2009), there are a total of 7,792 total decrees—3,860 proclamations, 1,522 orders, and 2,410 memoranda (see figure 4.3). The collection and coding of the dependent variable (i.e., decrees) is straightforward when it comes to executive orders and proclamations as they are numbered and easily accessible. A listing of orders and proclamations, their date, number, and title is provided by the American Presidency Project (Woolley and Peters 2010).[42] The task of collecting and accounting for presidential memoranda, however, is more complex and less absolute. Unlike executive orders and proclamations, memoranda are not numbered and are not required to be published in the *Federal Register.* It is important, therefore, to provide precise detail on methods of collection and coding.

In this study, memoranda are drawn from two sources—those appearing in the *Federal Register* and *Public Papers of the President.*[43] For the years under review, the *Federal Register* lists three subcategories under the heading "Presidential Documents: Executive Orders, Proclamations, and Administrative Orders." Any document, whether it be titled as a finding, presidential determination, notice, letter, or memorandum, listed under the heading "administrative orders" in the index of the *Federal Register,* is added to the database.[44] The archive of the American Presidency Project catalogues documents from the *Public Papers of the President.* In order to compile the most complete (and comparable) list of memoranda issued by presidents Jimmy Carter through George W. Bush, all documents of the project's database were retrieved by searching on the word "memorandum." Any document

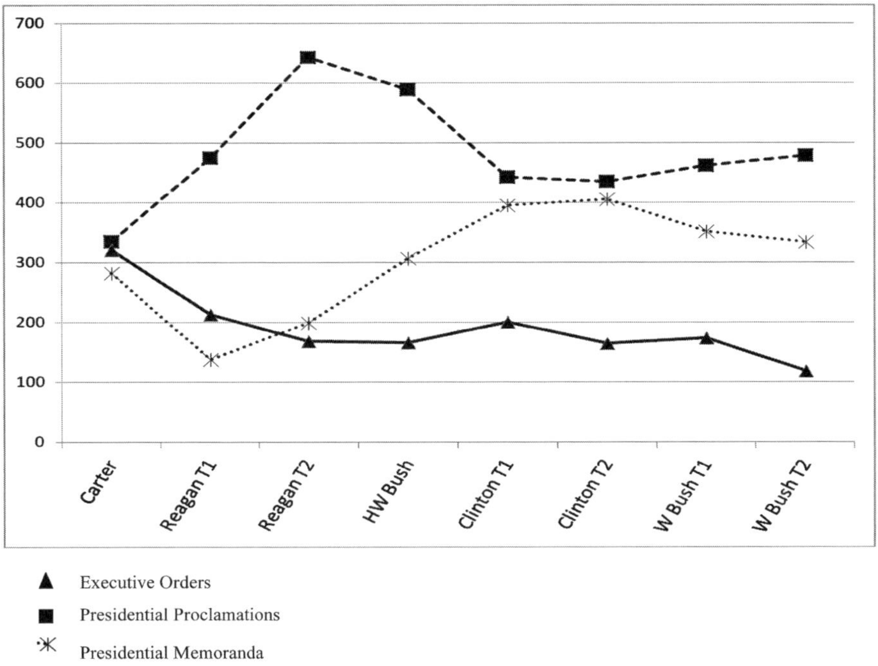

Figure 4.3. *Total count of executive orders, presidential proclamations, and presidential memoranda (1977–2009).*

that did not have the word "memorandum," "determination," or "notice" specifically listed in the title was then excluded. For instance, documents pertaining to presidential remarks made at news conferences and interviews with the press, as well as messages to Congress, including State of the Union addresses, turn up in the retrieval list. These are all excluded. Presidential determinations or hortatory declarations (so long as either "memorandum" or "determination" appeared in their title) were included. Recall that the *Federal Register* refers to memoranda as administrative orders. A document appearing in the *Federal Register* may or may not appear in the *Public Papers.* Although the project states that "documents such as Proclamations, Executive Orders, and similar documents that are published in the *Federal Register* and the Code of Federal Regulations, as required by law, are included [in the *Public Papers*] beginning with the administration of Jimmy Carter (1977)," this cannot be assumed to be the case for presidential memoranda.

Figures 4.4 and 4.5 show how the publication of memoranda has changed over the last thirty years and the past five presidents. President Carter published

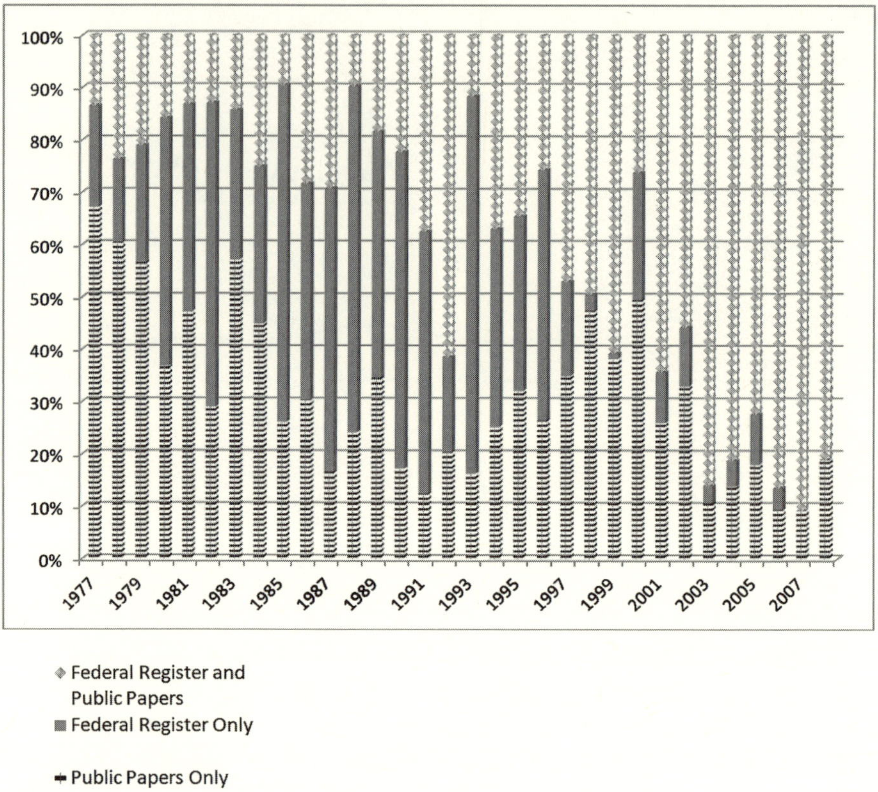

Figure 4.4. *Publication of presidential memoranda by year (1977–2008).*

most of his memoranda in the *Public Papers* (56 percent) and some in the *Federal Register* (25 percent), and a few can be found in both the *Federal Register* and the *Public Papers* (19 percent). Presidents Reagan and George H. W. Bush, on the other hand, published most of their memoranda in the *Federal Register* (49 percent and 45 percent, respectively) and some in the *Public Papers* (33 percent and 29 percent, respectively). Only a few were found in both places (18 percent and 19 percent, respectively). There appears to be little systematic pattern for publication during the Clinton administration. Sometimes his memoranda were published in just the *Federal Register* (29 percent), sometimes in just the *Public Papers* (34 percent), and other times in both places (37 percent). Moreover, these percentages vary over the course of Clinton's tenure—at times publishing more in the *Public Papers* and less in the *Federal Register* and vice versa. Certainly, each president faces a learning curve of where and when to publish, but the Clinton administra-

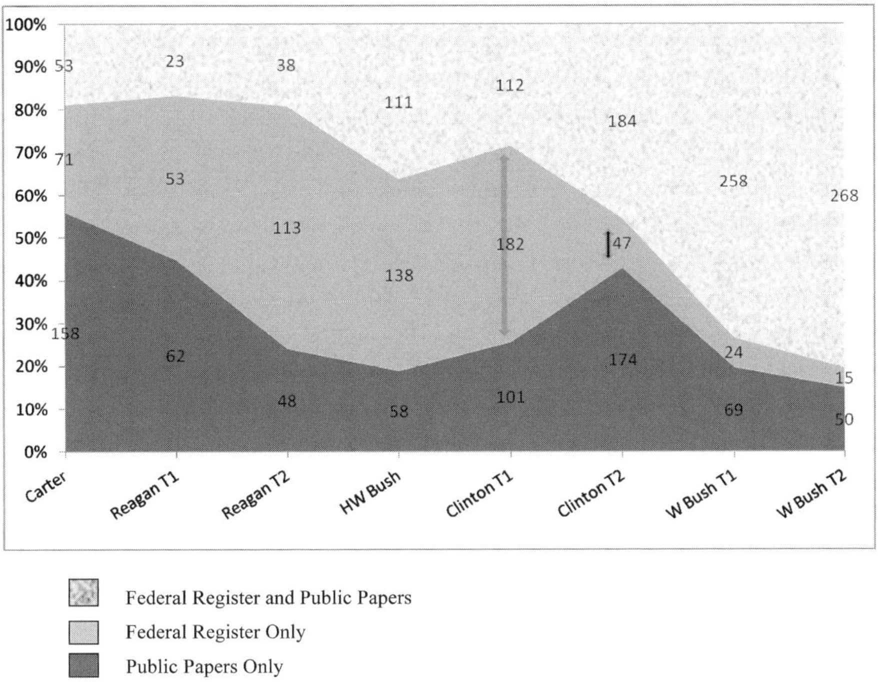

Figure 4.5. *The trend of memoranda publication by presidential term (cumulative proportion of each publication type), 1977–2009.*

tion remained inconsistent in its publishing over time. This is particularly interesting and possibly even alarming because President Clinton used memoranda (a total of eight hundred) more than any other president and in powerful and often controversial ways as described earlier in this chapter. An unmethodical and haphazard publication process clouds transparency. In comparison, the publication process under President George W. Bush was more systematized. During his administration, memoranda were published 77 percent of the time in both the *Public Papers* and the *Federal Register;* only 6 percent of the time did they appear in the *Federal Register* alone and 18 percent of the time in the *Public Papers* alone.

It is important to note that this analysis of memoranda publication does not include any count or estimate of how many memoranda go unpublished outside these sources. Cooper (2002, 246), for instance, mentions that some memoranda are published on the Internet site of the federal agency "most directly concerned with the issue at hand." Furthermore, there is no assessment of the level of con-

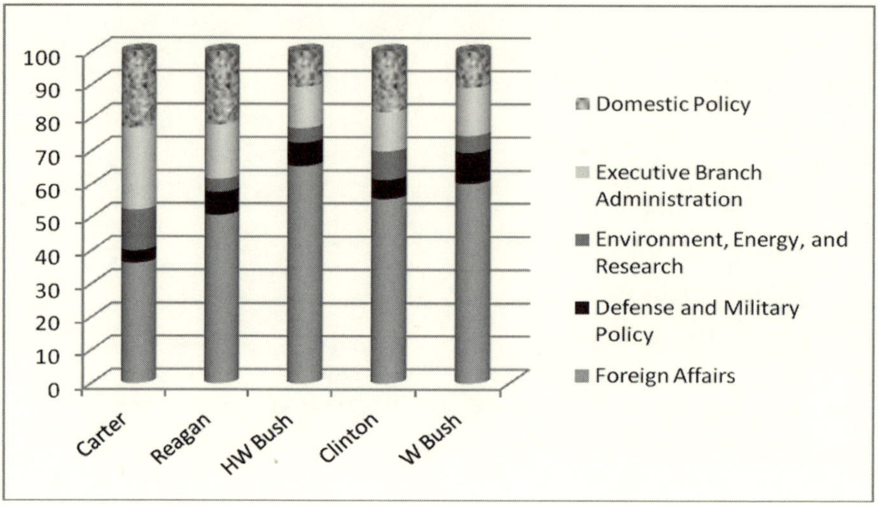

Figure 4.6. *Percentage of decrees by category for specific presidents (1977–2009).*

sequence of each memorandum, order, or proclamation. Perhaps the 18 percent of memoranda published by President George W. Bush in the *Public Papers* alone are those of greatest importance. Undoubtedly, this needs to be explored further. Recall that the overarching goal of this study is to measure presidential initiative of change—no matter how technical or significant that change may be.

Figure 4.6 shows the distribution of decrees across the five policy domains for each of the five presidents in this study.[45] Table 4.1 lists total counts of decrees according to type (proclamation, memorandum, order) and major policy domain (domestic, foreign, military and defense, environment, and executive branch administration). From here one can gather some general characteristics of the data. Table 4.2 outlines exactly what each category entails. I use a slightly modified version of Mayer's (2001, 80) policy categories. Decrees are coded according to the category that best describes their focus. Each category is exhaustive and mutually exclusive. A large portion of foreign policy decrees are memoranda, whereas orders constitute the majority of decrees related to defense and military policy, environmental policy, and domestic policy.

In Table 4.1, decrees are further subcategorized into smaller, more specific groups. These subcategories are meant to be purely illustrative. They are not subject to statistical analysis for several reasons. First, the N-counts within the subcategories are small. Second, placing decrees into the more specific categories leaves

Table 4.1. Policy issues covered by presidential proclamations, executive orders, and memoranda (1977—2009)

Policy Issue	Proclamation	(%)	Memorandum	(%)	Order	(%)	Total
Environment, Energy, and Research	**52**	(17.5)	**93**	(31.3)	**152**	(51.2)	**297**
conservation and resource protection	51		19		29		
public lands	0		6		7		
space	0		6		7		
energy	1		16		33		
research initiatives in science and technology	0		12		41		
other	0		34		35		
Domestic Policy	**19**	(2.6)	**313**	(42.9)	**397**	(54.5)	**729**
restoration of law and order	15		8		4		
health	0		28		29		
drugs	0		13		14		
education	0		25		40		
labor policy	0		2		87		
volunteer service	1		4		27		
pardons	3		0		1		
assistance for victims	0		5		9		

(*continued*)

Table 4.1. (*continued*)

Policy Issue	Proclamation	(%)	Memorandum	(%)	Order	(%)	Total
other (e.g., federal aid, industry regulation, reform)	0		213		150		
emergency preparedness	0		15		36		
Hortatory	**3,432**	**(98.2)**	**57**	**(1.6)**	**7**	**(0.2)**	**3,496**
Foreign Policy	**353**	**(15.2)**	**1,555**	**(67.1)**	**410**	**(17.7)**	**2,318**
foreign trade	213		355		98		
foreign aid	2		293		21		
international organizations	0		80		54		
US terr./commonwealths	7		6		11		
immigration	3		160		17		
nonproliferation	0		56		52		
diplomacy (general)	3		245		53		
nondiscrimination treatment of country or product (e.g., GSP, AGOA)	102		15		25		
sanctions (including suspension of entry)	23		47		68		
international drug control	0		46		0		
notice of emergency	0		252		11		

Defense and Military Policy	**2**	(0.6)	**105**	(36.0)	**185**	(63.4)	**292**
military personnel	2		15		88		
intelligence and national security	0		34		54		
military lands and facilities	0		7		4		
designation of combat zones	0		0		4		
administration	0		2		0		
other	0		47		35		
Executive Branch Administration	**2***	(.3)	**287**	(43.5)	**371**	(56.2)	**660**
appointments and nominations	0		8		20		
mandatory retirement exemptions	0		0		5		
federal pay	0		16		79		
civil service (rules of conduct)	0		85		60		
holiday designation	0		0		15		
civil service medal	0		4		2		
other	2		174		190		

* Census.

Proclamations refer to declaration of next decennial census. The US Constitution requires a census of the US population once every ten years.

Table 4.2. US decree categories

Category	Description
Foreign affairs	Decrees involving at least one nation outside the United States. Decrees dealing with export and import controls, foreign economic policy, foreign trade, foreign aid (including those titled as economic and security assistance and those related to preferential trade treatment, such as GSP, AGOA, and CBERA), sanctions (the blocking of individual persons from entering the United States or the blocking of individual agreements), foreign affairs and diplomatic relations generally (including those related to nonproliferation, world hunger, and drug-control efforts between countries), establishment of international or treaty-based organizations, management of territories (e.g., Philippines, Puerto Rico, the Canal Zone), and immigration
Defense and military policy	Decrees dealing with military personnel (issues pertaining to pay and benefits excluded from analysis), classified information (presidential records) and information sharing, organization of the intelligence community, creation and management of national/homeland security, rules regarding behavior on military lands and reservations, designation of combat zones (emergency and termination), and defense policy generally
Environment & research	Decrees dealing with environmental conservation, energy, space and resource protection (e.g., water and food security, monuments, national parks) Public lands: Decrees that regulate behavior on public lands (e.g., establish or alter the boundaries of public lands, migratory waterfowl refuges, fisheries, or airspace reservations) Research: Decrees dealing with initiatives in science and technology

(continued)

Table 4.2. (*continued*)

Category	Description
Domestic policy	Decrees dealing with domestic policy generally, including those that address civil rights, the economy (domestic industry/business), health, drugs, education, volunteer service, and assistance to US citizens who are victims of international events such as the Holocaust and terrorism. Also included are decrees granting pardons/clemency and decrees that address readiness for domestic natural disasters Labor policy: Decrees creating emergency boards and boards of inquiry to investigate labor disputes; orders managing federal government labor policy
Administration	Decrees creating boards, commissions, or interagency councils; decrees that deal with order of succession, delegation of presidential power or powers transferred from one agency to another, establishment of civilian awards, administration of tax policy (including inspection of tax returns), issues that affect the organization of the executive office of the president; commemorative orders; contracting Civil service: Decrees dealing with civil service appointments, retirement exemptions, administration of federal personnel, salary, holidays; rules regarding civil service (including foreign service) conduct, programs, training

This is a modified version of Mayer's (2001, 80) category configuration.

more room for interpretation, and since 7,792 observations were coded based on title alone, misspecification at the subcategory level likely breaches normal standards of error. Indeed, what these subcategories are intended to show is that specific decree types are not confined to broad domains or even to specific issues. Often it is the case that a policy issue is addressed by two or more of the decree types, lending credence to the notion that presidents mix one type with another—and can do so in deceptive ways.

4.6 CONCLUSION

In this chapter, I explain why studying proactive power initiatives, specifically decrees, is the proper avenue in which to test hypotheses about terminal logic behavior. Then I review three decree types used by US presidents—executive orders, presidential proclamations, and presidential memoranda—and show the validity of using such instruments as a measure of TLB in the United States. Orders, proclamations, and memoranda direct policy in almost every domain—foreign policy, domestic and environmental policy, and defense and military policy. Presidents use the three types interchangeably and oftentimes supplement one decree type with one or more of the others. A large portion of the chapter is spent discussing presidents' use of memoranda. This presidential tool has enormous potential to shape, even create policy under the radar—outside the Administrative Procedures Act. To be sure, little is known about this decree type's overall effect on presidential power and on the balance of power among the branches of government in general.

I call attention to the varying ways in which memoranda have been published over the past thirty years. Of the five presidents under study, President Clinton's pattern for publication was largely inconsistent over the course of his tenure. This should cause serious pause since he used memoranda more than any other president in this study and in powerful and often controversial ways. Finally, I describe the collection, coding, and counts of decrees with regard to their type and category. From this, one can gather basic features of the data used in the US case of the TLB analysis. This is our jumping-off point for chapter 5.

In chapter 5, I group the three decree types and explore how presidents alter their use of decrees over time in various policy domains. I test hypotheses linking presidential periods (transition, regular, and legacy) to presidents' use of decrees in three domains (foreign policy, environmental policy, domestic policy) and one specific issue—emergency power.

CHAPTER 5

Terminal Logic Behavior of US Presidents

> We've spent a lot of time . . . saying that the President's [Clinton] a lame duck, he doesn't have any power, he doesn't have any authority—it's nice to know that at least for one week during the course of this year, people find that differently. I suppose at the end of the day, we'll see what happens.
>
> —*Chief of Staff John Podesta speaking at a press briefing (September 5, 2000)*[1]

The period under review for the US analysis begins in January 1977 and ends in January 2009. In chapter 1 I explain why 1977 is the proper starting point for analysis. Recall that Congress passed the National Emergencies Act (NEA) in 1976 and the International Emergency Economic Powers Act (IEEPA) in 1977. With 1977 as our starting point, we can analyze presidents' use of emergency power—executive orders, memoranda, and proclamations issued pursuant to either the NEA or the IEEPA. What this study uncovers is significant. Analysis of public, unclassified data (executive orders, presidential proclamations, and presidential memoranda appearing in the *US Federal Register* and/or *Public Papers of the President*) indicates that the use of emergency power has not only increased over the last thirty years but also reveals a clear pattern. Presidents, in

Table 5.1. US presidents under study (1977—2009)

Name	# of Terms	Party Affiliation	Years Served
Jimmy Carter	1	Democrat	1977–1981
Ronald Reagan	2	Republican	1981–1989
George H. W. Bush	1	Republican	1989–1993
Bill Clinton	2	Democrat	1993–2001
George W. Bush	2	Republican	2001–2009

their last seventy-five days, invoke their authority under the NEA and the IEEPA at a substantially greater rate than previously in their tenure. In fact, across the board in all policy domains (foreign, environmental, and domestic policy, as well as emergency power), presidents increase their rate of decree issuance when they are in the final weeks of their last term, particularly when their successor has been named *and* that successor is from the opposing party.

5.1 THE MODEL: SOME EXPECTATIONS

For the period under review, two presidents served only one term; one is a Democrat, the other a Republican (see table 5.1). The predicted space of TLB activity is clear. When they fail to be reelected, they have less than two and a half months to act before the president-elect takes office. Three presidents served two terms—two Republicans and one Democrat. The predicted space of TLB for these presidents is not so clear-cut. For two-term presidents I test three points in time for TLB activity (legacy period): (1) the day after winning the second election, (2) the day after congressional midterm elections during their sixth year, and (3) the day after their successor has been named—their final ten weeks in office.

As discussed in chapter 3, I expect US presidents will attempt to fulfill their legacy agenda in foreign affairs. The main independent variable in this study is the legacy period. The dependent variables are the number of presidential decrees issued per week by the president in foreign policy, domestic policy, and environmental policy. Recall that each policy category is exhaustive and mutually exclusive. Table 4.2 in chapter 4 outlines what each category entails.

I compare the foreign policy model to both the domestic and the environmental policy models to look for evidence of terminal logic behavior effects. A number of authors point out that simply analyzing the number of decrees issued by presidents is problematic. Warber (2006, 13) notes that researchers need to distinguish between those decrees that establish major policy and those that "implement routine, bureaucratic matters or . . . accomplish symbolic acts."[2] Similarly, Carey and Shugart (1998, 4) warn that too often researchers lump together "more mundane incarnations of executive decree[s] . . . with 'calling out the tanks,' and as a result, the phenomenon of executive decree as a whole is misinterpreted." The total volume of presidential decrees does not necessarily reflect change in policy direction or expansion of executive power or even the existence of TLB.

Previous literature highlights the importance of differentiating policy type when analyzing presidential behavior, particularly because the audience costs of domestic policy decisions are considered to be much higher than those of foreign policy (see Farnham 2004). The importance of distinguishing between foreign and domestic policy is particularly evident in the Canes-Wrone and Shotts (2004) study of the effect of public opinion on presidential responsiveness in relation to a set of individual issues over time. They find substantial variation across domains. For three domestic issues (crime, health, and social security) the percentage of congruent observations, which are a function of the relationship between the survey data and the president's proposed budgetary authority for a given issue and year, is greater than 90 percent. In contrast, for the two foreign policy issues in their study (foreign aid and defense spending), congruent observations constitute only 32 percent of the observations. These authors speculate that this is due to the fact that "presidents are more likely to take popular positions on the issues that voters are likely to encounter in their daily lives. In comparison, on those matters on which citizens are less likely to be informed or have stable preferences, like foreign policy, presidents are much more willing to be out of step with public opinion" (ibid., 692). It is for this reason that I differentiate decrees according to specific policy domains.

With regard to the frequency of decree issuance, I expect to find the following:

> H_1: *One-term and two-term presidents:* Once presidents become aware of their endpoint (either by losing an election or in serv-

ing out their final term as stipulated by law), a higher level of policy activity occurs (i.e., decree issuance).

Additionally, for two-term presidents I test the following hypotheses:

H_2: *Two-term presidents:* Once presidents become aware of their endpoint (in serving out their final term as stipulated by law) *and the midterm congressional elections of the sixth year are over,* a higher level of policy activity occurs (i.e., decree issuance).
H_3: *Two-term presidents:* Once presidents become aware of their endpoint (in serving out their final term as stipulated by law) *and a successor has been chosen by the electorate,* a higher level of policy activity occurs (i.e., decree issuance).

I include a number of controls in the analysis. Researchers, both in US and comparative politics, argue that presidents in issuing decrees are egregiously usurping power and setting policy. They often point to presidents' lack of legislative support as evidence of such usurpation.[3] Yet when Mayer (2001), in his event count analysis of executive orders, looks at differences in rate issuance of those presidents who faced both a divided and a unified government during their presidency, he finds that, "in contrast to what the conventional wisdom predicted," more executive orders are issued under a unified government than under a divided government.[4] He cites President Clinton's behavior as a prime example. Mayer finds that President Clinton issued nearly 2.5 fewer orders per month after the Republicans took Congress in the 1994 midterm elections—noting that in 1998, following his impeachment trial, President Clinton issued only thirty-eight orders, the fewest in any previous year of his tenure, with the exception of 1997. Additionally, Mayhew (1991) argues that even presidents who face a divided government can make significant legislative gains.[5] For this reason, I include a simple dichotomous measure for *unified government* (1 during periods of each administration when the president's party controls both Houses; 0 otherwise). Following Mayer's results, I expect to find the following:

H_4: If a president's party controls both Houses, the president will issue more decrees, resulting in a higher level of policy activity.

I include a dichotomous measure for beginning-of-term effects when there is a change in presidential party. *First year, party change* is coded 1 if, during the first year of a new administration, party control has changed from that during the previous administration, 0 otherwise. According to Cooper (2002, 61), Reagan was the first to use executive orders "to shape a new administration." For instance, thirty-nine executive orders, mostly issued by Carter, were revoked by the end of 1981. I expect to find the following:

> H_5: If party control has changed with the new administration, presidents will issue more decrees, resulting in a higher level of policy activity.

I include a dichotomous measure concerning policy discontinuity. Since President Reagan is the only president that was succeeded by a member of his own party, this variable is named *final ten weeks-R.* Expectation of policy discontinuity is important as I hypothesize that it intensifies the legacy effect. Knowing one's successor is from the opposition party and likely oriented differently toward policy will create fervor to act, tie up loose ends, and solidify one's presidential mark on policy. Issuing decrees even in the last week or on the last day obligates successors to various courses of action until the successor issues a new decree revoking or replacing the former decree. For this reason, I expect to find the following:

> H_6: If presidents know the president-elect's party is different from their own, they will issue more decrees, resulting in a higher level of policy activity.

To test these hypotheses, I ran six separate event count models—two for each policy domain (foreign affairs, domestic policy, and environmental policy). The paired models for each policy domain test the count level of decrees with respect to different points in presidents' tenure. The paired models vary in only one aspect—the inclusion of President Reagan in the *final ten weeks.* Party turnover occurred in all but one case—when President Reagan was followed by his vice president, George H. W. Bush. Therefore, with the exception of President Reagan, the presidents in this study had a strong expectation of policy discontinuity in their last ten weeks in office. In Models 2, 4, and 6, the variable, *final ten weeks-R,* represents the last ten-week period for all presidents, excluding President Reagan. Conversely, in Models 1, 3, and 5, the variable, *final ten weeks,* represents the last ten-week period for all presidents, including President Reagan.

Since the number of decrees issued each week can take on only nonnegative integer values, an event count model is appropriate. Specifically, I use a negative binomial distribution, the common alternative to the Poisson distribution.[6] The underlying count process of decrees is not independent. Mayer (2001, 92) reminds us that the occurrence of one executive order increases the probability of another occurring in a given time period. Orders, he explains, are "commonly issued in clumps, external events that spur order issuance may well be responsible for multiple orders, and presidents often revise specific orders several times by issuing additional orders." This is also true of memoranda and proclamations.

I exclude decrees that are hortatory in nature. The focus here is on those that affect policy. I also exclude any decree that is related to the restoration of law and order in the United States, such as emergencies caused by natural disasters; shortages of energy or food supply; or domestic violence that involves and is caused by US citizens (see table 5.2).[7] I distinguish between two types of emergency decrees, restoration of law and order decrees and emergency power decrees. Emergency power decrees are issued under the NEA or the IEEPA. Most decrees of this type are issued in response to acts carried out by foreign nations and/or foreign nationals.[8] These are *not* excluded. Declaration of such an emergency allows presidents to take measures against nations and/or persons outside the borders of the United States.[9] The scope of emergency power decrees goes beyond the restoration of law and order in the United States.[10] A decree like Proclamation 6427, "Law and Order in the City and County of Los Angeles, and Other Districts of California," is defined as a restoration of law and order decree because the cause of such disorder is purely domestic.[11]

In sections 5.3 and 5.4 the reason for this distinction becomes clear. There is much dispute over the use of emergency power decrees by presidents, particularly because they allow presidents to direct activities against foreign nations or foreign nationals without congressional oversight. Scholars like Olson and Woll (1999) claim that presidents abuse their emergency powers to legislate and operate outside their constitutional limits. In section 5.4 I explore presidents' use of emergency power decrees and find a systematic pattern of use—indicating that there may be some truth to the allegations of abuse.

Table 5.2. US Decrees excluded from analysis

	Decree Type	Restoration of Law and Order (Domestic)	Hortatory/ Symbolic (Domestic)
Carter	Memorandum	6	13
	Proclamation	3	251
	Order	1	5
	Total	10	269
Reagan	Memorandum	0	18
	Proclamation	2	1,028
	Order	1	0
	Total	3	1046
H. W. Bush	Memorandum	1	6
	Proclamation	2	532
	Order	2	0
	Total	5	538
Clinton	Memorandum	1	13
	Proclamation	3	770
	Order	0	2
	Total	4	785
W. Bush	Memorandum	0	7
	Proclamation	2	851
	Order	0	0
	Total	2	858

Only twenty-four decrees fall into the category of restoration of law and order. These were issued purely as a result of external circumstance. Arguably, all decrees are a result of external circumstances to some degree—dictated by a president's domestic and foreign situations at the time. Yet I argue that the decrees included in the analysis were made with conscious deliberation and the mental construction of events and possible consequences. On the contrary, the excluded decrees were immediate responses to interruptions in domestic order and occurred as natural consequence, not as steps and turns in policy making.

5.2 DATA RESULTS

The results of the event count models appear in tables 5.3, 5.4, and 5.5. For all six models the likelihood ratio test that alpha equals zero (LR test against Poisson) strongly suggests that the negative binomial model is better than the more restrictive Poisson regression model, which requires independence between events. These models include the proper dispersion parameter α to account for the contagion in the order sequence.

Models 1 and 2 represent the foreign policy models; Models 3 and 4, the environmental policy models; and Models 5 and 6, the domestic policy models. Recall that the only difference between the paired models is the variables: *Final ten weeks* represents the last ten-week period for all presidents, while *final ten weeks-R* represents the same period for all presidents, excluding President Reagan. President Reagan is the only president in the analysis whose successor was not from the opposing party. The purpose of the paired models was to see whether his inclusion (or exclusion) makes a marked difference in the results.

First, we should consider a few points concerning the models and the three periods of interest where increased activity is hypothesized to occur (*from reelection day, from sixth-year midterm elections,* and *final ten weeks/final ten weeks-R*). In Models 1 and 2, only one period is significant—the last ten weeks of a presidential tenure, and this period remains significant and in the positive direction for all models except Model 6, which is discussed in more detail later. This indicates that across the board in foreign, environmental, and domestic policy, presidents increased their rate of decree issuance in their final ten weeks as they prepared to leave office. The variable that tests the period from reelection day (loss or win) to end of tenure, on the other hand, is not significant for all six models. Recall that

Table 5.3. **Event count results: dependent variable, foreign policy decrees (1977—2009)**

Foreign Policy Model 1			Foreign Policy Model 2
Final 10 Weeks	0.546***	0.550***	Final 10 Weeks-R
	(0.129)	(0.143)	
first year, party change	−0.254**	−0.255**	first year, party change
	(0.088)	(0.088)	
unified government	0.193**	0.206**	unified government
	(0.080)	(0.080)	
from 6th-year midterm elections	0.112	0.137*	from 6th-year midterm elections
	(0.083)	(0.083)	
from reelection bid (win or lose)	−0.091	−0.091	from reelection bid (win or lose)
	(0.071)	(0.071)	
Carter	−0.010	−0.037	Carter
	(0.120)	(0.121)	
H. W. Bush	0.488***	0.474***	H. W. Bush
	(0.095)	(0.096)	
Clinton	0.511***	0.487***	Clinton
	(0.077)	(0.077)	
W. Bush	0.360***	0.332***	W. Bush
	(0.087)	(0.088)	
constant	−0.016	−0.001	constant
	(0.069)	(0.069)	
chi-square	(9) 103.98	(9) 101.11	chi-square
significance	0.0000	0.0000	significance
log-likelihood	−2600.89	−2602.32	log-likelihood
R-squared	0.020	0.019	R-squared
N	1670	1670	N
LR test against Poisson	chi-squared (1) = 136.89, p < 0.001	chi-squared (1) = 138.12, p < 0.001	LR test against Poisson

* Significant at $p < 0.1$.
** Significant at $p < 0.05$.
*** Significant at $p < 0.000$ (standard errors are in parentheses).

Table 5.4. Event count results: dependent variable, environmental policy decrees (1977—2009)

	Environmental Policy Model 3	Environmental Policy Model 4	
Final 10 Weeks	1.028**	1.033**	Final 10 Weeks-R
	(0.333)	(0.362)	
first year, party change	−0.241	−0.245	first year, party change
	(0.251)	(0.251)	
unified government	0.189	0.219	unified government
	(0.253)	(0.255)	
from 6th-year midterm elections	0.585**	0.634**	from 6th-year midterm elections
	(0.253)	(0.252)	
from reelection bid (win or lose)	−0.286	−0.283	from reelection bid (win or lose)
	(0.232)	(0.232)	
Carter	1.490***	1.415***	Carter
	(0.339)	(0.343)	
H. W. Bush	0.368	0.321	H. W. Bush
	(0.329)	(0.330)	
Clinton	1.123***	1.051***	Clinton
	(0.243)	(0.244)	
W. Bush	0.407	0.329	W. Bush
	(0.288)	(0.289)	
constant	−2.614***	−2.568***	constant
	(0.230)	(0.230)	
chi-square	(9) 76.76	(9) 75.53	chi-square
significance	0.0000	0.0000	significance
log-likelihood	−766.64	−767.25	log-likelihood
R-squared	0.048	0.047	R-squared
N	1670	1670	N
LR test against Poisson	chi-squared (1) = 169.52, p < 0.001	chi-squared (1) = 169.84, p < 0.001	LR test against Poisson

* Significant at $p < 0.1$.
** Significant at $p < 0.05$.
*** Significant at $p < 0.000$ (standard errors are in parentheses)

Table 5.5. Event count results: dependent variable, domestic policy decrees (1977—2009)

Domestic Policy Model 5		Domestic Policy Model 6	
Final 10 Weeks	0.530** (0.217)	0.329 (0.255)	Final 10 Weeks-R
first year, party change	−0.381** (0.148)	−0.380** (0.148)	first year, party change
unified government	−0.081 (0.150)	−0.072 (0.151)	unified government
from 6th-year midterm elections	−0.009 (0.140)	0.024 (0.139)	from 6th-year midterm elections
from reelection bid (win or lose)	−0.155 (0.121)	−0.130 (0.122)	from reelection bid (win or lose)
Carter	0.565** (0.192)	0.566** (0.195)	Carter
H. W. Bush	−0.631** (0.182)	−0.620** (0.184)	H. W. Bush
Clinton	0.309** (0.120)	0.291** (0.120)	Clinton
W. Bush	−0.370** (0.158)	−0.390** (0.159)	W. Bush
constant	−0.799*** (0.105)	−0.798*** (0.105)	constant
chi-square	(9) 80.76	(9) 76.68	chi-square
significance	0.0000	0.0000	significance
log-likelihood	−1399.67	−1401.71	log-likelihood
R-squared	0.028	0.027	R-squared
N	1670	1670	N
LR test against Poisson	chi-squared (1) = 50.50, $p < 0.001$	chi-squared (1) = 51.56, $p < 0.001$	LR test against Poisson

* Significant at $p < 0.1$.
** Significant at $p < 0.05$.
*** Significant at $p < 0.000$ (standard errors are in parentheses).

this variable constitutes the final ten week period of one-term presidents (loss of reelection) like the previous variable, which is significant, but also includes the entire second term of two-term presidents.[12] From this we can deduce that no systematic rate of increase in decree issuance is detected during the second term in any of the three policy areas. The variable testing the third period of interest, the time following the sixth-year midterm elections to the end of tenure, is significant only in the environmental policy models (Models 3 and 4).

Looking at Model 1, we see that presidents issue decrees at a rate 0.546 higher in foreign policy during their last ten weeks. (The coefficient is slightly higher when Reagan is excluded in Model 2.) What does this increased rate of issuance actually mean or equate to in real numbers? There are 2,318 counts of total foreign policy decrees over the 1,670-week period (1977–2009), which equals an average of 1.388 foreign policy decrees per week; setting θ to this value (1.388 × 0.546) produces estimates of 0.758 more foreign policy decrees per week, or 3 more each month. Similarly, there are 297 counts of environmental policy decrees over a 1,670-week period, which equals 0.711 decrees per month; setting θ to the value in Model 3 (0.711 × 1.028) produces estimates of 0.7 more environmental policy decrees per month. There are 702 counts of total domestic policy decrees over the 1,670-week period, which equals 1.681 decrees per month; setting θ to the value in Model 5 (1.681 × 0.530) produces estimates of 0.9 more domestic policy decrees per month. These increased counts may seem negligible, but remember that decrees are generally issued in clumps—raising expectations that issuance may actually be at a much higher rate for specific presidents. Note that the increased rate of issuance in the *final ten weeks* of environmental policy decrees is quite high (1.028) in comparison to the rates of foreign (0.546) and domestic (0.530) policy decree issuance.

Next I take a closer look at the models with regard to each policy area and evaluate the effects of the other independent variables on decree issuance. The results for the *first-year party change* variable are unexpected. Here, as in all six models, the coefficient is negative. This variable is statistically significant in both the foreign policy and the domestic policy models, suggesting that presidents actually issue *fewer* decrees in these policy areas when they assume office and succeed a president of the opposition party. It is true that presidents usually issue a slew of executive orders revoking or modifying executive orders of the previous president. This result may be due to how orders that deal specifically with the revocation of previous orders are coded. For instance, on February 25, 1993, Clinton issued Executive Order 12836—Revocation of Certain Executive Orders concerning Federal Contracting. This order revoked two orders of H. W. Bush issued in April and October of the previous year. This order, however, is counted only once. Also, this result is not necessarily contrary to previous findings. Earlier studies, like that of Mayer (2001), test the issuance of total executive orders. It may be that presidents issue far more administration decrees in that first year than decrees in foreign and domestic policy. Clearly, this result requires further exploration.

Unified government is significant only in the foreign policy models, and, as expected, when the president's party controls both houses, this results in a higher issuance rate of foreign policy decrees. Although the increase is small, this further confirms the unexpected finding of Mayer's 2001 analysis of executive orders—that unified government may actually increase presidents' use of decrees. *Unified government* is not significant in either the environmental or domestic policy models, but in the domestic policy models the coefficients are negative, indicating that divided government may actually increase the rate of issuance in domestic policy.

These six models also show that presidents issue decrees at significantly different rates in different policy domains (see tables 5.3, 5.4, 5.5). Reagan is the omitted variable, so all of the presidents are oriented relative to his administration. Unsurprisingly, looking at Model 3, for both Democrats Carter and Clinton, the rates of environmental policy decree issuance are greater compared to their Republican counterparts—Carter (1.490) and Clinton (1.123) relative to H. W. Bush (0.368) and W. Bush (0.407). In Model 5, the rates of domestic policy decree issuance for Republicans, H. W. Bush (−0.631) and W. Bush (−0.370), are large and in the expected negative direction, as opposed to Carter (0.565) and Clinton (0.309). Here all presidents are statistically significant, showing that Democratic presidents are likely to issue more decrees in domestic policy than Republicans. In foreign policy, on the other hand, this differentiation cannot be made. In Model 1, the coefficients for Carter (−0.010), H. W. Bush (0.488), Clinton (0.511), and W. Bush (0.360) are large, and all are statistically significant except for Carter. Party difference in the rate of foreign policy decree issuance (relative to Reagan) is small, with the two Republicans issuing at a slightly higher rate.

As it turns out, for the most part only small differences exist between the paired models. Signs indicating positive or negative effects are in the same direction, and variables maintain the same significance levels—with one notable exception. In domestic policy, when President Reagan's final ten weeks are included, that time period becomes significant at the 0.05 level, showing some indication that President Reagan, even though he was to be replaced by a fellow Republican with whom he ran his administration, issued domestic policy decrees at a higher rate in those last ten weeks relative to the rest of his time in tenure. In the cases of foreign and environmental policy *final ten weeks-R,* however, the coefficient is slightly larger, consistent with evidence that the expectation of policy discontinuity has a strong effect.

In this section evidence is found that TLB is indeed in play—and not just among decrees that concern foreign policy. In the next section I continue to examine the hypothesized effects of terminal logic thinking on presidential behavior. I carry this examination to perhaps one of the most unexpected places—presidents' use of national emergency powers.

5.3 EMERGENCY POWER DECREES: AFTER THE 1976 NATIONAL EMERGENCIES ACT

The National Emergencies Act details the formal procedures presidents must use in invoking authority in times of national emergencies.[13] Prior to the NEA, the country was technically in four presidentially declared states of national emergency. According to the Special Senate Committee on the Termination of the National Emergency, which convened in 1973, these states of national emergencies, despite being obsolete, were still technically in effect. In March 1933, when the markets began crashing, President Roosevelt issued Proclamation 2039, which declared the existence of a national emergency and proclaimed a bank holiday. In December 1950, President Truman issued Proclamation 2914, proclaiming a national emergency during the Korean conflict. President Nixon declared two states of national emergency. The first came on March 23, 1970, in response to the US postal strike. No formal proclamation or executive order was issued to declare this national emergency. Instead, in public remarks, President Nixon stated the following:

> I directed the Attorney General to take whatever action he believes necessary to see that these court orders are obeyed and, working with local authorities, to see that no illegal picket lines interfere with workers returning to work.

> Secondly, I have just now directed the activation of the men of the various military organizations to begin in New York City the restoration of essential mail services. New York City is where the current illegal stoppages began; it is where the mail has been halted the longest; and it is where the resultant problems have become most acute. If the Postmaster General deems it necessary to act in other affected major cities, I will not hesitate to act . . . [14]

President Nixon declared his second national emergency in August of 1971. In Executive Order 11615, he explains that "in order to stabilize the economy, reduce inflation, and minimize unemployment, it is necessary to stabilize prices, rents, wages, and salaries . . ." These four proclaimed national emergencies activated 470 provisions of federal law, and since these emergencies had no specified termination date, subsequent presidents retained the extraordinary powers delegated to them under those provisions even though the emergency had long since passed.[15] The report of the Special Senate Committee explains that these 470 statutes "delegate to the President extraordinary powers, ordinarily exercised by the Congress, which affect the lives of American citizens in a host of all-encompassing manner." The report adds, "this vast range of powers, taken together, confer enough authority to rule the country without reference to normal constitutional processes."[16]

Emergencies can also be declared under the IEEPA. This act, passed by Congress in 1977, authorizes the president "to regulate the nation's international and domestic finance during periods of declared war or national emergency" (Relyea 2001, 17). It was an attempt to curb presidential powers conferred under the Trading with the Enemy Act, which gave presidents broad power in regulating US finances in times of declared war. Presidents seeking authority under the IEEPA must meet the provisions mandated by the NEA.

Since the passing of the NEA in 1976 and the IEEPA in 1977, presidents have issued more and more decrees, dictating action pursuant to these acts (see figure 5.1). Scholars like Olson and Woll (1999, 19) have called attention to the "explosive growth in the number of declared national emergencies." The black line in figure 5.1 is of particular interest. From 1977 to 2008 it traces the total count by year of decrees declaring national emergencies and initiating action pursuant to those declarations *and* presidentially issued continuances of national emergen-

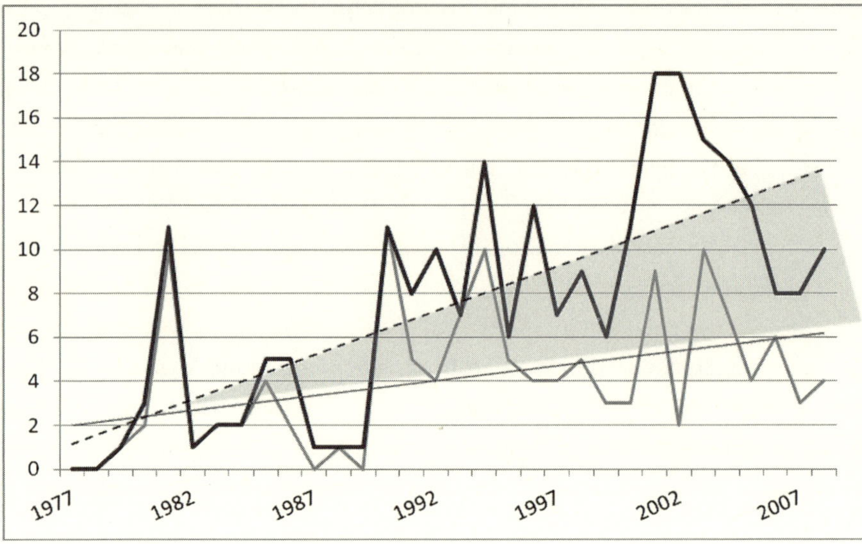

Counts of EOs, Proclamations, Memoranda, and *Notices* issued pursuant to NEA or IEEPA

Counts of EOs, Proclamations, Memoranda issued pursuant to NEA or IEEPA

Linear Trend of Black Line

Linear Trend of Gray Line

Figure 5.1. *Counts of executive orders, presidential proclamations, presidential memoranda, and notices issued pursuant to the NEA or the IEEPA (1977–2009).*

cies. Examining only instances in which presidents initiate emergencies and action pursuant to doing so (the gray line) tells only half the story. Presidents issue emergency continuances in the form of notices to extend their authority and control of the action, particularly that of action abroad.

The dotted trend line in figure 5.1 includes counts of notices of emergency continuances. Although not a perfect measure, the trend line's inclusion of notices uncovers the hidden dimension of duration in presidents' use of emergency powers over time. For instance, following the gray line, we see that the year of the September 11 terrorist attacks saw a spike in decrees issued pursuant to the NEA or the IEEPA—a total of nine (eight executive orders and one proclamation). Then, in 2002 it appears that President Bush decreased action under the

NEA and IEEPA—issuing only two decrees. Yet as the black line shows, he issued sixteen notices for emergency continuances, up from nine the previous year. So although the gray line shows only a slight increase in the use of emergency powers over time, the black line tells quite a different story. In the case of emergency powers, decree use has increased in the past thirty years. Perhaps this is because modern-day circumstances call on presidents to increase their invocation of emergency powers. Laura Blumenfeld of the *Washington Post* writes, "With two wars, multiple crises abroad and the threat of growing terrorism activity at home, these national security officials do not sleep in peace." Current Secretary of Defense Robert Gates protests that times are tougher and threats to US citizens are worse than they were thirty years ago. Gates tells Blumenfeld: "The actual physical threat to Americans today from abroad, in reality, is worse than it was during the Cold War. All you have to do is look at these repeated attempts to set off bombs in populated places."[17] This may be true. In the next section, however, I find evidence of TLB in presidents' use of emergency powers. Using an event count model, I find that, in their last seventy-five days, presidents invoke their emergency powers at a substantially greater rate than earlier in their tenure.

5.4 EMERGENCY POWERS AND TERMINAL LOGIC BEHAVIOR

One would not expect to find electoral trends or evidence of TLB in presidents' use of national emergency powers. The immediacy inherent in crises, which "are perceived to threaten life or well-being beyond tolerable limits," frustrates expectations of patterns associated with the cyclical model of time in tenure.[18] This is true if one assumes consistent presidential restraint in the face of great and awesome power such as that afforded to presidents in times of emergency. After all, an emergency declaration gives presidents the power

> to seize property; organize and control the means of production; seize commodities; assign military forces abroad; institute martial law; seize and control all transportation and communication; regulate the operation of private enterprise; restrict travel; and, in a plethora of particular ways, control the lives of all American citizens.[19]

For instance, recent presidents have taken advantage of a national emergency declaration by using them to prevent US residents from giving aid to groups of which they disapprove (Olson and Woll 1999, 19). Olson and Woll cite the following examples:

> [President Clinton] has declared a national emergency (annually renewed) with regard to UNITA (anticommunist participants in the Angolan civil war, who had received support during the Reagan administration,[20] certain residents of Bosnia-Herzegovina,[21] certain groups identified as Middle Eastern terrorists,[22] Colombian drug traffickers,[23] certain Cubans,[24] certain Burmese,[25] and certain Sudanese[26] . . . Previously, President Bush had followed the same path in order to ban aid to certain Iraqis,[27] Haitians,[28] and Yugoslavians.[29]

I ran another event count model using a negative binomial distribution testing the same hypotheses cited in section 5.1. The main independent variables are the same as those in the models described in the previous section, which constitute the three periods of interest where increased activity was hypothesized to occur (*from reelection day*, *from sixth-year midterm elections*, and *final ten weeks/final ten weeks-R*). Again I tested the effects of *first-year party change* and *unified government* and used dummy variables for individual presidents. The dependent variable was the number of presidential decrees issued by the president that invoked either the NEA of 1976 or the IEEPA of 1977 as warrants for their authority. The unit of analysis was presidential week. The results of the event count models appear in table 5.6. For these models the likelihood ratio test that alpha equals zero (LR test against Poisson) strongly suggests that the negative binomial model is better than the more restrictive Poisson regression model, which requires independence between events. These models, like the previous six, include the proper dispersion parameter α to account for the contagion in the order sequence.

Presidents issue decrees at a rate 1.287 higher in emergency powers in the last ten weeks of their tenure. This means that presidents issue such decrees at nearly a 130 percent higher rate than in their prior period of tenure. This is a surprising and unexpected result. There are only 238 counts of emergency power

Table 5.6. **Event count results: dependent variable, emergency power decrees (Orders, Memoranda, Proclamations, and Notices), 1977—2009**

Emergency Power Decrees Model 7		Emergency Power Decrees Model 8	
Final 10 Weeks	1.287***	1.383***	Final 10 Weeks-R
	(0.320)	(0.327)	
first year, party change	−0.220	−0.224	first year, party change
	(0.249)	(0.249)	
unified government	−0.394 **	−0.379*	unified government
	(0.194)	(0.195)	
from 6th-year midterm elections	−0.587**	−0.567**	from 6th-year midterm elections
	(0.239)	(0.240)	
from reelection bid (win or lose)	−0.094	−0.109	from reelection bid (win or lose)
	(0.185)	(0.185)	
Carter	0.373	0.297	Carter
	(0.414)	(0.420)	
H. W. Bush	0.931**	0.879**	H. W. Bush
	(0.316)	(0.318)	
Clinton	1.460 ***	1.414 ***	Clinton
	(0.269)	(0.271)	
W. Bush	1.901***	1.850***	W. Bush
	(0.280)	(0.282)	
constant	−2.938***	−2.895***	constant
	(0.252)	(0.252)	
chi-square	(9) 88.72	(9) 90.32	chi-square
significance	0.0000	0.0000	significance
log-likelihood	−672.820	−672.021	log-likelihood
R-squared	0.062	0.063	R-squared
N	1670	1670	N
LR test against Poisson	chi-squared (1) = 19.09, p < 0.001	chi-squared (1) = 19.21, p < 0.001	LR test against Poisson

* Significant at p < 0.1.
** Significant at p < 0.05.
*** Significant at p < 0.000 (standard errors are in parentheses).

decrees over a 1,670 week period (1977–2009) in this study. This equals an average of 0.7 emergency power decrees per month; setting θ to this value (0.7 x 1.287) produces estimates of 0.9 more emergency power decrees per month. This count may seem negligible with presidents issuing on average two to three more decrees in their final ten weeks. Yet one decree initiating or continuing a state of national emergency greatly expands the breadth and depth of presidential power. These decrees grant presidents great unilateral discretion in action abroad and at home to do as they wish. As noted earlier, moreover, decrees are generally issued in clumps—raising expectations that issuance may actually be at a much higher rate for specific presidents. Under the NEA/IEEPA President Carter issued ten executive orders on his last day in office (Iranian hostage crisis), and President Clinton issued four notices and one executive order in his last ten weeks.

Like the previous six models, the variable testing the period from reelection day (loss or win) to end of tenure is not significant, and the coefficient estimates are rather small in the negative direction. Curiously, the variable that tests the third period of interest, the time following the sixth-year midterm elections to end of tenure is significant but in the negative direction, running contrary to hypothesis 2. Furthermore, the coefficient estimates are rather high for both Models 7 and 8.

First-year party change is not significant. *Unified government,* however, is significant, and the coefficient estimates are negative, indicating that divided government may actually increase the rate of issuance in emergency power decrees. As for the individual presidents, President Reagan is the omitted variable, so all of the presidents are oriented relative to his administration. Coefficient estimates show that over time, for each successive president, the rate of issuance increases, as shown in figure 5.1.

One would hope *not* to find electoral trends or evidence of TLB in presidents' use of national emergency powers, which are meant to be reserved for times of inherent crisis. Yet the evidence provided in this section shows that a systematic pattern of use indeed exists for decrees of this nature. Even more surprising is that the rate of increase in emergency power decrees is substantial over a rather compressed period and occurs during a rather provisional period in presidential tenure. Again, more research and further exploration of the conditions by which presidents issue emergency power decrees need to be done.

5.5 CONCLUSION

All presidents close out their tenure in the unique circumstance of their time—in different contexts and facing dissimilar sets of contingencies. Presidents come from different backgrounds, subscribe to diverse concepts of leadership and ideology, and exercise a variety of executive styles. Moreover, they devote more time and resources to some policy areas and less to others. Nonetheless, this study provides evidence that presidents, with respect to specific policy domains, increase or decrease their involvement depending not only on political context (unified government) but also on whether they understand themselves to be terminal. Using increased decree issuance as a proxy for TLB, the models show that TLB indeed exists, when TLB is most likely to begin, and the relative degree of its effect. Moreover, the results of the models reveal the importance of differentiating between policy types when analyzing presidential behavior. Such differentiation allows us to test the effects of TLB on decrees that have similar characteristics—either in policy outcomes or in the source of authority that allowed for their issuance in the first place. When isolating decrees issued exclusively under the NEA and the IEEPA, for instance, a systematic pattern of use becomes clear (Models 7 and 8).

I find that TLB has its strongest effect on presidents who are in the final weeks of their term, particularly when their successor has been named *and* that successor is from the opposing party. This supports expectations and prior empirical analyses. Both Cochran (2001) and de Rugy and Davies (2009), using *Federal Register* page counts, find that presidential activity soars during transitions, particularly when party changeover is to occur.[30] Mayer (2001) finds that presidents (1939–1999) issue twice as many executive orders in their final weeks when the outgoing presidents know their successor is from the opposing party.[31] Higher rates of issuance are found even among "significant" executive orders in those final weeks when it is known that the successor is from the opposing party (Mayer and Price 2002).[32] The analysis here includes only one president, President Reagan, who did not face a successor from the opposing party. When Reagan is excluded from the foreign, environmental, and emergency power models, the rate of issuance in those last ten weeks increases slightly—confirming prior findings. During these final weeks, one's end of tenure is most clearly felt, and as a result presidents react. The increased contact, involvement, and press of presidents-elect bent on changing the way things are done in Washington all motivate outgoing presidents to fight in those last days and secure *their* policies and *their* initiatives. Their mark in history depends on it.

One wonders whether this pattern of increased decree issuance may be more severe if a broader universe of presidential action were included in the analysis. Arguably public, unclassified data like those used in this analysis are representative of more "scrubbed"—cleaner—less contentious presidential initiatives than those that we might find behind classified walls. This is not to say that many of these last-minute decrees, although unclassified and public, are *not* egregious examples of presidents' unilateral power to dismiss, protect, prohibit, and allow whatever they see fit—outside of the Founders' instituted checks and balances.[33] This study calls attention to presidents' use of memoranda, executive orders, and proclamations in conjunction with each other and the importance of accounting for all three in presidential studies of direct action. Accounting for only executive orders likely skews analysis. Jack Beerman (2003, 996), in his analysis of presidents Bill Clinton and George W. Bush's midnight regulations, writes: "Although it would seem that executive orders can be a useful instrument for an administration in assuming the reins of power, they do not appear to be widely used in that way . . . Interestingly, the executive order does not appear to be a major instrument for midnight regulation or presidential consolidation of power over the executive branch." Beerman's analysis is incomplete. Executive orders evaluated in isolation from memoranda and proclamations tell only half the tale.

Without doubt, the power of presidents to make decisions unilaterally without consulting Congress is seen most vividly in their issuance of last-minute decrees. Last-minute decrees tie successors, often unwillingly, to domestic and international commitments. For instance, President Carter committed the United States to international agreements known as the Algiers Accords.[34] In exchange for Iran's freeing of American hostages, the United States was to unfreeze $7.9 billion of Iranian assets, grant Iran immunity from US lawsuits, and pledge that "it is and from now on will be the policy of the United States not to intervene, directly or indirectly, politically or militarily, in Iran's internal affairs."[35] An external tribunal, the Iran–United States Claims Tribunal, was put in place to resolve disputes between the two countries. President Carter committed the United States to international law on his very last day in office, and this made for a treacherous legal situation for President Reagan if he denied these obligations. In December of 1992, President George H. W. Bush sent twenty-five thousand troops to Somalia on a humanitarian mission, and although he assured US citizens the troops would be out before Clinton took office, they were not (Johnson 2008). In fact, US forces were not removed in entirety until March of 1994.[36] In late December of 2000, just twenty days shy of leaving office, President Clinton made the United States a signatory to the Treaty of Rome and in effect the International Criminal Court (ICC). Although in May of 2002, under President George W. Bush, the United States "unsign[ed] the treaty and renounced all obligations as a signatory," Howell and Mayer (2005, 544) argue that "the move did (and continues to) complicate foreign policy, requiring the Bush administration to expend political capital that it might otherwise have been able to devote to other purposes."

The importance of policy continuity to presidents' conception of legacy cannot be overstated. Yet it is important to remember that it may not be the only driving force behind TLB. Take President Clinton's case, for instance. In an extraordinary event the outcome of the 2000 presidential election was unclear, and the winner was not formally declared until a month after the election took place. In that month President Clinton was not sure who his successor would be—his vice president, Al Gore, or his rival, George W. Bush. This circumstance, however, did not stop Clinton's flurry of presidential activity. Also, it is worth mentioning that in President Reagan's case, there was some debate over his health and when exactly Alzheimer's disease began to affect his mental capacity. Former CBS White House correspondent Lesley Stahl, after an interview with President Reagan, claimed that "a vacant Reagan barely seemed to realize anyone else was in the room." She recalled, moreover, that before he "reemerged into alertness . . . 'I had come *that* close to reporting that Reagan was senile'" (Rouse 2006).[37] Most recently the son of President Reagan, Ron Reagan, suggested in his memoir, *My Father at 100,* that his father did indeed suffer from the beginning stages of Alzheimer's disease while still in office. The *Washington Post* reports as follows:

> The younger Reagan recalls how his father became uncharacteristically lost for words and looked "lost and bewildered" during the 1984 presidential debates with Democratic rival Walter Mondale. He says his father may have suspected the onset of Alzheimer's in 1986 when he was flying over familiar canyons

> north of Los Angeles and became alarmed that he could no longer remember their names.[38]

If true (his doctors, colleagues, and eldest son deny this), the effect of TLB particularly in those final weeks may not have followed normal patterns.

Although these findings imply that the two-term executive structure instigates disruption in policy continuity by motivating presidents to sharp aggressiveness at the end of their term, this is far from conclusive. Perhaps by tracking one president's efforts on specific issues (e.g., foreign aid) or in specific regions (e.g., Middle East), more on this effect will come to light. Also, quite telling might be an analysis of how often such decrees are amended, modified, suspended, or revoked. Do presidents live up to the obligations placed on them by outgoing presidents' executive orders, proclamations, memoranda, appointments, and the like? From this, interesting questions arise. When and why would a president choose not to live up to those obligations? When would such efforts become too costly—at home or internationally? Also, I use event count analysis to test the data. This allows for easy comparison to prior research that also used this form of analysis. Other empirical tests may bring new insights and draw us to different data sources.

The models here show clear, consistent patterns of terminal logic behavior in presidents' issuance of decrees. Presidents experience a sort of pure cognitive clarity that discounts, even disregards, the game of politics—the partisanship, the honed relationships, the horse-trading tactics that all go with the game of statecraft. It is then that presidents turn toward their vision of legacy and issue foreign, domestic, and environmental decrees—even emergency power decrees at increased rates.

In chapters 6 and 7 I take my examination of terminal logic a step further—to contexts outside the United States. I explore the use of decree power by Brazilian and Argentinean presidents, probing further the assumptions and conclusions drawn here concerning the use of decrees by US presidents.

CHAPTER 6

Decree Power in Argentina and Brazil

6.1 INTRODUCTION

In chapter 4, I briefly discussed the link between proactive power and presidential initiative and the reasons that such powers, specifically decrees, make for valid data in determining the existence of TLB. Recall that proactive presidential powers are associated with change in the status quo, specifically change that Congress would not have brought about on its own. Although presidents may possess a number of tools that allow them to exercise proactive power, I focus on their issuance of decrees because it is the most visible form of presidential choice.

Determining whether TLB exists in other countries necessarily suggests that the presidency as an institution is not completely unique—in all its facets—to one country, one time, or one place. The assumption is that common traits exist among presidents by virtue of the fact that they are all limited to serving a fixed term or set of terms. I hypothesize that terminal logic thinking affects the behavior of presidents even though they may operate in different contexts. Constitutional rules, party discipline, the number of parties, and even the level of centralization may differ, but as long as presidents may serve for only a predetermined period, TLB can be expected to exist. As Hart (1998, 396) points out, "the comparative perspectives open up possibilities for research on the big picture questions about the American presidency." Exploring the use of decree power by presidents of other countries allows us to probe further the assumptions and conclusions we draw concerning the use of decrees by US presidents. Comparative analysis allows for the development of a more nuanced understanding of the various institutions that drive the policy process.

The political institutions of Argentina, Brazil, and the United States have similar characteristics: in their division of powers between the executive, legislative, and judicial branches of government; in their electoral system; and in their institutional capacities. Both Argentina and Brazil have been heavily influenced by the model of the United States and have developed "somewhat less centralized regimes" (Watts 2008, 25–27). Like the United States, in Argentina and Brazil "there have often been historical and economic regional differences among the constituent units [states/provinces], but *not* the depth of distinctiveness engendered by ethnicity, language or religion" (ibid.; emphasis added). See table 6.1 for more common characteristics shared by these federal political systems.

The number of historical parallels between Argentina and Brazil on the one hand and the United States on the other is striking. From the 1860s to the 1920s Argentina was perhaps the most like the United States in its early era. Romero (1963, xiii) declares that "ethnically and ecologically Argentina in this era was astonishingly similar to the US." Just as the United States had the "Wild West," Argentina, too, had a large expanse of space, a rugged wilderness that made it difficult to unify the country. Hundreds of thousands of immigrants flooded Argentina and actually numbered more proportionately than in the United States during this same era. Argentines fought a civil war at the same time as the United States and did so for a similar reason: "the growing domination of one region of the country over another (ibid., xii). The attack on Fort Sumter occurred just five months before the decisive Argentine civil war battle at Pavón. An end to civil war made it possible for Argentina to organize an effective national government and to seed the foundation it needed for economic development, which was patterned on Europe and the United States. Argentina maintained the same constitution from 1853 to 1920 and made both political and economic advances ahead of other Latin American countries. Romero (ibid., xiv) comments that "from these pinnacles of progress in the 1920s, Argentina and the United States could look back on their matching evolution: the austere colonial eras, the wars for independence, the establishment of constitutional order, the years of pioneering, the Indian fighting, the growth of the big cities, the conquest of foreign markets."

Table 6.1. Characteristics of the federal political systems under review

Country	Current Constituent Units	Year Originally Founded as Federation[1]	Current Constitution	Type of Federation[2]	Federal Executive-Legislature Relationship	Head of Government/ Head of State	Legislature	Political Party System
United States	50 states + 1 federal district + 2 federacies + 3 associated states + 3 local home-rule territories + 3 unincorporated territories + 130 Native American domestic dependent nations	1789	1789	mature	separated: president-Congress	directly elected president/ president	bicameral[3]	two-party
Argentine Republic	23 provinces + 1 federal district + 6 regions	1853	1994	emergent	separated: president-Congress	directly elected president/ president	bicameral[3]	multiparty
Brazil, Federative Republic of	26 states + 1 federal capital district	1891	1988	emergent	separated: president-Congress	directly elected president/ president	bicameral[3]	multiparty
Mexico (United Mexican States)	31 states + 1 federal district	1824	1917	emergent	separated: president-Congress	directly elected president/ president	bicameral[3]	single party (up to 2000)

Source: Watts (2008).

1. Federations are defined as "compound polities, combining strong constituent units and a strong general government, each possessing powers delegated to it by the people through a constitution, and each empowered to deal directly with the citizens in the exercise of its legislative, administrative and taxing powers, and each with major institutions directly elected by the citizens" (Watts 2008, 10).

2. A mature federation is one that has functioned continuously as a federation for more than a century. Argentina, Brazil, and Mexico are all classified as emergent federations because, even though their history with federal institutions spans more than a century, they have experienced "either lengthy periods of military and autocratic rule or of one-party dominance" (Watts 2008, 25).

3. Both houses of the federal legislature have directly elected members, but different electoral rules or terms apply to the two houses (Watts 2008, 145).

Argentina, Brazil, and the United States all began as colonies, and when independence was won, they all began anew—as disjointed confederations of states. The wars of independence—Argentina in 1810 and Brazil in 1822—like that of the United States were influenced by eighteenth-century Enlightenment and its theories of natural law and utilitarianism. The newly independent nations were plagued by regionalism's politics, and an effective national government became possible only after much blood was spilled. Yet when compared to the United States, democracy in Argentina and Brazil has been short lived, punctured by long bouts of authoritarianism. A common observation is that many Latin American countries were not prepared for the foreign liberal constitutional models. Lane (1996, 67) notes that the copied constitutions often led to military governments either by presidential action or a coup d'état.[1] During a Senate discussion more than twenty years after Brazil's constitution, based on the US model, was adopted, Ruy Barbosa, one of the crafters of that constitution, explained as follows:

> When we adopted the American form of government and endeavored to adapt its delicate and complex mechanism to our political customs, it became evident that our training, especially among the generation who first constituted the Republic, was as yet imperfect in its understanding of American organization, politics, and jurisprudence." (Turner 1945, 112, citing Barbosa, Discurso na Senado, January 20, 1915)

It is important to highlight the long struggle that Brazil and Argentina have undergone in trying to consolidate democracy under a presidential system of governance. Both of their most recent constitutions emerged during or immediately following periods of economic crisis. In the 1990s Brazil followed Argentina's lead in addressing economic crisis with reforms based on neoliberal, market-based policies (as opposed to the state-led, import-substitution-industrialization models of economic development). Economic crisis, moreover, sparked their presidents' use of decrees.

Whereas the United States represents a mature industrialized nation with established formal market structures, Argentina and Brazil represent emerging market nations for the periods under review—from 1989 to 1999 for Argentina and from 1995 to 2010 for Brazil. Martínez and Santiso (2003, 365) define "emerging market" as "an economy whose political outcomes and uncertainties (such as a presidential election or a cabinet reshuffle) tend to have high impacts on financial variables and therefore on stock markets." In these countries weak economic fundamentals and political-institutional instability create a situation in which politics and economics are intimately linked.[2] Undoubtedly, presidents of emerging market economies face similar obstacles. The size of their economies is substantial, but so is the size of their debt. In fact, in the 1980s Argentina and Brazil were two of the largest debtor societies in the world (Kaufman 1985). Presidents of Argentina and Brazil find themselves walking the same dangerous tightrope. They must deal with the demands of both international creditors and their own citizenry—and oftentimes the demands of the two are at odds.[3] On the one hand, presidents must satisfy the requirements of international creditors, such as demands for stabilization measures, so that their country can have access to international financial markets. On the other hand, due to a fundamental collective action problem, presidents can expect great resistance from groups within the populace to those stabilization measures (devaluations, wage and credit restrictions, and fiscal deficit reductions) needed to satisfy creditors (ibid.).[4]

This makes for a politically dangerous situation for presidents. For one, labor organizations have acquired an extensive political presence in both Brazil and Argentina. Furthermore, labor (as opposed to businesses) bears a disproportionate share of the short-term risk and "must attach a significantly greater discount for long-term benefits" (Kaufman 1985). To be sure, the internal political and economic conditions cannot be separated from the management of economic policies at the international level.[5] Discounting external factors and succumbing to domestic demands can cause great harm to the long-term health of the national economy.

Both Argentina and Brazil are presidential democracies that run under federal systems with similar executive term structures. Given their similar political frame set amid like economic conditions, they are ideal cases for comparative analysis. Most important, their similarities in effect act as a control by allowing us to look closely at some of their key differences—differences that have been found in previous research to affect presidents' use of proactive power. In this chapter, I address the country specifics of Argentina and Brazil with regard to the party system, the legislative process, and the role of the courts, which pattern interaction between the branches of government and in turn influence presidential choice in the use of decrees. I review recent constitutional changes in the executive term structure and in the decree power of Brazilian and Argentinean presidents, addressing the legal provisions of decrees as defined by their constitutions, congressional laws, and the cases adjudicated in their nations' courts. This gives us a framework for the subsequent analysis of TLB (chapter 7).

6.2 TERM LIMITS AND DECREE POWER

Table 6.2 shows the executive term structure for presidential republics in Latin America. A cursory look reveals that the executive's term ranges from four to six years, and most countries maintain limits on reelection. Furthermore, reelection can be prohibited altogether, prohibited until a specified number of years (i.e., an interim term) has passed, or prohibited after a president has served a specified number of terms.

A few comments are in order regarding table 6.2. First and foremost, its scope is limited. The precise rules of reelection are not necessarily evident from the information provided there. For instance, the 1993 Constitution of Peru held that the president could be elected to two consecutive terms and could serve another term once an interim term had passed following the first two consecutive terms. Table 6.2 does not clearly describe this exact structure. Moreover, it is important to note that the text of a constitution can be unclear as to whether reelection is allowed and, if so, under what circumstances another term may be permitted. This may be because the term structure can be amended by a law passed by Congress rather than by an amendment to the constitution. This was done, for example, in Peru in November of 2000. Law no. 27365 prohibited the immediate reelection of the president, and this provision was not officially adopted into the constitution until 2005. Second, recall that constitutional reform of the executive's term in Latin America is frequent—changing sometimes as often as a new president comes into office. Table 6.2 is merely meant to show term length and the range of limits placed on presidents' ability to be reelected in Latin America.

Although the current Argentine and Brazilian constitutions allow their presidents to serve two consecutive four-year terms as in the United States, this term structure is rather new for both countries. Table 6.3 shows the changing nature of the executive term structure for Brazil, Argentina, and the United States. It was not until the mid-1990s that Argentina traded its nonrenewable six-year presidential term for a renewable, four-year one. According to the 1994 constitutional amendment, presidents may serve two consecutive terms and may seek reelection to a third term once an interim term has passed.

Section 90 states the following:

> The President and Vice-President shall hold their offices for the term of four years; and they may be reelected or may succeed each other for only one consecutive term. If they have been reelected or they have succeeded each other, they cannot be elected for either of these two positions but with the interval of one term.

The nonrenewable six-year term dates back to the Argentinean Constitution of 1853. This changed in 1994. A year earlier, President Carlos Menem and former president Raúl R. Alfonsin, serving as the president of the National Committee of the Radical Civil Union, made an agreement known as the Olivos Pact, based on "a set of mutual concessions" (Sagüës 1996, 44). This led to the constitutional reform of 1994.[6] In exchange for allowing Menem to run for reelection and making past decrees lawful, the executive term would be shortened to four years, and a number of constitutional changes would curtail presidential influence over the other branches of government.[7] I discuss this in more depth later in this section.

As noted earlier, Brazilian presidents are currently allowed to serve two consecutive four-year terms. Brazilian president Fernando Henrique Cardoso won a constitutional amendment on June 4, 1997, allowing him to run for a second four-year term. The constitutional amendment also allowed governors of the states, federal district, and prefects to run for reelection. Prior to 1997, these posts, like that of the presidency, had all been barred from reelection to a subsequent term (Rosenn 2008).[8] Initially, Brazil's 1988 constitution stipulated that the term of office for the president was five years, with no right to reelection. In 1994, Constitutional Amendment no. 5 changed the five-year term to a four-year term, and three years later presidents won the right to run for reelection to a second term.[9]

Constitutional change is not a rare occurrence in Latin America, particularly for Brazil. In the past twenty years, the Brazilian Constitution has been modified by sixty-two amendments, expanding to 250 articles in the main text. Rosenn (2008) describes the Brazilian Constitution as "incredibly lengthy, detailed, pro-

Table 6.2. Executive term structure for presidential republics in Latin America

Country	Term Duration	No Limit on Reelection	Two-Term Limit	No Reelection	Reelection Prohibited by Specified Number of Years	Reelection Prohibited for Interim Term	Constitution
Mexico	6	–	–	x	–	–	1917–1934
Uruguay	5	–	–	–	x	–	1967
Venezuela	5	–	x	–	–	–	1961
Venezuela	5	–	x	–	–	x	1992
Venezuela	6	x	–	–	–	–	2009
Peru	5	x	–	–	–	x	1993
Peru	5	–	x	–	–	x	2005
Paraguay	5	–	–	x	–	–	1992
Ecuador	4	–	–	x	–	–	1998
Ecuador	4	–	x	–	–	–	2008
Colombia	4	–	–	x	–	–	1991
Bolivia	4	–	–	–	x	–	1967

Country	Term Duration	No Limit on Reelection	Two-Term Limit	No Reelection	Reelection Prohibited by Specified Number of Years	Reelection Prohibited for Interim Term	Constitution
Bolivia	5	–	–	–	–	x	1994
Bolivia	5	–	x	–	–	–	2008
Chile	4	–	–	–	–	x	1980
Dom. Rep.	4	x	–	–	–	x	1966
Honduras	4	–	–	x	–	–	1982
Guatemala	5	–	–	–	–	–	1985
Guatemala	4	–	x	–	–	x	1993
El Salvador	5	–	–	x	–	–	1996
Costa Rica	4	x	–	–	–	x	1949
Panama	5	–	x	–	–	x	1978
Nicaragua	5	–	x	–	–	x	1995

Note: An “x” marks the term structure to which the country ascribes.

Table 6.3. Recent history of executive term structure for Brazil, Argentina, and the United States

Country	Term Duration	No Limit on Reelection	Two-Term Limit	No Reelection	Reelection Prohibited by Specified Number of Years	Reelection Prohibited for Interim Term	Constitution/ Amendment
Brazil	5	–	–	x	–	–	1988
Brazil	4	–	–	x	–	–	1994
Brazil	4	–	x	–	–	–	1997
Argentina	6	–	–	–	–	x	1853–1860
Argentina*	4	–	x	–	–	–	1994
United States	4	x	–	–	–	–	1788
United States	4	–	x	–	–	–	1951

* Argentine presidents can seek reelection to a third term once an interim term has passed.

Note: An "x" marks the term structure to which the country ascribes.

grammatic and problematic." He adds: "With rare exception, the style of constitutional change has been to modify or to add to the huge text by amendment rather than to deconstitutionalize subjects, many of which should never have been constitutionalized in the first place." As a point of reference, Brazil's constitution has a word count of 70,000, whereas Argentina's has 12,600, and the United States' has only 5,000 (Palanza 2009). Entrenching detailed policy in the constitution has its upsides as it can serve as a constraining mechanism in efforts to change policy—whether by decree or through ordinary legislative channels. The Argentine Constitution, on the other hand, which dates back to 1853 (with extensive amendment in 1860), has undergone relatively minor changes up until the 1994 constitutional revision.[10] The 1994 revision kept the fundamental political system intact but made substantial procedural changes, some of which are discussed in the following sections as the revision pertains to the president's decree power. The constitutional reform of 1994 increased the number of articles from 110 to 129 and added seventeen complementary rules. According to Sagüës (1996, 52), the 1994 constitution is nearly 70 percent longer since the new articles and rules are quite lengthy compared to "the brief and concise language of the Constitution of 1853/60."

The most recent amending of the Brazilian and Argentine constitutions, in 2001 and 1994, respectively, has brought more specificity and, consequently, procedural changes in presidents' use of decrees. This provides a unique avenue of exploration since the presidents chosen for analysis were in office during these constitutional changes. Questions arise such as the following: How did presidents react to the constitutional change? Has the change been effective? And in what ways did the constitutional change manipulate conditions that are assumed to affect the rate of decree use? Before we tackle these questions, it is necessary to define what is meant by the term *decree* within the context of each country and to detail exactly how their respective rules governing decree use have changed in the past two decades. As defined in chapter 3, a decree is a written statement of instruction or declaration issued by the president that effectively becomes law without previous deliberation by Congress. Following earlier research for Brazil, I equate the term *decree* with the presidential instrument of direct action—*medidas provisórias com força de lei* (MPVs) in Brazilian legislative terminology.[11] For Argentina I equate the term *decree* with *decretos de necesidad y urgencia* (decrees of necessity and urgency), or DNUs.

Unlike the US Constitution, the current constitutions of both Brazil and Argentina specifically state that exigent circumstances are needed to warrant the use of such decrees.

Article 62 of Brazil's 1988 constitution states the following:

> In *relevant and urgent cases,* the President of the Republic may *adopt provisional measures with the force of law;* such measures shall be submitted immediately to the National Congress . . . (emphasis added)

Article 99.3 of Argentina's 1994 constitution states the following:

> He [The president of the nation] takes part in the making of laws according to the Constitution, promulgates them and has them published.
>
> The Executive Power shall in no event issue provisions of legislative nature, in which case they shall be absolutely and irreparably null and void.
>
> Only when *due to exceptional circumstances* the ordinary procedures foreseen by this Constitution for the enactment of laws are impossible to be followed, and when rules are not referred to criminal issues, taxation, electoral matters, or the system of political parties, he shall issue decrees *on grounds of necessity and urgency,* which shall be decided by a general agreement of ministers who shall countersign them together with the Chief of the Ministerial Cabinet . . . (emphasis added)

According to Negretto (2004, 535), in Brazil and Argentina this urgency "generally refers to domestic crisis, usually economic, that requires an immediate solution, and Congress is either unable to act or its action would be inappropriate given the urgency of the circumstances." As in the United States, Brazilian and Argentinean presidents declare an emergency based on their justification of fact.[12] Recall that "presidential determinations" are needed in order for US presidents to decree certain action. These determinations declare that proper conditions set by the US Congress have been met, and therefore action is permissible. And recall that the US Supreme Court excludes these findings from judicial review, making presidential determinations virtually exempt from scrutiny. During the time periods under review the courts in both Argentina and Brazil more often than not chose to defer judgment on presidents' issuance of MPVs and DNUs. On occasion, however, they have stepped in and ruled against an issuance. I return to a discussion of the judiciary later in this chapter.

In addition, DNUs are only a subset of decrees used by Argentinean presidents. The Argentine Constitution of 1853/1860 and the presently reformed Constitution of 1994 recognize two types of standard decrees—what Scribner (2004, 283) describes as *decrees of execution* and *autonomous regulatory decrees. Decrees of execution* detail how the laws made by Congress are to be instituted.[13] Decrees of this type are subordinate to the constitution and the congressional laws from which they derive their authority.[14] *Autonomous regulatory decrees* regulate administrative matters and procedure required for the "general administration of the country" (Article 100.1 of the 1994 Constitution). However, DNUs stand apart from these decree types in that they decree emergency action without any legal foundation in emergency legislation passed by Congress (Scribner 2004, 391). Presidents legislate without statutory warrant, and up until 1994 they did so without constitutional warrant.[15] In this way DNUs are the most outright exercise of proactive power. Operating on the fringe of legality, Argentine presidents, particularly prior to 1994, are pushing the limits of decree issuance as permitted under democratic governance.

What makes MPVs and DNUs ideal subjects of study is that they, like emergency power decrees in the United States, are issued when an emergency situation makes them compelling (e.g., "in relevant and urgent cases," "due to exceptional circumstances," and "on grounds of necessity and urgency"). The emergency goes beyond the declaration of war, internal armed conflict, or even civil unrest to encompass all that is considered a serious effect on the nation's state of affairs. What we will see, particularly in Argentina's case, is that the *very* projection of a situation as an emergency facilitates legislative and judicial deference to presidential choice. Because the declaration of an emergency is a subjective evaluation, it becomes a political question, which denies judicial review. Kapiszewski (2007, 269) explains that "one way to think about Emergency . . . is as a tool that the elected branches provided to the high court to facilitate deference—to create a justification to which the court could point when endorsing the exercise of emergency power." Moreover, Congress is constrained from intervening since the declaration is usually based on information monopolized by the executive. The lack of constitutional and legal definition of what constitutes an emergency, combined with the lack of legislative and judicial oversight, creates a slippery slope that has the potential to lead to the normalization of extraordinary powers.[16] A finding that substantiates terminal logic thinking in the use of DNUs and MPVs should invoke critical reflection on the meaning of "emergency" and the existing provisions governing their use.[17]

6.3 THE CHANGING CONSTITUTIONAL BOUNDARIES OF MPVs AND DNUs

When US presidents issue an order, a proclamation, or a memorandum, the statement has the immediate effect of law. The US Congress must then enact a statute that modifies or nullifies the decree; this may involve repealing statutory authority retroactively, putting in a date of expiration of such authority, or passing legislation that outright contradicts the decree. No explicit approval by Congress is needed for the decree to become permanent law. In the case of Brazil, a decree has immediate—but only temporary—legal effect. Legislative approval of an MPV is needed in order for it to become permanent law. From the 1988 adoption of the constitution to 2001, Article 62 stated that a decree would have immediate legal effect for thirty days and would expire following that thirty-day period if Congress did not address it. Yet, prior to 2001, this rule was easily circumvented, which often happened. From 1995 to 2001 decrees were reissued an average of fifteen times and were therefore in effect for nearly two and a half years. In that same period 12 percent of all decrees were reissued more than forty times, having the effect of law for more than seven years (Pachón-Buitrago 2008, 77). Presidents simply continued to reissue a decree once it had expired—and were able to continually do so as long as Congress had not rejected it. This began with President Sarney's issuance of MPV 29/89, and as table 6.4 shows, President Cardoso was particularly fond of this practice. In theory, Brazilian presidents needed the explicit approval of Congress in order for decrees to remain valid. Yet, in reality, presidents' practice of continual reissuance became a way to circumvent this requirement of congressional approval (Figueiredo and Limongi 1997, 141).[18]

Passed on September 11, 2001, Constitutional Amendment 32 (EC32) is an attempt by legislators to limit presidents' use of MPVs.[19] First, EC32 stipu-

Table 6.4. Count of Medidas Provisórias (MPVs) (1989—2000)

MPVs	Sarney (Jan. 1989—Mar. 1990)	Collor (Mar. 1990—Oct. 1992)	Franco (Oct. 1992—Dec. 1994)	Cardoso, First Term (Jan. 1995—Dec. 1998)	Cardoso, Second Term, (Jan. 1999—Dec. 2000)	Total (1989—2000)
total per period	133	164	506	2,612	2,121	5,536
original	110	89	142	160	70	571
reissued	23	75	364	2,452	2,051	4,965 (90%)[a]
reissued with modifications	2	22	50	454	222	750 (15%)
expired (not reissued)	5	5	15	3	2	30 (5%)[b]
rejected	9	11	–	1	–	21 (4%)[b]
made into laws	79	69	74	101	55	378 (66%)[b]
amended	40	47	28	36	5	156 (41%)
vetoes	8	19	7	13	2	49 (13%)

Note: A dash (–) indicates that no MPVs were rejected during this period.
Table reprinted from Negretto (2004, 543).
a. Percentage calculated from the total number of decrees (original plus reissued).
b. MPVs that were not reissued after the expiration of the deadline for approval.

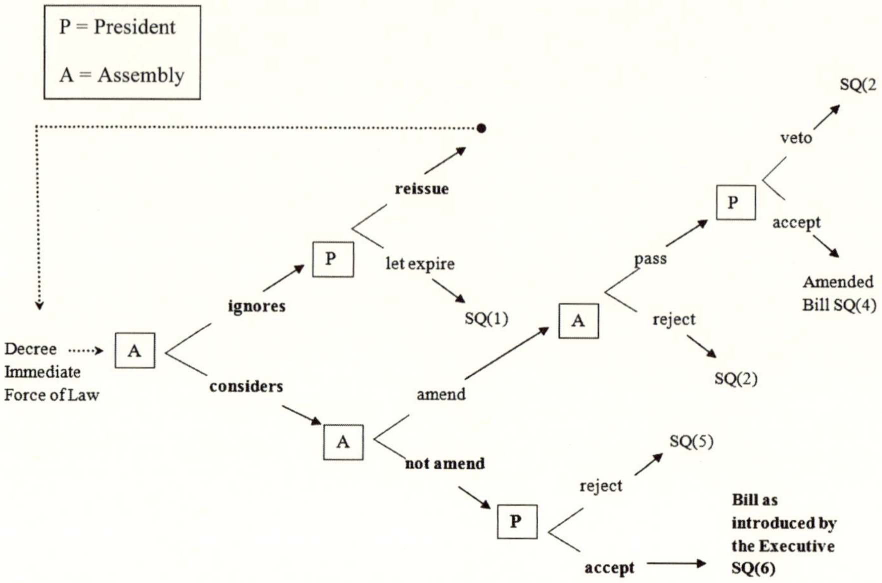

Figure 6.1. Pre-EC32, *reissuance game before the approval of Constitutional Reform no. 32/2001. Reproduced by permission from Monica Pachón-Buitrago, "Cross-Avenue Politics: The Case of Colombia and Brazil" (PhD diss., Political Science and International Affairs Department, University of California at San Diego, 2008), 77, Figures 3.1;* emphasis added.

lates that if Congress does not act, the MPV can be reissued only once after sixty days of its enactment—meaning that the MPV will be valid for up to 120 days unless Congress acts; Congress must vote on any decree seeking a second reissuance. Second, forty-five days after its initial enactment, if Congress has not yet addressed it, the MPV becomes *regime de urgência.* Congress must consider the MPV before all other issues, and, according to Pachón-Buitrago (2008, 159), "there is no possibility for the Board of Directors to negotiate an avenue of 'no consideration.'"[20] This forces Congress to be proactive, giving legislators more opportunity to deliberate on policy pushed by the president. Figures 6.1 and 6.2 illustrate the procedural differences pre- and post-reform. Figure 6.1 shows the two pathways by which a decree could remain in its original form, as introduced by the president. Figure 6.2 shows that only one pathway remains, one that requires Congress to actively choose not to amend the MPV and pass it as is. Congressional passivity (i.e., ignoring the MPV) is no longer an option.

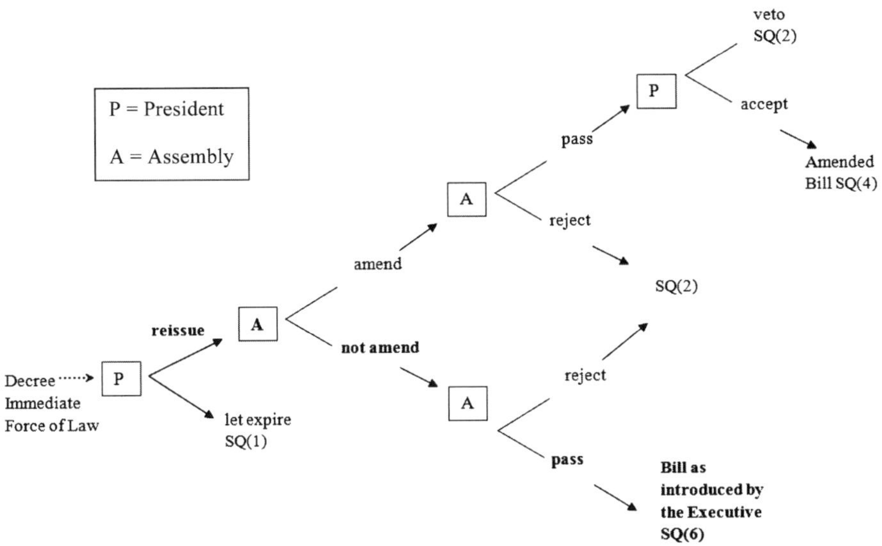

Figure 6.2. Post-EC32, *reissuance game after the approval of Constitutional Reform no. 32/2001. Reproduced by permission from Monica Pachón-Buitrago, "Cross-Avenue Politics: The Case of Colombia and Brazil" (PhD diss., Political Science and International Affairs Department, University of California at San Diego, 2008), 79, Figures 3.2;* emphasis added.

Third, EC32 does not require Congress to meet in a joint session in order for an MPV to be considered. The chambers can meet and approve versions separately.[21] Finally, the amendment also stipulates specific issues that are off limits to presidents' issuance of decrees. These include nationality, citizenship, political rights, political parties, and electoral law; criminal law, criminal procedure, and civil procedure; organization of the judiciary and the public ministry, as well as the careers and guarantees of their members; multiyear plans, budgetary directives, budget, and additional and supplementary credits;[22] issues that deal with detention or sequestration of property, people's savings, or any other financial assets; issues reserved for a complementary law; and issues that have already been regulated in a bill approved by the National Congress and which is awaiting the approval or veto of the president of the republic (see appendix).[23]

In contrast to the Brazilian case, Argentinean presidents have the power to pass *permanent* law without the consent of Congress.[24] In fact, Argentinean presidents issued DNUs long before the Argentine Constitution even mentioned them. It was not until 1994 that the Argentine Constitution recognized DNUs as a valid presidential tool and set some limits on their use.[25] The 1994 Constitution declares that DNUs are constitutionally forbidden to address issues involving crimes, taxes, elections, or political parties. Furthermore, it states a process of congressional review with a specified timetable. The executive must submit DNUs within ten days for consideration by the Permanent Bicameral Commission of the Congress. This commission is to send a report to each chamber as to how the DNU should be addressed. Then, an absolute majority of each chamber is to approve a special law regulating the procedure and the scope of Congress's intervention within a ten-day period.[26]

Four years prior to the constitutional reform, just after President Carlos Menem took office, the judiciary did recognize DNUs as a "constitutionally valid instruments of legislation" and took steps to condition their use. The Supreme Court claimed that a DNU was valid in the following instances: (1) if "the existence of a 'serious social danger' . . . makes necessary the adoption of rapid measures" and (2) if "Congress does not adopt decisions different from the decree on the involved issues of economic policy" (Negretto 2004, 551–52). Yet, although the court spelled out these conditions, like the US Supreme Court, it has traditionally declined to consider whether presidents have actually met them—giving no teeth to its stipulations. The court instead has put the burden of review on Congress. According to the court, in order to negate a decree, Congress needs to pass a new law. Yet even if Congress is able to garner the necessary votes and enacts a new law, it would become subject to a presidential veto either in part (line-item veto) or as a whole. And in order to override the presidential veto, a two-thirds majority must be obtained in both the 72-member Senate and the 257-member Chamber of Deputies.

Recall that Brazilian presidents, unlike their US and Argentine counterparts, must obtain majority support in each chamber, the Chamber of Deputies and the Federal Senate, in order to convert MPVs into permanent law. Decrees issued by US and Argentinean presidents become permanent law without previous deliberation by Congress. This is particularly true since the passing of EC32. In Brazil, moreover, legislative rejection of a decree is not subject to a presidential veto. Compared to their Brazilian counterparts, Argentine presidents can more easily protect decrees in their original form from amendments by legislators (Negretto 2004, 552).

The next section explores the particulars of Congress and the court's interplay with the executive branch; the purpose is to better define their role in executive decree issuance. Presidents' use of decrees is at least a partial function of behavior of the other two branches of government. Congressional acquiescence and the practice of judicial accommodation have allowed both Brazilian and Argentinean presidents to decree with great latitude during the periods under review.

6.4 HOW THE COURT AND CONGRESS HANDLE MPVs AND DNUs

The preceding section outlined Brazilian and Argentinean presidents' constitutional authority to issue decrees. Yet this says little about how decree issuance is actually realized within the overall legislative process in Brazil and Argentina or how legislators react when a president issues a decree. As Eaton (2000, 363) reminds us, "the first step in policy analysis is identification of all the relevant actors who have stakes in and the power to affect the outcome of a policy process." The institutional setting determines the extent to which presidents must consider Congress and the court in their decisions to decree. If, for instance, institutional factors make it difficult for Congress to articulate its preferences, punish the president, or legislate in general, the president will likely have more opportunity and freedom to decree at will. Similarly, if the court is likely to find decrees to be outside the bounds of judicial review or to favor presidential policies in general, the president, exempt from judicial control, is more at liberty to choose when and how to decree.

Interestingly, scholarly discussion concerning US presidents' use of executive orders has for the most part revolved around the question of legislative delegation, that is, whether presidents' exercise of decree authority is an outright usurpation of the legislature's power or instead a result of the legislature's tacit consent. This is perhaps due to the fact that the presidential system of the United States is unique in that all legislation is required to be initiated from within Congress—whereas in most other presidential systems a variety of actors can initiate legislation (Cheibub 2009).[27]

As the following sections show, research on non-US presidential systems puts emphasis instead on presidential choice a priori (i.e., why presidents choose to pursue policy via decree rather than by traditional legislative means) (Palanza 2009, 10). In Brazil, for instance, presidents are equipped with a broad range of legislative tools. Moreover, they face more restrictions on the passage of decrees than either their Argentinean or US counterparts. The Brazilian case allows us to see how constitutional rules can successfully *or unsuccessfully* (as the case may be) curb presidents' use of decrees—and why presidents may choose to issue a decree rather than utilize other legislative means.

The next two sections highlight important aspects of the court and Congress that come into play, affecting presidents' use of decrees.

The Case of Brazil

Democracy has been in place for nearly twenty-five years in Brazil, and the current constitution has been in place since 1988.[28] According to the purchasing power parity used by the World Bank, Brazil's economy as of 2005 was the ninth largest market-based center of production, having a gross domestic product (GDP) more than three times that of Argentina (Moniz Bandeira 2006, 13). Yet such was not always the case for Brazil. Like Argentina, during the 1990s and early twenty-first century Brazil faced economic crisis. During this period President Cardoso maintained surprisingly high levels of party discipline among his coalition (Amorim Neto 2000) and enjoyed "solid congressional backing not only for measures of stabilization and fiscal adjustment but also for constitutional amendments in 1995, 1996, and 1997 that made possible a relatively far-reaching program of structural reforms," reforms implemented by ordinary bills and MPVs (Negretto 2004, 550).

Maintaining a solid base of congressional support in Brazil is no easy feat. For one thing, relative to Argentina and the United States, Brazil has weak national parties, meaning legislators in general are more interested in state and municipal matters than national affairs. Provincial interests commonly structure legislative careers. Samuels (2003, 210) finds that "for the vast majority of congressional deputies national partisan images are relatively unimportant, and few politicians see a career in the legislature as a way to influence policy." Party switching is rampant, and, according to Power (1997), there is great confusion among the populace regarding the identifiability and accountability of elected representatives.[29] Although both Samuels (2003) and Schmidt (1999) find that legislators are often punished for switching parties in the middle of a legislative term, they still do it—and do it often. The policy process is less driven by national party organization and more by subnational forces. Presidents must consider how local and regional politics matter to legislative support and negotiate accordingly.

Table 6.5. Distribution of seats in Brazilian Senate (1995—2007)

Party	1995—1999 Cardoso/PSDB	1999—2003 Cardoso/PSDB	2003—2007 Lula/PT
PDS/PPR	4.9	4.9	2.5
PMDB	27.2	32.1	25.9
PDT	6.2	4.9	4.9
PTB	8.6	3.7	2.5
PFL	23.5	19.8	23.5
PSDB	12.3	16.0	14.8
PRN	2.5	–	–
PT	6.2	8.6	16.0
PST/PP	4.9	4.9	–
PSB	1.2	2.5	4.9
PL	1.2	1.2	2.5
All others	1.3	1.4	2.5

Reprinted from Kapiszewski (2007, 538, table 7.3).
a. Senators hold eight-year terms.
b. Elections are held every four years, replacing one-third of senators in 1998 and two-thirds in 1994 and 2002.
c. There have been a total of eighty-one senators since 1995.
d. A dash (–) indicates "0" or no seats.

Second, Brazil has a large number of parties active in Congress. Tables 6.5 and 6.6 illustrate just how fragmented the Brazilian party system is. Arguably, systems that are more inclusive of multiple parties are in fact more representative of the population's parochial and sectoral interests. The growth of political parties, in effect, increases the opportunity for the articulation of minority viewpoints; parochial concerns about classes and other bases of societal cleavages are likely to be present in Congress and the cabinet (Shugart and Carey 1992, 18). Yet scholars like Mainwaring (1990) and Linz (1978) find that the combination of multipartism and presidentialism leads to legislative deadlock.[30] Indeed, legislative deadlock was the case for Brazil prior to 1993, but since then presidents, particularly Cardoso, have constructed a relatively large and cohesive governing coalition. This was even the case for President Lula. His ability to form coalitions was at times "uneven"

Table 6.6. **Distribution of seats in Brazilian Chamber of Deputies (1995—2007)**

Party	1995—1999 Cardoso/PSDB	1999—2003 Cardoso/PSDB	2003—2007 Lula/PT
PDS/PPR	10.0	–	–
PMDB	20.9	16.2	14.4
PDT	6.8	4.9	4.1
PTB	6.0	6.0	5.1
PT	9.6	11.3	17.7
PFL	17.3	20.5	16.4
PL	2.5	2.3	5.1
PCdoB	1.9	1.4	2.3
PSB	2.9	3.7	4.3
PRN	0.2	–	–
PSDB	12.1	19.3	13.8
PPB	–	11.7	9.6
PPS	–	0.6	2.9
All Others	9.8	2.1	4.3

Reprinted from Kapiszewski (2007, 538, table 7.4).
1. Deputies hold four-year terms.
2. Elections are held every four years for the entire chamber.
3. A dash (–) indicates "0" or no seats.

(Kapiszewski 2007, 539n798), but he managed to maintain the "ability to negotiate a deal, whatever the circumstances."[31] He leaves his successor, President-elect Dilma Rousseff, with a coalition that will control 70 percent of votes in both houses.[32]

In Brazil, presidents have a wide range of legislative tools at their disposal. They have exclusive power to propose the budget, can influence the timing of legislative bills as well as introduce bills through ordinary means, and maintain great discretion over patronage jobs. In addition, the executive controls more than forty thousand jobs, which are often used to reward those who are loyal to the administration (Alston and Mueller 2006).

This has prompted Brazilian scholars to focus on executive-legislative exchange and link MPV issuance to the process of statute enactment.[33] Research focuses on the gains legislators and presidents alike perceive they will extract from any decree issuance over the introduction of a bill by ordinary means. Palanza (2009), for instance, links legislator indifference to the payoff structure they experience in presidents' use of MPVs over statutes.[34] This, along with the fundamentals of Brazilian politics (i.e., the undisciplined, fragmented party system and the relative strength of local and regional interests) may all play to legislators' indifference to presidents' use of MPVs.

Strikingly, research shows that EC32 has neither deterred the use of MPVs nor prompted more resistance from legislators. This may be due to the MPV process itself imposed by EC32. Pereira, Power, and Rennó (2008) argue that EC32 may have actually made MPVs a more powerful and efficient presidential tool to push presidential policy. Congress must make the president's agenda items its priority. If Congress does not consider a decree within its first forty-five days, it must be discussed before all other agenda items. This results in *trancamento da pauta,* or "a lockdown of the agenda." Congress must evaluate the policy quickly and move on. Pereira, Power, and Rennó (2008, 26) claim that, as a consequence, the process by which MPVs become permanent has "greatly accelerated." They calculate a conversion rate from temporary to permanent at 79 percent for the period following the reform—up from a rate of 43 percent for the period before the reform.[35] After all, Congress it seems has had little choice. Blocked congressional sessions have come to be more common than unblocked ones (Rennó 2010, 217).[36]

Yet there is still more to this story. In March 2009 the president of the Chamber of Deputies, Michel Temer, declared that EC32 applied to only one type of legislative proposal—ordinary law proposals. Resolution proposals, constitutional amendment proposals, complementary law proposals, and legislative decree proposals were excluded, he maintained. Ordinary law proposals are the only type of legislative proposal that is subject to blockage by congressional votes on MPVs. Said differently, legislators could now vote on *non*ordinary law proposals—independently of the presence of an MPV on the agenda (*ordem do día,* or order of the day) (Rennó 2010, 215). Rennó (ibid., 227) contends that Temer's oral clarification has "reduced its [the executive branch's] propensity to govern through Provisional Measures [MPVs]." There is some empirical support for this claim.[37]

In the case of Brazil, it is difficult to argue that decrees are purposeful acts of congressional circumvention. Note the low percentage of MPV rejection by Congress prior to the passing of EC32 (see table 6.4).[38] Negretto's data show that, from 1989 to 2000, 66 percent of original MPVs were made into law. Moreover, 41 percent of MPVs were approved with amendments.[39] Amorim Neto and Tafner (2002) show that President Cardoso, throughout both of his terms, reintroduced decrees with changes as a way to cooperate with the coalition that he had created in Congress. For example, Cardoso continually reissued MPVs associated with the new currency (the *real*) until they obtained approval one year later. In fact, many of Cardoso's reissued decrees deal with the Real Plan, his 1994 economic stabilization plan, which was begun prior to his presidency, during his tenure as finance minister. The argument of congressional circumvention is even harder to make with EC32 in effect. Congress now plays an active role in the process. Legislators must approve or deny each MPV. Clearly EC32 has not obstructed the presidents' ability to issue MPVs. Since MPVs have relatively high approval rates and high rates of conversion to permanent law pre- and post-EC32, presidents Cardoso and Lula certainly did not issue more decrees in response to an obstructive Congress.[40] Cheibub (2009, 12) adds: "Legislative behavior in the Brazilian Congress has exhibited remarkably high levels of partisanship, with presidents capable of relying on a stable coalition who supported them on most of their legislative agenda." Survey evidence[41] and a 2005 proposal for a constitutional amendment (PEC 72) requiring decrees to be approved first by the Justice Committees of each house before hitting the floor in Congress may indicate some legislative frustration with presidents' MPV power. Nevertheless, this does not deny the *unified government* hypothesis.[42] The fact remains that presidents Cardoso and Lula issued MPVs—and a significant number of them—and Congress did not stand in their way before or after the passing of EC32.

There is also little evidence that the judiciary poses a threat to presidents in their issuance of MPVs. Moreover, if there were a branch of government to oppose MPVs, Brazil's judiciary certainly maintains the independence, opportunity, and power to do so. The court is powerful and enjoys a high level of autonomy.[43] Federal judges are granted life tenure and a constitutionally protected salary and are difficult to impeach (Rios-Figueroa and Taylor 2006). Judges in the lower courts also enjoy great latitude in decision making due to the judiciary's weak hierarchical structure and guarantees of tenure.[44] The public holds the court in high regard, whereas corruption in the other branches of government remains an ongoing concern. As of 2003, polls conducted by Latinobarómetro ranked Brazil the fourth highest of seventeen countries in trust afforded the judiciary by the public.[45] Moreover, in contrast to Argentina, Brazil's federal judiciary is "widely known to contain the elite of the legal profession," as they are required among other things to pass rigorous and competitive examinations rather than simply being appointed (Ballard 1999, 246; Kapiszewski 2007, 107).[46] And outside the United States, Brazil's federal court system is the highest funded in the western hemisphere (see Taylor 2006, 353n12). Most important of all, presidents and legislators do not challenge the court's decisions. They adhere to them (Taylor 2006).

In addition to power and independence, the court has ample opportunity to address the constitutionality of MPVs. To start with, the Brazilian Constitution follows a "dirigiste," or "directed," model, where it is excessively detailed on public policy, "prescrib[ing] a program intended to produce political, economic, and social transformation" (Ballard 1999, 247). This puts the court in a principal position to evaluate all sorts of federal programs put into place by the other two branches of government. Brazil's constitution also includes an extensive and broad list of individual rights. Article 5 alone uses seventy-eight different clauses to describe the ways in which Brazilian citizens are "ensured of inviolability of the right to life, to liberty, to equality, to security and to property" (Kapiszewski 2007, 128). Moreover, Brazil has "one of the broadest grants of group standing in the world" (next to Costa Rica and Colombia), such that parties of all types able to petition the court for judicial review, including the president, federal and state legislators, state governors, the federal procurator-general, the Brazilian Bar Association (OAB), unions and various associations, political parties, and citizens (Rios-Figueroa and Taylor 2006, 753).[47] This broad grant of group standing, along with the character of the Brazilian Constitution, with its treatise on public policy and broadly defined rights and guarantees, grants the judiciary a long arm of judicial review under which legislative and executive action are subject to its scrutiny.

On a related note, the federal courts' caseload in response to implemented economic and social policies has exploded in the past two decades. Figure 6.3 illustrates the great increase in the number of cases filed with the Supreme Federal Tribunal (STF) from 1990 to 2002. As recent as May 2009, the *Economist* declared the STF "the most overburdened court in the world" and attributed this to "a plethora of rights and privileges entrenched in the country's 1988 constitution."[48] Constitutional Amendment 45 was passed in December 2004 in an attempt to curb the rise in court cases.[49] Despite these reforms, however, the number of filed cases remains high, with a total of 100,781 cases filed in 2008 alone.[50]

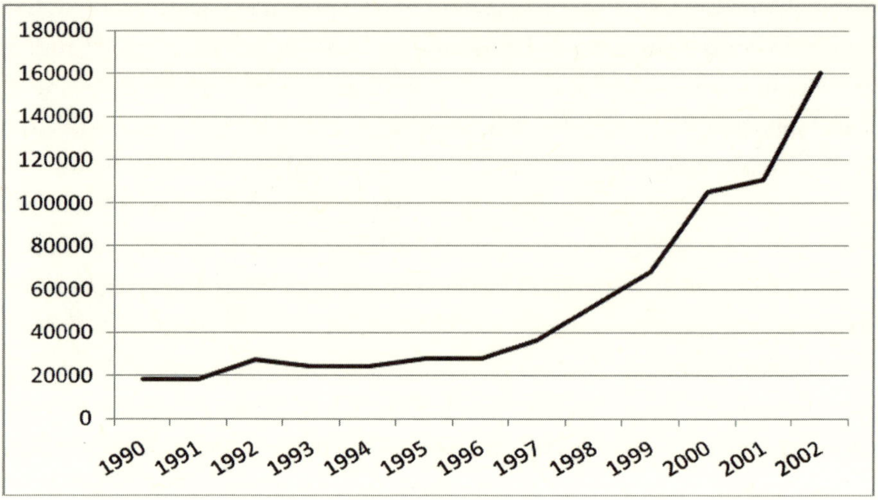

Source: Data drawn from Kapiszewski's (2007) Appendix 3.1.

Figure 6.3. *Number of cases filed with Brazil's Supreme Federal Tribunal (1990–2002).*

Many times the court could step up and rule against an MPV. It has both the opportunity and the power to do so. Yet the court appears to view *this manner* of implementing law as constitutional and supported as other forms. In fact, empirical analysis of cases reveals that the court is less likely to issue an injunction against executive decrees than against other forms of laws.[51] Kapiszewski (2007) finds that in 22 of the most important cases regarding economic policy, only 4 are MPVs (18 percent of the time).[52] The object of cases is more often a complementary or an ordinary law (36 percent of the time) or a constitutional amendment (27 percent of the time). She adds: "[I]t was much more often the *content* rather than *form* of policies that was questioned: policy content was questioned in 17 cases (or 65 percent of the time), and both form and content were questioned in 4 cases (or 15 percent of the time)" (ibid., 336). Similarly, using a sample of more than one thousand cases in which the plaintiffs charged direct action of unconstitutionality (*ação direta de inconstitucionalidade*, or ADIn) against laws passed by the three branches of federal government. Taylor (2006, 175–76) finds that "ordinary laws, which require far more deliberation than executive measures, are roughly twice as likely to face successful injunctive challenges as executive decrees. In addition, non-executive decrees by either Congress or the Judiciary are 1.8 times more likely to face successful injunction requests than executive decrees."[53] As a result, he concludes that this "knocks down any assumption that the STF views the use of provisional measures (MPVs) as inherently more arbitrary or less constitutional than the use of other forms of legislation" (ibid., 179).

Not only is the court less likely to issue a successful injunction against MPVs than other forms of law, but on notable occasions it has flat out refused to grant review of cases associated with them. For instance, in a sweeping display of presidential power President Collor decreed the freezing of Brazilian accounts. Then he made subsequent decrees prohibiting courts from placing injunctions against decrees related to the Collor Plan. The court refused to review petitions associated with any of these decrees (Ballard 1999, 255).

This is not to say that the court does not hear cases questioning executive action. It hears such cases and has "reversed important decisions [made] by powerful presidents" (Taylor 2006, 338).[54] In Kapiszewski's sample, executive action in the form of "some sort of administrative policy or decision" is questioned in 31 percent of the cases. And the court did step in when presidents began to reissue MPVs after they had been disapproved by Congress. The court ended this practice in 1991. Moreover, there are some signs that the court is beginning to change its tune. The court appears to support Temer's interpretation of EC32, which restricts the application of legislative blockage to ordinary law proposals (Rennó 2010, 219–21).[55] Another instance of the court's "change in tune" is a 2008 case, in which the court ruled that MPVs could be used to reallocate budgetary funds only in moments of crisis—not for routine budgetary transfers.[56]

Recent developments aside, the court, given the breadth of its judicial powers, has shown deference and remarkable restraint with regard to presidents' use of MPVs during the period under review (1995 to 2010). Perhaps this is due to their temporary nature; after all, permanence in law is achieved only after congressional approval, and a check on power is already in place. It is worth noting that even though Argentina's judiciary has found itself under the thumb of presidents, presidential decrees still represent a larger portion of questioned policies in Argentina than in Brazil (Kapiszewski 2007, 337).

To review, in Brazil presidents can issue a decree, and it has the immediate effect of law, but only temporarily. Legislative approval of an MPV is needed in order for it to become permanent law. Although EC32, passed in 2001, curbed the presidential practice of continual reissuance, evidence shows that MPVs continue to maintain high rates of approval by Congress and may in fact have a faster conversion rate to permanent law as a result of the reform, making MPVs perhaps an even more powerful legislative tool for presidents than before. There is, however, some preliminary evidence that Michel Temer's March 2009 oral clarification of EC32 reduces the number of presidential issuances of MPVs. Because this development is recent, more time is needed to evaluate its repercussions. There is also little evidence that the judiciary poses a threat to presidents in their issuance of MPVs even though Brazil's judiciary maintains the independence, opportunity, and power to do so. The court in Brazil is no more likely to rule on an MPV than on a complementary law, an ordinary law, or a constitutional amendment. Moreover, when a case does concern an MPV, the court is less likely to issue a successful injunction against it than other forms of law.

In Brazil, both the Congress and its court are equipped to restrict the effect of MPVs if they so choose.[57] Whether it is due to utility costs or concern about infringement on the executive's separate and independent powers, both branches of government generally choose to oblige the president when it comes to MPVs. Given the need for congressional approval, divided government, one in which the president stands opposed to a majority coalition, most likely poses the greatest threat to decree issuance. The Brazilian presidents under review in this study, Presidents Cardoso and Lula, maintained somewhat stable coalitions throughout their tenure, so further analysis of divided-government effects cannot be properly tested.

As we will see in chapter 7, both presidents Cardoso and Lula have taken advantage of the other branches' reluctance to oppose MPVs. They have decreed freely and often. For this reason, despite facing more restrictions than presidents of Argentina or the United States, these Brazilian presidents, in their use of MPVs, qualify as appropriate and comparable test cases of TLB. Now I turn to the Argentine case of decree use—where presidents' latitude to decree is even broader than in Brazil.

The Case of Argentina

From a comparative perspective, Argentinean presidents enjoy a more solid basis of partisan support in the legislature, a stronger veto, and less demanding requirements for legislative approval as compared to their Brazilian counterparts (Negretto 2004, 532). In fact, President Menem enjoyed unprecedented support in Congress as his party, Partido Justicialista (PJ), controlled both chambers for most of his tenure (see tables 6.7 and 6.8).[58] It was not until the midterm congressional elections in October of 1997 that an opposition party, Alianza, won a majority of the congressional seats up for reelection, and as a result the PJs no longer had an absolute majority.[59] Menem enjoyed the unprecedented support not only of Congress but of the court as well, allowing him to decree with great freedom. In fact, according to Ferreira Rubio and Goretti (1998), Congress took no action on 90 percent of those decrees actually submitted.

This is not to say that Menem religiously adhered to constitutional standards and traditional rules of conduct to garner such support. In fact, his administration is often accused of corruption and underhanded tactics, and as we will see, these accusations are not without merit.

Experts and the public alike generally agree that the Supreme Court during Menem's tenure was not one of judicial independence and that decisions were more products of political pressure and government loyalty than of "administering justice well and faithfully, and in conformity with what the Constitution prescribes."[60] During the 1990s the public consistently ranked the Supreme Court and the judiciary as a whole as one of the least respected institutions. Estimates of little or no confidence ran as high as 70 percent in 1991 and 92 percent in 1997.[61] This lack of confidence is not unfounded. For one, justices faced the threat of removal.[62] Between 1994 and 1995, three justices were forced to retire and were replaced with those loyal to Menem's administration. He removed the chief of the Federal Prosecutor's Office and appointed new federal appeals court judges. This took place after Menem packed the court in 1990, expanding the number of justices from five to nine so that a majority would rule in his favor.[63] After all, it was Menem himself who famously asked, "Why should I be the only president in fifty years who hasn't had his own court?" (Kapiszewski 2007, 64, citing quote from Prillaman 2000, 111).

Just as Brazilian presidents Cardoso and Lula often used MPVs to impose economic reform, so, too, did President Menem. As a consequence, Argentina's Supreme Court, or Corte Suprema de Justicia de la Nacíon (CSJN), was often put in the position of evaluating the content of the economic reform and the process by which it was being imposed. At some points, the court did challenge Menem but did so significantly less often than it challenged presidents preceding or following Menem. In fact, Kapiszewski (2007, 251) finds that, during Menem's ten-

Table 6.7. Argentine Chamber of Deputies: distribution of seats between two major parties (1989—1999)

Period*	Total Number of Seats	Justicialist Party (PJ) Seats	Radical Party (UCR) Seats
July 1989–Dec. 1989	254	106 (42%)	114 (45%)
Dec. 1989–Dec. 1989	254	112 (44.5%)	90 (35.5%)
Dec. 1991–Dec. 1993	257**	117 (46%)	84 (33%)
Dec. 1993–Dec. 1995	257	128 (49.8%)	83 (32.5%)
Dec. 1995–Dec. 1997	257	131 (50.9%)	68 (26.5%)
Dec. 1997–Dec. 1999	257	119 (46.3%)	106 (41.2%)***

Reprinted from Ferreira Rubio and Goretti (2000).
* Half of the seats in the Chamber of Deputies are renewed every two years.
** The increase in the total number of seats was due to the creation of a new province: Tierra del Fuego.
*** These seats correspond to the ALIANZA (UCR + FREPASO).

Table 6.8. Argentine Senate: seat distribution between two major parties (1989—1999)

Period*	Total Number of Seats	Justicialist Party (PJ) Seats	Radical Party (UCR) Seats
July 1989–Dec. 1989	46	20 (43.5%)	19 (41.5%)
Dec. 1989–Dec. 1992	46	26 (57%)	14 (30.5%)
Dec. 1992–Dec. 1995	48**	30 (62.5%)	11 (23%)
Dec. 1995–Dec. 1998	72***	37 (51.4%)	20 (27.7%)
Dec. 1998–Dec. 2001	72***	38 (52.7%)	20 (27.7%)****

Reprinted from Ferreira Rubio and Goretti (2000).
* A third of the Senate's seats were renewed every three years, according to the 1853 constitution.
** The increase in the total number of seats was due to the creation of a new province: Tierra del Fuego.
*** The Constitutional Reform of 1994 increased the number of seats per district to three instead of the previous two.
**** These seats correspond to the ALIANZA (UCR + FREPASO).

ure, "of the 12 cases decided between 1989 and 1999, the high court endorsed the exercise of government power on eight occasions, "twice as often as it challenged," and of those four challenging decisions the high court "accorded with elected branch preferences and/or regarded laws that were no longer in effect." One of the most crucial cases was that of *Peralta,* decided in late 1990.[64] With a DNU, Menem imposed the Bonex Plan, which took fixed-term private savings accounts worth at least US $610 and converted them to ten-year government bonds that the government could temporarily use to cover the nation's internal debt. Luis A. Peralta and Sara Foralledo, two owners of the affected private savings accounts, filed suit. The court denied their claim and upheld the government's stabilization plan. Here the court sanctioned the president's infringement of property rights, encouraging Menem to "rule by decree throughout the 1990s" (Kapiszewski 2007, 280, citing Gargarella 1998, 442; Pellet Lastra 2001, 26). In another case, the court sanctioned the executive's use of legislative power, which ordinarily fell under Congress's domain, explaining that the executive is able to solve problems "more efficiently and expeditiously" (Manzetti, 2003, 336).[65] In another case, Menem issued a decree privatizing national airports. Ten legislators challenged the decree in courts, claiming it to be a constitutional violation of executive power. A lower court invalidated the decree. Menem then issued another DNU, this one reinstating the previous decree. A lower court invalidated Menem's second decree as well. The Supreme Court then invalidated both of the lower courts' orders, declaring the first moot due to the issuance of the second, and the second invalid, claiming that the legislators did not have standing to bring suit. This decision was especially significant because the court issued a blanket statement to the effect that DNUs are "inherently political and thus inappropriate for judicial interference" (Bowen and Rose-Ackerman 2003, 176).[66]

There is clear evidence of the judiciary's political partiality during Menem's tenure, when justices formed a voting bloc, supportive of government interests. This bloc voted together 70 percent of the time, particularly in politically crucial cases.[67] It was not until Menem became a lame duck that the court began to rule in opposition to government policy.[68]

The type of aggressive conduct, such as "the packing of the court," by which Menem ensured support, was not confined to his dealings with the judiciary. According to Manzetti (2003), Menem misused federal funds to expand patronage networks and secure congressional support.[69] The peripheral provinces controlled

83 percent of the Senate and 52 percent of the Chamber of Deputies, "thus holding the key to legislative approval of any reform agenda" (ibid., 349). Menem poured money into these peripheral regions; after all, buying votes here was cheaper than in urban areas, where votes were more costly due to intense party competition. Manzetti's data show that funds more than doubled between 1990 and 1995, and this trend continued until the end of Menem's presidency. The *Washington Post* calculates that $2.2 billion per year was lost to political patronage jobs. As of 2001, public spending on salaries had grown to a staggering $9 billion a year.[70]

The buying of congressional support worked for Menem. Of the 335 decrees issued during Menem's first term only four were repealed by the legislature, and two of those were overridden by presidential veto (Bowen and Rose-Ackerman 2003, 170).[71] The opposition was outgunned. As Böhmer (2000, 28) explains, "[T]he specter of the president simply decreeing policy change hung over the opposition during congressional negotiation of every important policy decision, and the imposition of decrees often allowed the government to bypass congressional debate and confrontation."[72]

Finally, the institutional bodies charged with fiscal oversight were ineffective and served more for the purpose of appearance.[73] This was enhanced by the fact that the public was left without access to information about either the courts or the political process at the federal level. The lack of transparency made effective oversight "extremely difficult" (Bowen and Rose-Ackerman 2003, 177).[74]

On a related note, corruption and exploitation of government funds in Argentina are not unique to Menem or even to his era. According to a *Washington Post* article published in February of 2002,

> Although almost half of Argentines live on less than $2 a day, legislators make as much as $5,400 a month, enjoy $3,000 monthly travel budgets, receive gasoline and car insurance allotments of $1,200 a month, and have additional budgets for as many as seven staff members. A Senate investigating committee recently found the government spent $1.5 million last year to maintain the Senate's fleet of 50 cars, more than enough to buy 50 new ones.
>
> Former officials have been accused of bilking the national health care system for the aged for an estimated $1 billion, and

> dozens of legislators have been accused of taking bribes from the failed administration of President Fernando de la Rua to approve a controversial labor reform law last year. And although several politicians, judges and government ministers have been charged with corruption, they rarely face punishment.[75]

The public, hurting from the early 2000 economic downturn and fed up with government corruption, took to the streets and began harassing government officials. A remark by one Argentinean may be indicative of public sentiment. Sergio Tobal, a real estate agent who helped organize a neighborhood assembly in the middle-class Buenos Aires neighborhood of Palermo Viejo, stated: "If you ask why Argentines are harassing politicians, the answer is because in this country, it is the only way to make them pay for their arrogance . . . We know they will never be punished by the courts. So the streets are being made unsafe for them. At least that way they will be prisoners in their own homes."[76] As it turns out, Menem was arrested in 2001 for arms trafficking charges but released soon thereafter by the Supreme Court, which happened to be headed by one of his former law partners.

Argentina during Menem's tenure serves as a case in which the judiciary and Congress lacked commitment to constitutional rules intended to regulate DNUs. Admittedly, the constitutional rules that are in place do not make it easy to obstruct a decree. Recall that in order to negate a decree, the Argentine Congress has to pass a new law, and even if Congress is able to garner the necessary votes, the new law is subject to a presidential veto either in part (line-item veto) or as a whole. And in order to override the presidential veto, a two-thirds majority must be obtained in both the Senate and the Chamber of Deputies. These rules may indeed favor the executive, but they at least provide Congress with a way to intervene. Moreover, the 1994 constitutional reform specified a number of reforms centered on institutional checks on the executive. Of particular note is the creation of a new position, the chief of the Cabinet of Ministers.[77] The chief of the cabinet is to oversee the general administration of the country, to issue acts and regulations in accordance with the constitution or that which is delegated to him by the president, and convene sessions of the Cabinet of Ministers in the absence of the president. Furthermore, the chief of the cabinet is to approve "jointly with the other Ministers, decrees of necessity and urgency and decrees that partially promulgate laws" and to "personally submit these decrees for consideration by the Standing Bicameral Committee within ten days of their enactment."[78] Although the chief of the cabinet was one of the showpieces of the reform, it has turned out to be a powerless position, and the bicameral committee that was to review DNUs did not come into being until 2006. Similarly, the National Judicial Council, created in 1994 and given assorted powers to oversee the judiciary, did not actually begin operating until early 1999.[79] Thanks to delays put in place by Menem, judges appointed by this independent council did not take the bench until after the close of Menem's tenure (Finkel 2004).

In short, the constitutional reforms of 1994 had little if any effect on Menem's issuance of DNUs, and he retained a court and a congress that were committed to him, a result largely attributable to Menem's backdoor deal making. Menem could, therefore, decree with great latitude, and the variables generally assumed to constrain the level of decree issuance by presidents (particularly the variable of *unified/divided government*) were effectively removed from the equation—making Menem's case particularly ideal for the study of TLB. It allows us to focus on the primary variable of interest—his tenure in office with regard to his decree issuance.

6.5 CONCLUSION

In this chapter I present a large body of literature on the constitutional boundaries of decree use in Brazil and Argentina for the periods under study and the reforms that have affected those boundaries. I also review how Congress and the court in each country respond to decree issuance given the workings of domestic politics peculiar to their state. This chapter makes the following three important points:

1. First, presidents Cardoso, Lula, and Menem maintained solid bases of congressional support throughout the majority of their tenure. Although support at times varied in degree and short bouts of abandonment did occur, it is fair to say that all three constructed and acted in cooperation with cohesive propresidential coalitions. Because Congress rarely stood in the way of decree issuance and because variance in presidents' congressional support is difficult to detect, these country cases offer only anecdotal evidence as to the causal relationship between unified government and executive decree issuance.[80] Recall that evidence from the case of the United States is mixed as to the role that unified/divided government plays in presidents' use of decrees. Coefficient estimates for *unified government* in the US

foreign policy models are positive and significant, indicating that unified government may actually increase the rate of issuance in decrees related to foreign affairs. In the case of US emergency power decrees, coefficients for *unified government* remain significant but in the negative direction, supporting the alternative hypothesis that higher issuance occurs in the wake of divided government. What is important to remember is that in all three countries during the periods under review, the legislative body or Congress did not stand in the way of a president's ability to issue decrees. This remains true even for the case of Brazil, where congressional approval is needed for any decree to transfer from temporary to permanent law.

2. There is little evidence that judiciary poses a threat to either Brazilian or Argentinean presidents in their issuance of decrees. The Argentine court is politicized and corrupt. The Brazilian court, in contrast, is powerful and independent and maintains ample opportunity to oppose executive decrees. Still, in both cases, as different as they are, the court rarely rules against a decree.

3. Certain reforms, specifically Brazil's EC32 and the associated Temer clarification and Argentina's 1994 constitutional reform, need to be considered and accounted for in the subsequent analysis of executive decree issuance. Most important, these reforms allow us to see if and what kinds of constitutional rules can successfully curb presidents' use of decrees.

What makes decrees in Brazil and Argentina (i.e., MPVs and DNUs) ideal subjects of study is that they, like emergency power decrees in the United States, are issued in actual emergency situations or under the guise of an emergency. Their current constitutions specifically state that exigent circumstances are needed to warrant their use. A finding that substantiates terminal logic thinking in the use of DNUs and MPVs should among other things invoke critical reflection on the meaning of "emergency" and "urgency." The immediacy inherent in crises should deny expectations of patterns associated with the cyclical model of time in tenure. When they do not, the abuse of executive power begins to look like the rule instead of the exception. And recall that one of the principle causes of democratic breakdown is the abuse of executive power (Diamond 2000).

Compared to the United States, Brazil and Argentina are nascent democracies. Although their history with federal institutions goes back more than a century, both countries have experienced long periods of autocratic rule. It is only recently (i.e., since the 1980s) that they have returned to the fold of democracy. Many Latin American scholars have long argued that the very context of political instability strengthens the stature of presidents at the expense of Congress and the judiciary.[81] O'Donnell (1994, 56) labels countries like Argentina and Brazil "delegative democracies." He explains that these countries are not institutionalized democracies, although there is "no sign either of any imminent threat of an authoritarian regression, or of advances toward representative democracy." Yet the combination of crisis, both economic and social, and a history of authoritarianism pushes them to rely on institutions that champion strong and powerful presidents. Scholars have kept a keen eye on how presidents of these countries use powerful presidential tools like decrees—and for good reason. Certainly, the concern for democracy in term-limit overstep is real and serious.

In chapter 7 I reveal evidence of TLB, showing that this is indeed a phenomenon to which leaders ascribe. I find a peculiar pattern of decree use—one that is best explained *not* by the occurrence of relevant or urgent events but instead by a behavioral idiosyncrasy that occurs in presidents' decision making. This behavioral idiosyncrasy is best explained by the theory of terminal logic behavior.

CHAPTER 7

Terminal Logic Behavior in Argentina and Brazil

A Comparative Look

7.1 INTRODUCTION

What we find in this chapter is that the TLB hypothesis also works for presidential behavior outside the United States. Presidents Cardoso, Lula, Menem, and Kirchner drastically increased their use of decrees during their final month in office—just as the presidents of the United States did. Presidents may be from different parties and stand ideologically opposed. They may issue decrees under different sets of legal provisions. Some may leave office highly popular with the public, whereas others finish their days being criticized as the worst president in the nation's recent memory. Congressional support may come and go—just as inflation rates rise and fall. Legacy most likely means something different to each president. What remains constant, however, is that presidents issue decrees in record numbers in their final month as president.

Recall that I expect US presidents will likely seek to fulfill their legacy agenda in foreign affairs. In contrast, I expect the legacy agenda of Argentine and Brazilian presidents to be more directly related to domestic issues and less so to issues surrounding the country's interests in world politics. As discussed in chapters 2 and 5, Argentina and Brazil represent emerging market nations for the periods under review. In these countries weak economic fundamentals and political-institutional instability create a situation where politics and economics are intimately linked. Their recent constitutions emerged during or immediately following periods of economic crisis. In the 1990s Brazil followed Argentina's lead in addressing economic crises with reforms based on neoliberal, market-based policies (as opposed to the state-led import-substitution-industrialization models of economic development). In the midst of democratization Brazilian and Argentinean presidents have used decrees to set up stabilization plans and structural reforms in an attempt to bring stability to the economy. I assume that the legacy agenda of presidents of emerging market nations is fixed on economic policy, specifically in the addressing of internal institutional arrangements that obstruct the performance of their country's financial markets. This is not to say that presidents do not see foreign relations or even environmental policy as important to their country's economic success. It is not uncommon for Latin American presidents to publically link their country's problems to the behavior of foreign powers. Faro de Castro and Valladão de Carvalho (2003, 465) note a clear example of this:

> In a trip to Uruguay, in early March 2000, the Brazilian President, Fernando Henrique Cardoso, declared to newspapers that the tariffs imposed by the American government on imports of steel and orange juice from Brazil were directly connected to poor social conditions in his country. Cardoso asked: "What is the responsibility that American or European markets have in keeping economies closed, in keeping a situation of hunger here?" The president also declared that US trade policies had a direct impact on "employment here [in Brazil]" and on "Brazilians' life conditions."

Yet Argentine and Brazilian presidents are less in a position to build a legacy out of involvement in affairs abroad than are US presidents. They must first fix their sights on domestic arrangements before moving on to make a meaningful mark in the international arena.

Indeed in Argentina and Brazil, presidential decrees mainly address issues of domestic policy and government administration, whereas in the United States, the majority of decrees issued concern foreign affairs. Ferreira Rubio and Goretti

Table 7.1. Policies covered by Argentina's DNUs (1989—1994)

Policy Area	Total	Percentage
Taxes	72	21.4%
Salaries	39	11.6%
Public debt	29	8.6%
Trade	10	3.0%
Transport	21	6.3%
Nation/Provinces	6	1.8%
Real estate privatization	22	6.5%
Civil and political rights	8	2.4%
Public agencies	32	9.5%
Proceedings against state	5	1.5%
Electric energy	8	2.4%
Promotion of industry	8	2.4%
Mega-NUD 435/90	14	4.2%
Mega-NUD 1930/90	22	6.5%
Others	32	9.5%
Total	336	97.6%

Reprinted from Ferreira Rubio and Goretti (1998, 46, table 2.3).

(1998, 43–51) identify sixteen categories covered by Menem's DNUs (see table 7.1). The last four categories describe three mega-DNUs that cover a broad range of policies, most of which are domestic in nature (related to taxation policy and deregulation of the economy) and one category that the authors describe as a "residual category." By Ferreira Rubio and Goretti's count, the majority of DNUs issued during Menem's tenure involve policies associated with taxation, public agencies and salaries, public debt, and deregulation of the economy.[1]

Similarly, most MPVs for the period under review involve policies associated with economic stabilization packages (e.g., the Real Plan and the PAC [Programa de Aceleração do Crescimento, or Growth Acceleration Program]), domestic market deregulation and privatization, civil rights, the economy generally (domestic industry/business), health, education, and labor. Refer to table 7.2, Reich's (2002) classification of MPVs from the 1989 to 1998 time frame.

Table 7.2. **Policies covered by Brazil's MPVs, (1989—1998)**

Policy Area	Number of MPVs made into law
Reorganization of executive branch offices	56
Extraordinary/emergency authorization of funds to specified agencies	38
Pay/regulations regarding civil servants	38
Transfer of funds between federal agencies	29
Income tax regulations	27
Monetary policy (banking, credit)	26
Taxes on manufactured and imported goods	22
Social security	20
Wages	19
Miscellaneous	17
Trade	14
Agricultural policy	10
Commerce	10
Energy	9
Closure of executive branch agency	9
Indexation of prices and wages	9
Labor code	8
Education	8
Privatization	8
Poverty programs	5
Consumer Protection	5
Minimum wage	5
Environment	4
Public safety/crime	4
Transfer of funds between central government and states and municipalities	4
Federal housing program	4
Taxes on financial transaction	3

(continued)

Table 7.2. *(continued)*

Policy Area	Number of MPVs made into law
Monetary conversion (new currency)	3
Public health	2

Data from Reich (2002, 18–19, table 2). The right column does not represent a total count of MPVs for the 1989–1998 time period. Reich did not exclusively assign each MPV to one category if assignment to two or more was warranted. Also, 28 percent of the 323 decrees were coded into two categories, and just over 1 percent of decrees were coded into three categories.

The majority of MPVs from the early 1990s on had to do with either domestic policy or organization of the executive branch. Amorim Neto and Tafner (2002) confirm that issues addressed by MPVs have remained consistent regardless of the government in power from 1988 to 2000.[2] Pereira, Power, and Rennó (2008) then remind us that "the first-order executive priorities of Cardoso and Lula have so far been interchangeable: defending the *real* with similar monetary policies, pursuing social security and tax reform with similar goals, and combating poverty and inequality with similar social programs. In fact, from November 1998 through December 2005 (two dates that bookend the reform of presidential decree authority) an unbroken series of agreements with the International Monetary Fund homogenized Brazilian macroeconomic management to a significant degree, so much so that Lula's government has been referred to as 'the third term of President Cardoso.'" For this reason, it is fair to assume that MPVs issued during Lula's terms in office did not take on issues entirely different from those cited in table 7.2.

Since MPVs and DNUs address primarily issues of domestic policy and government administration, I do not differentiate by policy type. Recall that, in the United States, domestic policy and government administration decrees account for only 23.9 percent of the overall total number of decrees issued from 1977 to 2008. This percentage jumps to 39 percent if environmental and research policy is included in the calculation. Foreign affairs decrees, on the other hand, account for 54 percent of all decrees issued in the United States for this period (see tabulations in chapter 4). And recall that the models presented in chapter 5 did in some cases yield notably different results. Indeed, testing the effects of TLB on decrees that share similar characteristics, either in policy outcomes or in the source of authority that allowed for their issuance in the first place, can produce meaningful results. Differentiating MPVs and DNUs by policy type is a promising avenue of inquiry for future research.

7.2 USING THE CASE STUDY METHOD

I examine the use of decrees by presidents of Argentina and Brazil who have completed full terms within the 1989 to 2009 time frame—two Brazilian presidents, Fernando Henrique Cardoso (January 1995–December 2002) and Luiz Inácio Lula da Silva (January 2003–December 2010), and two Argentinean presidents, Carlos Saúl Menem (July 1989–December 1999) and Néstor Carlos Kirchner (May 2003–December 2007).[3] For Brazil the time frame spans fifteen years; for Argentina, seventeen years.[4] Brazil and Argentina represent two of the three federal presidential democratic republics in the Americas.[5] In chapter 6 I reviewed the similarities and differences of the cases concerning their country's political institutions and presidents' power to decree.

In this chapter I analyze three cases using the case study method, specifically process tracing to uncover evidence of TLB. This is a deductive study, in which events and sequences within each case are carefully analyzed. I focus on key variables that were found in previous research to affect the level of decree issuance (e.g., legislative support, the economy, presidential popularity, and legal provisions governing decree use). I cast a wide net, allowing for the possibility of alternative explanations. Then, step by step, I pinpoint how and the extent to which these variables change over time with regard to the cases under review. Comparative analysis reveals that variation in levels of popularity, legislative support, economic indicators, and legal provisions governing decree use do not account for the consistent increase in levels of decree issuance at the end of each president's tenure. According to the hypothesis of TLB, alternative variables should not prevent the occurrence of increased decree issuance at the end of presidents' tenure. This is not to say that they have no effect on such issuance. Instead, these cases are meant to demonstrate that the single, common independent variable, *legacy period,* helps account for the common dependent variable, *rate of decree issuance.* These cases show that TLB is a plausible causal pathway and that other residual similarities between the cases are not.

A number of issues make these cases more amenable to the case study method than to statistical and formal methods. First and foremost, the rules governing decree use changed in the tenure of each of the presidents under study, and evidence indicates that all three of these reforms changed the way decrees could be issued (in content or in procedure) and as a consequence affected presidents' rate of decree issuance. The next section presents evidence of the reforms' effects on decree use. In September 2001 EC32 went into effect. President Cardoso completed his second term in December 2002. The Temer Reform went into effect in March of 2009. President Lula completed his term in December of 2010. Similarly, constitutional reform in Argentina took place in 1994 midway through President Menem's tenure. Not one of the presidencies under examination acted under the same set of legal provisions throughout the entire course of their tenure. Moreover, in the cases of Cardoso and Lula, the reforms were put in place during the most critical period of analysis for this study of TLB—during the last eighteen months of their tenures.

There is also the problem of changing reelection dynamics. Discussed at length in chapters 2 and 5 is the cycle of presidential periods, which includes the periods of *transition, regular,* and *legacy.* To review, the transition period denotes presidents' first year in office, when standing and influence are at their highest peak with Congress and the public.[6] Then presidents move to the regular period, which is assumed to be largely dictated by reelection behavior. This period stands in contrast to the legacy period. Presidents understand themselves to be terminal and as a result decide, act, and execute in light of the immediate prospect of termination. When Menem and Cardoso were first elected to serve as their countries' president, neither of their constitutions allowed for reelection. Cardoso won a constitutional amendment in June of 1997, allowing him to run for a second four-year term at the end of that year. Similarly, Menem won a chance to run for reelection in August of 1994, allowing him to run for a second term at the end of that year. Both of these presidents spent considerable time and political capital to obtain a constitutional amendment giving them the right to run for reelection. These presidents were technically terminal, but during that period both were amassing their efforts toward reelection, not toward solidifying their legacy. The assumption that the first term of presidents Cardoso and Menem is either a regular or a terminal period is problematic. The theory of TLB requires that presidents truly see their final period in tenure as exactly that. The theoretical construct of this research design requires this condition to be met.

On the one hand these reforms make it difficult to test count levels of decrees with respect to different points in presidents' tenure using statistical methods such as event count models. On the other hand, if other methods can unveil evidence of TLB across presidents even when those presidents are issuing decrees in different legal landscapes, this tells us that the behavioral tendency of TLB is fairly robust. For this reason, I use the case study method with the understanding of the trade-offs that come with doing so. I am not able to measure the magnitude of TLB's effects or the level of uncertainty that accompanies the causal inference as statistical methods like those used in chapter 5 could. Yet with this method I can achieve a higher level of *construct validity*, which is the "ability to measure in a case the indicators that best represent the theoretical concept we intend to measure" (Bennett 2007, 42). Given the problems noted earlier, the changing reelection dynamics and the changing legal provisions governing decree use, it would be difficult to achieve an acceptable level of construct validity using statistical methods.

Keeping these points in mind, see figures 7.1, 7.2, 7.3, and 7.4. These figures show timelines for presidents Menem, Kirchner, Cardoso, and Lula, respectively, from their first day in office to their reelection (with the exception of Kirchner) to their successor's election and then to their last day in office. More important, these figures illustrate when a reform affecting decree use and reelection possibilities took place in relation to these key dates.

7.3 THE EFFECT OF REFORMS ON DECREE ISSUANCE: THE EVIDENCE IN BRIEF

There is ample evidence that EC32 and the Temer Reform affected Brazilian presidents' use of MPVs and that Argentina's 1994 constitutional reform affected Menem's use of DNUs.

Brazil's EC32

First, the reform forbids key issues from being addressed by MPVs—issues such as taxation, which many MPVs prior to the reform addressed. Second, recall the difference that Pereira, Power, and Rennó (2008) find in the pre- and post-EC32 periods with regard to conversion rates when MPVs move from temporary to

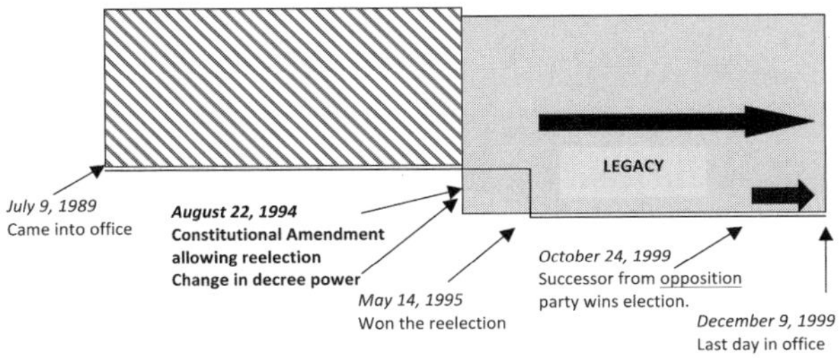

Figure 7.1. *The presidential cycle of Carlos Menem.*

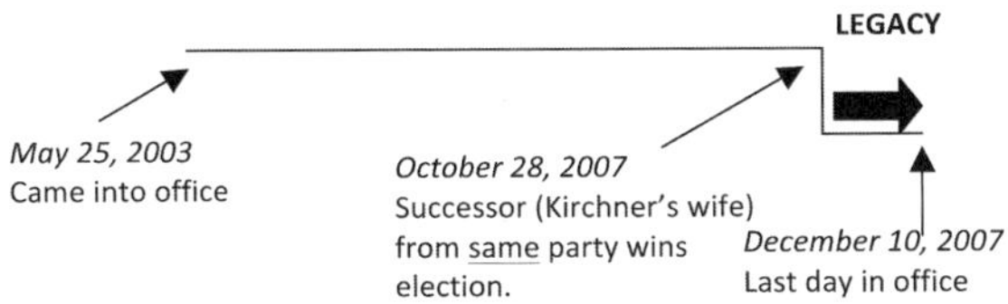

Figure 7.2. *The presidential cycle of Néstor Kirchner.*

KEY

- Post-Reform Period
- Terminal President Seeking Reelection

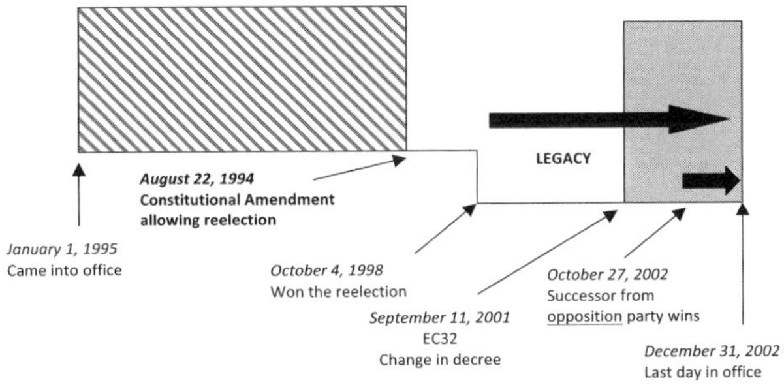

Figure 7.3. *The presidential cycle of Fernando Henrique Cardoso.*

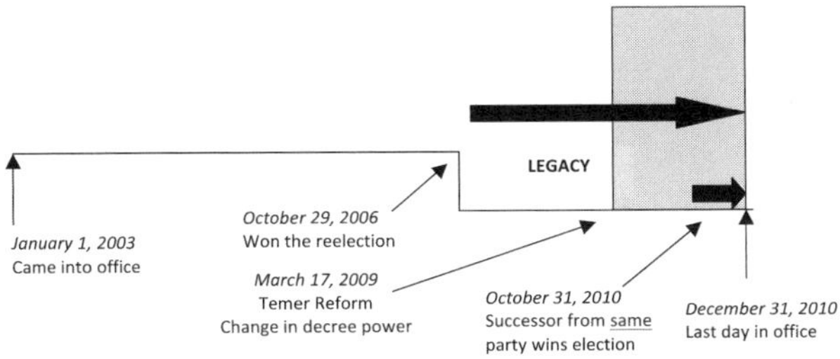

Figure 7.4. *The presidential cycle of Luiz Inácio Lula da Silva.*

permanent status. Prior to the reform the rate stood around 43 percent, and then in the post-EC32 period it jumped to nearly 79 percent (ibid., 26). Third, Palanza (2009) and Pereira, Power, and Rennó (2008) both obtain drastically different results when their data are partitioned between the two periods. For instance, the independent variables of Pereira, Power, and Rennó's (2008) negative binomial regression (i.e., variables measuring presidential popularity, legislative support, cabinet size, cabinet coalescence, and cabinet management) are not statistically significant when testing their effect on decree counts prior to EC32. For the period after EC32 these same variables spring to life and become statistically significant. In a similar analysis Palanza (2009, 147) finds "enormous variability" in effect of both political context variables and economic variables on decree issuance.[7]

Brazil's Temer Reform

Rennó (2010) demonstrates that the Temer Reform reduced presidents' issuance of MPVs using a simple *t*-test of difference in means contrasting the periods before and after the Temer Reform.[8] The mean for the fourteen months prior to the reform is 3.14. For the ten months following the reform the mean is 2.1—a difference of 1.04. He finds the difference to be statistically significant at the 0.11 level in a one-tailed test. Moreover, using similar testing procedures Rennó finds no discernable pattern for ordinary law proposals as a result of this reform.

Argentina's 1994 Constitutional Reform

Although many of the rules instituted under Argentina's 1994 reform have failed to regulate the use and process of DNU enactment as intended, there is evidence that the reform did in fact affect Menem's level of issuance. The dotted portion of the line in figure 7.5 represents the monthly average of DNUs following the 1994 reform. As we can see, DNUs decreased on average after the passing of the 1994 constitutional reform. Recall that the 1994 reform forbids presidents from issuing DNUs in relation to crime, taxes, elections, and political parties. Although this did not prevent Menem from issuing decrees addressing these areas, it did reduce them (Ferreira Rubio and Goretti 1998). For instance, as mentioned earlier, prior to the reform Menem issued more DNUs with regard to taxation than any other category (see table 7.1). According to Ferreira Rubio and Goretti (2000), DNUs related to taxation greatly diminished following the reform. The 1994 category

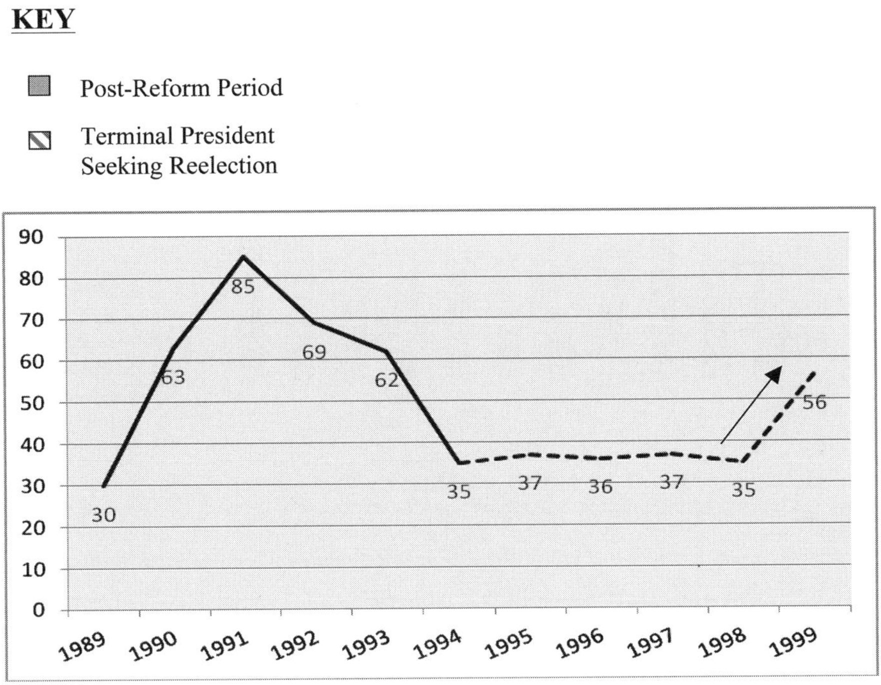

Figure 7.5. *Number of DNUs by year, before and after the 1994 constitutional reform (1989–1999).*

limitations may account for the reduced number of DNUs in the period following the 1994 reform (1995–1999).

For the yearly counts of DNUs, I use Ferreira Rubio and Goretti's (2000) data, which include both recognized and unrecognized DNUs. According to these authors, prior to 1994 only 166 of the 335 (47.2 percent) of DNUs were recognized as such, and following the reform only 110 of the 210 (52.4 percent) were recognized. Figure 7.6 shows total counts of recognized and unrecognized decrees for the period under review. Ferreira Rubio and Goretti (1998, 2000) classify a decree as a DNU if (1) it "modif[ies] or repeal[s] Acts of Congress in the absence of lawmaking authority or delegation or in any way impl[ies] the use of congressional legislative authority" or (2) it modifies or repeals another DNU. They explain that the Argentine legal system stipulates that a DNU can be modified or repealed only by a rule of the same or superior status. Therefore, a DNU can be modified or repealed only by another DNU or by an act of Con-

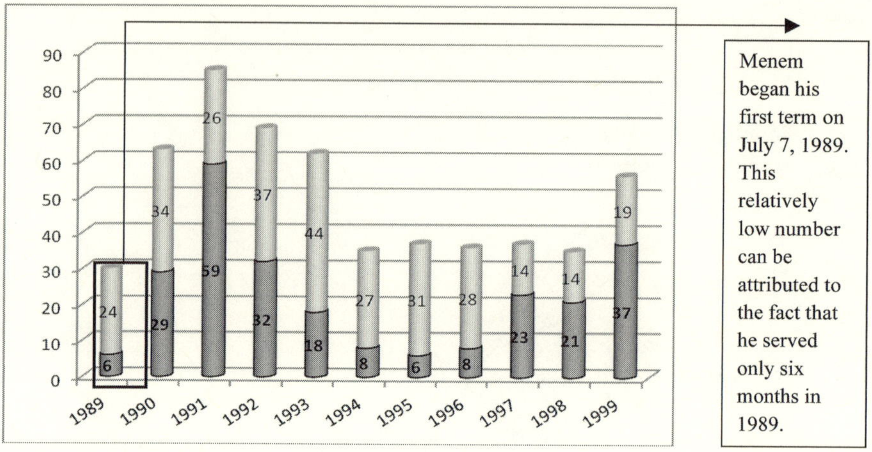

Data drawn from Rubio and Goretti (2000) and Palanza (2009).
*Top numbers represent "unrecognized" decrees and bottom numbers represent "recognized" decrees.

Figure 7.6. *Monthly average of DNUs by year during President Carlos Menem's tenure (1989–1999).*

gress. Others like Negretto (2004, 554) use only the "official" count of DNUs, arguing that the legal nature of Ferreira Rubio and Goretti's decree count is disputable. Yet the Argentine Constitution did not recognize the existence of DNUs until 1994, and since 1994 there has been no requirement for their listing or publication. For these reasons, I use Ferreira Rubio and Goretti's count of DNUs.[9]

7.4 DATA AND ANALYSIS: EXPLAINING TRENDS OF FREQUENCY

The point of analysis begins with figures 7.7, 7.8, and 7.9, which show the proportion of decrees passed by presidents Cardoso and Lula each month relative to the total count of decrees passed for the period. In Menem's case, figure 7.7 shows the proportion of decrees passed each year relative to the total count of decrees passed for the period. The data for the yearly counts of DNUs are drawn from Ferreira Rubio and Goretti (2000), which includes both recognized and unrecognized DNUs as explained in the previous section. Complete data for President Kirchner were not readily available. For the monthly counts of MPVs I use data from the Presidência da República Federativa do Brasil (Presidency of the

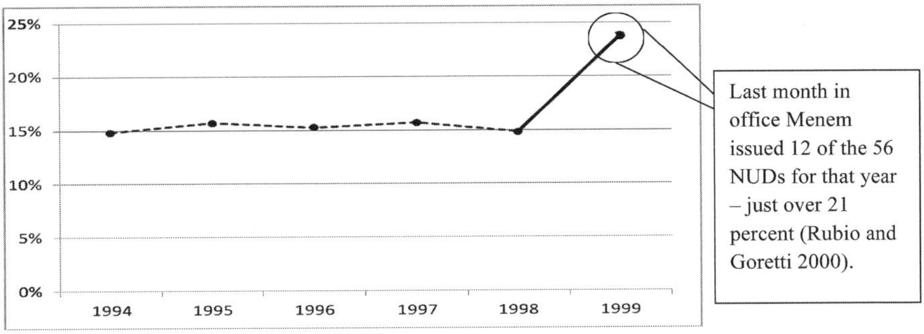

Figure 7.7. *Percentage of DNUs by year during President Menem's tenure after the 1994 reform (1995–1999).*

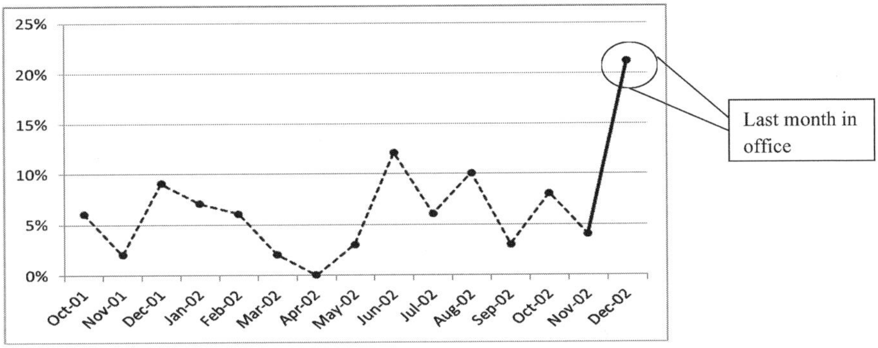

Figure 7.8. *Percentage of original MPVs by month during President Cardoso's tenure after the EC32 reform (October 2001–December 2002).*

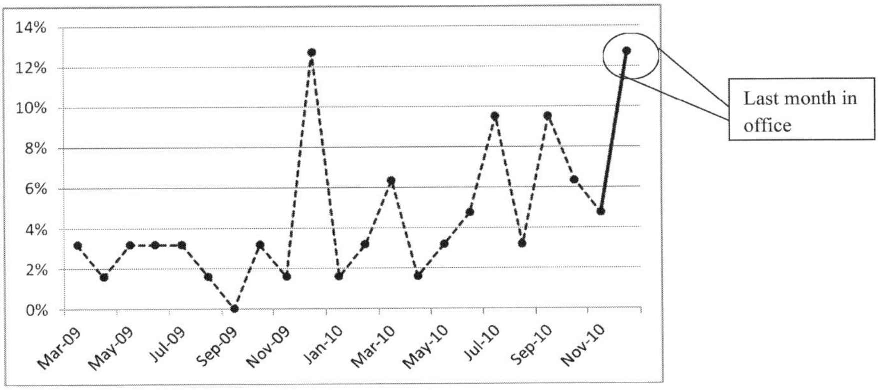

Figure 7.9. *Percentage of original MPVs by month during President Lula's tenure after the Temer Reform (March 2009–December 2010)*

Republic) website,[10] which provides a listing of MPVs, their date, number, title, legal standing, and accompanying documents.

These counts illustrate the post-reform period for each presidency. The reforms for Menem, Cardoso, and Lula (e.g., 1994 Constitutional Amendment, EC32, and the Temer Reform, respectively) are reforms that changed in some significant way the rules governing decree issuance. More important, they all occurred midtenure. Figures 7.7, 7.8, and 7.9 clearly show an end-of-tenure trend—increased decree issuance, particularly in the final month of each presidency. For Menem, when the final year is excluded, the average yearly count of decrees in the postreform period is 36.25. In his final year, he increased his decree use by 35 percent, issuing 56. The trend continues with Cardoso and Lula. For Cardoso, when the final month is excluded, the average monthly count of decrees in the postreform period is 5.57. In his final month, he increased his decree use nearly 74 percent, issuing 21. For Lula, when the final month is excluded, the average monthly count of decrees in the postreform period is 3.66. Again the final month represents a jump in decree use, a 54 percent hike with an issuance of 8 decrees.

Capriata's data (2008) shed light on Kirchner's last-minute activity. He reports that Kirchner issued 13 DNUs in the final month of his administration. Capriata also reports that Kirchner, a one-term Argentinean president from May 2003 to December 2007, averaged 60 DNUs per year, or 5 per month, for a total of 270 in his four and a half years as president. According to this data, Kirchner more than doubled his output of decrees in his final month. Kirchner was succeeded by his wife in office, and reports show that he planned on running for office again after her term was up. Yet even these conditions, which hold promise to continued presidential power, did not stop him from issuing a flurry of last-minute decrees.

Researchers have tested a broad range of variables—political, economic, and temporal in nature—thought to affect the level of decree issuance during a given period (e.g., presidential popularity, legislative support, size and coalescence of the cabinet, honeymoon period, reelection, inflation, currency fluctuation, period when major economic stabilization package was introduced, period when reform was introduced, type of issue addressed by decree (high versus low contested policy), and the number of bills sponsored by the executive). Researchers often neglect to use an end-of-term variable in their analysis. Palanza (2009) is an exception. Her analysis of Brazilian decrees utilizes a dataset of all MPVs and statutes from 1988 to 2005. Her logit analysis of two split samples, pre-EC32 and post-EC32, reveals that in the three months preceding an election, there is a systematic increase in the use of decrees, and this increase is statistically significant in both sample sets. Palanza's variable, *election,* however, does not denote the last three months of a president's tenure. It represents the three months preceding *any* presidential election. Moreover, the *election* effect increases nearly twofold in her post-EC32 sample. Since her post-EC32 sample contains data only through 2005, the effect accounts only for the preelection months of October, November, and December of 2002—Cardoso's final months in office.

Clearly, the effects of the political, economic, and temporal variables mentioned earlier are hard to pin down and are not yet understood. Specifying all the causal mechanisms that may affect the level of decree issuance is beyond the scope of this book. Instead, I seek to present evidence that the *legacy period* is a variable worthy of inclusion in analyses of decree use, one whose exclusion likely results in models with distorted results.

For the increased issuance of decrees in Menem's, Cardoso's, and Lula's final months let us consider alternative explanations that could hold greater explanatory power than terminal logic behavior.

(1) Presidential Popularity

Public approval ratings usually decline as presidential administrations come to their end. President Lula defied this expectation, leaving office at the height of his popularity with an approval rating above 80 percent. This end-of-term rating is even more impressive considering that Lula's lowest rating stood at 28 percent during his first term in 2005. Instead of falling, approval numbers climbed in Lula's second term—from 52 percent (December 2006) to 50 percent (2007) to 55 percent (March 2008) to 70 percent (November 2008) to 72 percent (December 2009) to 76 percent (May 2010) to a record 83 percent after seven years and eleven months in office. Kirchner, too, "left office as the most popular outgoing president in modern Argentine history" with an approval rating of 43 percent (Levitsky and Murillo 2008, 17).[11] Cardoso and Menem, on the other hand, closed out office with the lowest approval ratings of their tenure, 26 percent and 14 percent, respectively. We have presidents that left office at the peak of popularity and presidents that left with the lowest approval ratings in their tenure. Such evidence indicates that presidential popularity as a variable is not uniform in its effects on presidents' issuance of decrees.

(2) Congressional Support

Brazilian scholars have tested a number of variables such as the following in an attempt to connect empirics to hypotheses of congressional agency and support: the percentage of legislators following the vote recommendation of the leader of the governmental coalition in a congressional chamber; the percentage of seats held in a congressional chamber by parties represented in the president's cabinet; correspondence between share of cabinet ministers and share of intracoalitional legislative seats held by parties supportive of the president; or simply a dichotomous measure of divided government, where parties or coalitions different from the president have a majority in at least one chamber.[12] We have already seen evidence in chapter 5 supportive of the unified government hypothesis in the case of the United States. The cases of Brazil and Argentina also provide support to this claim that presidents issue more decrees under a unified government than a divided one. Palanza (2009) finds that issuance of DNUs is 5 percent more likely during periods of unified government. Similarly, Pereira, Power, and Rennó (2008) find that after the enactment of EC32 the size of a given legislative coalition in Congress and the degree of political investment presidents put into it are directly related to MPV issuance. Said differently, the successful management of congressional support leads to increased decree issuance—particularly after EC32.

But how does the unified government hypothesis square with evidence that suggests that as presidential administrations age, presidents lose the ability to bargain, negotiate, and persuade Congress? Lame-duck Brazilian presidents face a higher rate of MPV rejection by Congress. Cardoso, for instance, faced a higher rejection rate in the final six months of his presidency, when the rate of rejection increased approximately 3 percent.[13] Moreover, legislative discipline in roll call votes diminishes as Brazilian presidents come closer to the end of their tenure (Amorim Neto 2000).[14] What these conflicting hypotheses, each with their own supportive evidence, tell us is that the level of congressional support does not explain end-of-term decree behavior.

The unified government hypothesis may have some explanatory power when testing entire periods of presidential tenure. It does not, however, fully explain the jump in decree issuance at the end of a president's tenure. There are deep contrasts between presidents. For instance, using Palanza's (2009) measure of unified government, Menem only briefly experienced unified government between 1995 and 1997. Lula maintained a strong coalition at the end of this tenure, allowing his handpicked successor to capture the presidency. Cardoso's coalition, on the other hand, broke apart at the end of his term. Moreover, legislative support, particularly in Menem's case, may not necessarily correlate with whether the president's party or a coalition has a majority.[15] In fact, Mustapic (2002) shows that Menem's party (PJ), relatively speaking, did not unify on issues of economic reform.

Policy conflict still occurs under unified government. To assume that policy discord is minimized when two branches are controlled by the same party may be overly presumptuous. After all, Eaton (2000, 359) adds that "presidents and legislators are still elected by different rules and in districts of different sizes." Lack of party discipline on the one hand and strength of regional and local interests on the other counter the unified government hypothesis, which is based on party control of both the executive and the legislative branches. This surely attributes to the unsettled debate as to whether the executive is actually usurping power Congress's when issuing decrees or merely acting in the face of congressional acquiescence.

(3) Economic Context

Another rival explanation of increased decree issuance at the end of presidents' tenure is that something economic in nature necessitated a greater number of decrees. Indeed, economic turbulence came to Brazil in 2001/2002 at the end of Cardoso's presidency and at the end of Menem's presidency in 1999. Yet Treisman (2004) finds no link between the timing of stabilization measures and the electoral calendar. In Argentina, stabilization plans were instituted during the first, third (three times), fifth, and sixth year of the six-year presidential term. In Brazil, plans were instituted during the first, second, third, fourth, and fifth year in the five-year presidential term. During Menem's tenure a major stabilization package was introduced from August of 1989 to August of 1992. In Brazil, the last major economic stabilization plan introduced was Cardoso's Plano Real in July of 1994.

It is worth recalling that Lula's government is often referred to as the third term of President Cardoso. Although Lula was a member of the opposition party, his policies were strikingly like Cardoso's policies on issues of monetary policy, social security, taxes, and social programs and carried the policies out in a similar manner—with the use of MPVs. Increased decree issuance by Menem, Cardoso, and Lula in their final month cannot be chalked up to a drastic change in economic environment that necessitated such decree use. Issues of inflation and currency control do not arise overnight. They are part of larger cyclical processes, detected and addressed over longer periods of time.

7.5 CONCLUDING REMARKS: MOVING BEYOND INDIVIDUAL DIFFERENCES

As stated in the introduction, I do not dispute the premise that each president has a particular motivational structure and that in many instances no two presidents will likely make the same choice on similar issues not only because of their uniqueness in time and the political environment in which they each find themselves but also because of their individual uniqueness. Each likely has different conceptions of social causality, human nature, and the like. Presidents come from different backgrounds. For instance, compare the backgrounds of Cardoso and Lula. Cardoso has a doctorate in sociology and has written more than a dozen books—even publishing scholarly work while president.[16] He is the son and grandson of army generals. He has taught at Stanford and Cambridge. Lula, on the other hand, never finished elementary school. In an interview with *Newsweek,* he recalls his childhood poverty:

> I remember that I ate bread for the first time in my life when I was seven years old. Till then, I drank black coffee and mixed flour in the coffee along with porridge for breakfast. In those days a lot of children starved before reaching the age of one. I managed to survive.[17]

Regardless of whether one is a president, all individuals discount things at different rates. Much variability exists in their backgrounds and in the political, economic, and social dynamics that surround the office of the presidency over time. Yet despite such differences, because all presidents know they are limited to a fixed period of time within which to achieve their goals—similar behaviors emerge. The substance of the decrees issued in those final months and the issues they address are likely to be quite different. What remains constant, however, is that presidents issue decrees in record numbers in their final month as president. It is a time when reelection constraints have been removed, presidents' organizational motivation structure has been reformulated, sights have been set on legacy, and the end is most acutely felt.

CHAPTER 8

Anticipating the Effects of Terminal Logic Behavior

Avenues of Future Inquiry

Why do some countries succeed where others fail? Why do the budding democratic waves of some countries fall into chaos while other countries embrace the processes of modernization and the social change that comes with them? In his analysis of the global state of democracy, Diamond (2000, 418) states that "no period in world history has a wider expansion of the democratic form of government and of the ability of citizens, armed with universal suffrage, to change their political leaders in relatively free and fair elections." Yet he adds that "if the reach of democracy is greater than ever, it is also thinner and more vulnerable." Although this last wave of democracy has brought only three apparent democratic reversals in states of more than twenty million people (Nigeria, Sudan, and Thailand), democratic breakdowns have occurred in more than twelve states with smaller populations during the 1990s. The jury is still out on the success of the most recent revolutionary movement of unrest against autocratic governance, which began in the Arab world in late 2010.

The fragility of democracy, young or old, cannot be underestimated. Certainly, there are many questions to which we do not have answers. Yet the success of democracy seems to depend greatly on the answer to one question: which set of political institutions best promises a democratic government such that a democratic state can grow and persist even in the face of poverty, ethnic and religious divisions, and traditions of authoritarian rule? The executive office is one such institution whose design largely influences which way a state will swing.

This book focuses on how preferences become dynamically channeled by a structure instilled by term limits. If presidents serve a set time period of four years and can be reelected to only one subsequent four-year term, I hypothesize that they operate in two distinct frames of choice and desire. Simply put, they operate in one frame whose boundaries are set by terminal logic and in another whose boundaries are not. I hypothesize that this change in the imperative for action causes a sense of urgency in completing one's work—resulting in a rapid and otherwise unexplainable increase in policy activity. Evidence garnered in support of these hypotheses may help to explain why presidential systems, in general, face less chance of democratic achievement than do their parliamentary counterparts.

I begin my analysis of terminal logic behavior with the case of the United States. I use the decree dataset to test US presidents' rate of decree issuance over the course of their tenure with respect to domestic, foreign, and environmental policy. For each policy domain I run event count models to determine the count levels of decrees with respect to different points in presidents' tenure. Using increased decree issuance as a proxy for TLB, the models show that TLB exists, when it is most likely to begin, and the relative degree of its effect. In particular, the models show the following:

1. Across the board in all policy domains (foreign, environmental, and domestic policy, as well as decrees of emergency power), presidents increase their rate of decree issuance when they are in the final weeks of their last term, particularly when their successor has been named *and* that successor is from the opposing party.

2. Presidents consider their level of legislative support when issuing decrees. The models show a systematic effect of legislative support on rates of foreign policy and emergency power decree issuance. In the foreign policy models, the effect is as expected. When the president's party controls both houses, the result is a higher issuance rate of foreign policy decrees. This confirms previous findings that unified government may actually increase presidents' use of decrees. The emergency power models, however, show that divided government may actually increase the rate of issuance of emergency power decrees.

3. The rates of increase in emergency power decrees and environmental policy decrees are substantial during the final ten-week period. This is surprising, particularly for the use of national emergency powers.

4. Presidents issue decrees at significantly different rates in different policy domains. Democratic presidents are likely to issue more decrees than Republicans in domestic and environmental policy. In foreign policy and in emergency power, however, this differentiation cannot be made.

5. The rate of issuance for emergency power decrees, in general, has increased with each successive president.

I believe that a number of reasons account for why US presidents in particular feel the pressure of being acutely "terminal"—and why we can expect this pressure to grow in time. From its beginning, the United States, as compared to other societies, had few obstacles to mobility. Although there have always been "vestiges of hierarchy" present in US society (Young 1996) and "an array of other fixed, ascriptive systems of unequal status" present at the time of the American Revolution (Smith 1993, 549), it is hard to dispute the statement that, when compared to the varying political and economic statuses of people in Europe (e.g., monarchs, indigents, and farmers), the United States at its founding was unusually free.[1] Colonial America lacked a great many institutional structures that were present in its mother country. Wood (1969, 44) points out that, without "elaborate institutions of society—from hospitals and nursing homes to prisons and asylums" to regulate behavior, informal social networks had to step in to fill the void. The absence of formal institutions and the presence of informal social networks in their place allowed a new understanding of *what community meant* to take form.[2] It is from this that Americans' perception of themselves as connected to one another vertically rather than horizontally was born. North America never experienced a feudalistic era. This omission, if it can be so conceived, sheltered a certain innocence or purity of thought so that, as Hartz (1955, 9) argues, a phenomenon of "fixed, dogmatic liberalism" captured the United States at its earliest stages. In this sense, the political ideology of classical liberalism became synonymous with the North American way of life. Individual identity was championed, and terms such as *freedom* and *bootstraps* became deeply ingrained in the American psyche.

The US polity, present and past, is based on "the axiom of the irreducibility of the individual and hence the sovereignty of his [the individual's] passions" (Cropsey 1955, 124). Believing in the achievement of individual action fuels ambition of the strongest type. "Nowhere is this idea more pronounced than in the American presidency," for as King (2013) of the *Washington Post* reminds us, one can quickly go "from rags to riches, log house to White House, community organizer to commander in chief."[3]

We now live in a world where presidents use social media like YouTube, Twitter, and Facebook to attract and maintain followers. Current president Barack Obama uses others, too, such as Google+ and the social photo-sharing site Instagram. Social media help presidents increase their public appearances and lay claim to their policy initiatives in greater detail (Kumar 2010b). This platform of communication is evolving rapidly.[4] No one can be sure where the digital platform will take us in politics. What we do know, however, is that it allows for more personal engagement between leaders and their constituents through their respective digital identities. This personal engagement creates a more intimate connection between leaders and their populace—and, arguably, the new kind of personalization that comes from social media will only further imbue presidents with the feeling of independent power.

This personalization of power, matched with the increase in presidential transition activities, particularly the contact and involvement of presidents-elect in state affairs, exerts great pressure on outgoing presidents. It is quite inconceivable to imagine a transition today like that prior to the Eisenhower/Kennedy transition in 1960–1961, when presidents-elect were expected to stay away from Washington until inauguration day and have minimal contact with the outgoing administration. Presidents-elect now join the inner circle of information about military and foreign policy decisions. A large swath of transition staffers and volunteers stalks Washington as they ready the incoming administration for power.[5] Perhaps national security demands that presidents-elect jump into the fray months before inauguration. Both the National Academy of Public Administration and the Homeland Security Advisory Council recommend this. Indeed, more than seven thousand noncompetitive appointments must be made, of which over a thousand are political appointees requiring Senate confirmation (Kumar et al. 2000, 5). Background checks and security clearances must be done. Without doubt, prevention of both staffing gaps and disorganization of leadership should remain the priority. Yet we must recognize the increased pressure this puts on outgoing presidents and anticipate the behavioral changes as a result—specifically the power grab that outgoing presidents are likely to make.

As the comparative cases of Argentina and Brazil show (chapter 7), this is also true for leaders outside the United States. Increased policy activity happens despite presidents' standing with the public, despite their standing with Congress, despite their country's economic condition, and despite the makeup of their character or their ideological leanings. What is surprising is that researchers often neglect to use an end-of-term variable in their analyses of decree use. What this book shows is that it is a variable worthy of inclusion in the study of decrees. Moreover, it is easy to conceive how excluding an end-of-term variable in any analysis of presidential behavior risks producing distorted results.

This study is important for a number of reasons. First, it tells us a great deal about executive decision making in presidential systems. The findings here show that term limits channel the preferences and choices of executive leaders in such a way that their behavioral tendencies become more predictable. For instance, we now know that presidents in their final hour in office are more likely to order measures affecting the environment. Environmentalists lobbying to protect land from mining or timber harvesting might choose to step up their efforts toward the end of a president's tenure because their efforts stand a greater chance of success at that time. President George W. Bush designated large sections of the Mariana Islands, the Marianas Trench, Pacific remote islands, and Samoan islands as monuments (protected lands) in his final days.[6] Similarly, President Clinton proclaimed twenty-one monuments in his last nine months as president. And in a grand sweep of presidential power, Brazil's President Cardoso decreed "the biggest conservation program for tropical rain forests in the planet's history" three months before leaving office.[7] This study gives us a baseline and helps us understand why presidents make some decisions when they do. Presidents are likely to approach their legacy projects with the greatest intensity in those last ten weeks after their successor has been named. If a president cares about a particular issue or policy, it is best to begin by examining the president's behavior in that period with respect to that issue or policy.

Second, this study shows that democracy, although it is built on great intentions, is, like all other forms of government, still susceptible to the abuse of power. In particular, I want to call special attention to presidents' use of emergency power decrees. Linking this type of decree to TLB is not only theoretically intriguing but also normatively important. As reviewed in chapter 6, Brazilian and Argentine presidential decrees are much like emergency power decrees issued in the United States because they, too, are issued as the result of an actual emergency or under the guise of an emergency. The current constitutions of both Brazil and Argentina specifically state that exigent circumstances are needed to warrant the use of decrees. Recall that, among other things, emergency power allows presidents to seize property, organize and control means of production, seize commodities, assign military forces abroad, institute martial law, seize and control all modes of transportation and communication, regulate the operation of private enterprise, and restrict travel.[8] I find little evidence in all three country contexts that either Congress or the courts have been willing to stand up to presidents in their issuance of emergency power decrees. The very projection of a situation as an emergency facilitates legislative and judicial deference to presidential choice. Because the declaration of an emergency is a subjective evaluation, it becomes a political question, which denies review. I also find that the models of the five US presidents and the data collected in the two Brazilian cases and the two Argentine cases all show that emergency power is associated with the cyclical model of time in tenure. This should invoke critical reflection on the meaning of emergency and on the provisions governing its use.

Certainly, the conceptions of emergency and war in the modern era are quite different from those of times past. War on drugs, war on crime, and war on terrorism, for instance, are not like war against Nazi Germany.[9] Ackerman (2004, 1042) explains that "the realities of globalization, mass transportation, and miniaturization of the means of destruction suggest that bombs will go off too frequently for the common law cycle to manage crises effectively." The term *war* has evolved to denote less definite states in time. The margins of war's end are at best unclear and at worst nonexistent. For instance, it is hard to imagine a definitive end to the War on Terror or to cyberwarfare. Presidents' use of emergency power is likely to expand as realms unbound by fixed territory (in the traditional sense) become part of the landscape of war.

Curiously, as the concept of war has changed, so, too, has presidents' conception of urgency. The threshold of duress has become quite low—encompassing all types of events that have some power to change the course of a nation's state of affairs. In the case of MPVs and DNUs, presidents pass legislation, claiming the press of "urgency," which covers "all kinds of policy areas in any context"—health, education, even fishing rights in the Amazon River.[10] Certainly, the survival of the state need not be at risk for an issue to be proclaimed "on grounds of necessity and urgency." Consequently, this has led to the creation of many "emergencies."

Scholars like Olson and Woll (1999, 19) have called attention to the "explosive growth in the number of declared national emergencies" in the United States. Indeed, the models in this study show an increased use of emergency power decrees with each successive US president. What this tells us is that, even for the United States, the most long-standing presidential system of government, rules and boundaries of power must be recognized and properly set. Because presidential systems are particularly vulnerable to instability and breakdown, we need to understand how certain rules in these systems may affect the behavior of their leaders.[11] If we have learned anything from this study, it is that presidents even in the most established democracies have a hard time letting go. The president is acutely aware that the public identifies him or her, this *one* person, as the symbolic head of the state and holds that person accountable for the state's progress or decay.[12] Presidents scramble to right wrongs, tie up loose ends, and with all their might strive for achievements with principled purpose. Their history is all but a fait accompli.

Laws need to be designed properly so that this power can be held in check. This is far from an easy task. Thomas Eagleton's (1974) account of how the War Resolution Act of 1973 came to be makes this clear.[13] Crafting legislative language is a tricky business. On the one hand, legislative language that is too restrictive could hamstring presidents so much so that they are unable to carry out the necessary action required of them as commander in chief. On the other hand, legislative language that is too vague invites abuse that could be corrosive to the state's democracy. Ackerman (2004) may offer us a way forward. He suggests a new construction of the US Constitution whereby mechanisms for short-term emergency measures are installed and restricted in scope and time. In Canada, for instance, legal differentiation is made between types of emergencies (e.g., natural disasters, threats to public order, international crises, and states of war), and, as a consequence, each receives separate treatment in the eyes of the law (ibid., 1061–62).

As mentioned in chapter 2, the field of executive term limits remains largely unexplored. Most of the work in this area is speculative and remains unsubstantiated. This study is an attempt to reset the course by connecting term structure effects to empirically observed evidence in presidential behavior. Many of these issues surrounding term limits may seem self-evident. On closer look, however, it becomes clear that the situation is much more complicated. Term limit structure is connected to larger issues that matter most in the construction of democratic government. Characteristics of the term structure (e.g., mode of appointment, length of the term, reeligibility) are intimately linked to political configurations (i.e., separation of power issues) and the patterns of power that determine state behavior. After all, the term structure shapes and regulates the cycling of individuals and parties in and out of office, producing the continuous political competition that sets a democracy apart from a dictatorship.

Understanding how the two four-year executive term structure came to be in the United States is important. Here we learn that the US Constitutional Convention of 1787 gives us little reason to tether ourselves to the four-year term. As discussed in chapter 2, the tenure design was an "unanticipated by-product" resulting from a patchwork of compromises made between competing factions (Robertson 2005, 226) that hinged largely on the mode of presidential election. It was not that such a design was ill or well intentioned but that it was not so much intentioned at all.

Changing the executive term structure in the United States would be a mammoth task requiring two-thirds majorities in both Houses of Congress and the approval of three-fourths of state legislatures. The current US political system does not have the internal structure needed to foster the kind of unity required for such an amendment. Until it does, we need to press forward to learn more about term effects and other term structures, remembering that here we have the potential to better the whole of a political system with a one-line change to the Constitution. We have the potential to reign in campaign finance and bring efficiency and productivity to the legislative process all in one fell swoop. Imagine that, instead of two four-year terms, presidents would serve a single six-year term. Mexico, whose presidents serve under this condition, may hold interesting insights into the nature of midterm elections; in their role as national referendums on presidential administrations, they may affect presidential behavior in a domain where presidents can always be described as *terminal.* Moreover, some political scientists in the United States view Mexico's executive term structure as ideal or "more perfect" than the US executive term structure.[14] Perhaps instead of looking at decree frequency, we should look at the changing substance of the decrees themselves. Data can be gathered and analyzed from other presidential case studies—presidents who serve under different executive term structures.

This study is concerned more with how policy is made, not the kinds of policies actually created. Focusing on decree content instead of decree frequency yields other interesting questions. For instance, as presidents become terminal, are they more or less apt to seek peaceful cooperation and more or less likely to commit resources for an arms buildup? As presidencies age and become terminal, they may be more likely to favor a pragmatic approach to economic policy over a populist one (e.g., favor a removal of trade barriers over an endorsement of them or a move away from a state-administered, inward-oriented model of development to a more market-oriented model.). Moreover, decree use is only one possible indicator of terminal logic behavior. Other legislative tools could be examined, especially in relation to each other. Do presidents turn to different policy instruments as they enter their legacy period? For instance, O'Connell (2008, 901) finds that "although the press feasted on President Clinton's midnight regulatory activity, President George H. W. Bush started nearly 50 percent more notice-and-comment rulemakings in the final quarter of his term than did President Clinton and nearly 40 percent more than did President Reagan."[15] Presidents may use a variety of legislative tools to further their legacy objectives. This is another promising avenue for future research. Without a doubt, much meaningful work remains to be done.

In closing, this book would be incomplete without a brief note about current president Barack Obama, who presents a particularly interesting case. For one thing, his rapid ascent to power was extraordinary. In the words of *Frontline*'s Jim Gilmore, "I mean, he's so young. He's so green. And all of a sudden, bam, bam, bam."[16] He served less than four years in a national office before taking on the presidency at age forty-seven, making him the fifth youngest president in US history. He is also the first African American to hold the office. It is easy to see why expectations have been high. Certainly, his early life was not one of privilege. From community organizer to commander in chief, he rose with what Harvard law professor and Obama mentor Laurence Tribe describes as "a burning sense of obligation and ambition . . . an ambition to make a difference."[17]

Obama's second and final inaugural address was indeed a bold statement of his liberal vision. He called for the advancement of gay and women's rights, tolerance toward illegal immigrants, gun controls, preservation of the social welfare safety net, and action to stop climate change. *Politico*'s John Harris and Jonathan Martin (2013) call it "the most ideologically ambitious speech since Ronald Reagan's first inaugural address a generation and a half ago."[18] Clarence Page of the *Chicago Tribune* writes: "[Obama] sounded like a man who knows his clock is running out."[19] In the three months since then, Obama has been aggressive on a number of fronts. He has named nearly three dozen judicial candidates—"a significant departure from the sluggish pace of appointments throughout much of his first term."[20] In the realm of economic and trade policy, he has begun pursuing "the most aggressive talks in a generation." Bruce Stokes, head of the global economic program at Pew Research Center, claims that "If Obama pulls this off, it will be pathbreaking, precedent-shattering . . ."[21]

There is also evidence that a blurring of formal distinctions between executive orders and presidential memoranda is taking place under Obama. For instance, Obama signed what the White House press secretary called "23 new executive actions" related to gun control in January 2013. *Bloomberg News,* the *Huffington Post,* and *Forbes* also mistook these twenty-three "executive actions" as twenty-three "executive orders." A reporter, Meredith Dake, explains the cause of confusion: "Vice-President Biden and President Obama both referred to the orders as 'executive actions' during their speeches, but at the end of President Obama's speech the President said 'let's sign these orders.' In the White House official transcript it reads "(The executive orders are signed)."[22] Obama, flanked by children and with Biden standing close by, signed only three presidential memoranda. The administration counts signed reports to agency heads and broad pronouncements such as "launch a national dialogue led by secretaries Sebelius and Duncan on mental health" as its "executive actions."

Perhaps the most telling of what we can expect of an end-of-tenure Obama is what he has said in private conversation. According to an official who spoke to the *Washington Post* on the condition of anonymity, Obama said, "Let's not focus on what's possible or doable . . . Tell me what our goal should be, and let me worry about the politics." Consider also the open microphone moment with Russian president Dmitry Medvedev noted in the introduction of this book. It is worth quoting again here. Obama said, "On all these issues, but particularly missile defense, this can be solved, but it's important for him [Putin] to give me space . . . This is my last election. After my election, I have more flexibility."[23] Everything points to the conclusion that in Obama we have the making of a soaring eagle—not of a lame duck. Undoubtedly, an end-of-tenure Obama may be the most aggressive end-of-tenure president that we have seen yet.

Appendix

Formal Decree Power as Stipulated by Brazil's 1988 Constitution
The Constitution of the Federative Republic of Brazil, 1988
(as amended to 2002)

ART. 62. *In relevant and urgent cases, the President of the Republic may adopt provisional measures with the force of law; such measures shall be submitted immediately to the National Congress.*

§ 1°. Provisional measures may not be issued on matters:

I—with respect to:

a) nationality, citizenship, political rights, political parties, and electoral law;

b) criminal law, criminal procedure, and civil procedure;

c) organization of the Judiciary and the Public Ministry, as well as the careers and guarantees of their members;

d) multiyear plans, budgetary directives, budget and additional and supplementary credits, except as provided for in art. 167, § 3°;

II—that deal with detention or sequestration of property, popular savings, or any other financial assets;

III—that are reserved for a complementary law;

IV—that have already been regulated in a bill approved by the National Congress which is awaiting the approval or veto of the President of the Republic.

§ 2°. A provisional measure that involves institution of or an increase in taxes, except as provided for in arts. 153, I, II, IV, V, and 154, II, shall only produce effects in the following fiscal year if it has been converted into law by the last day of the [fiscal year] in which it was issued.

§ 3°. Except as provided for in § 11° and 12°, provisional measures shall lose their effectiveness as of the day of their issuance if they are not converted into law within a period of sixty days, which may be extended once, in the terms of § 7°, for an equal period. It is the responsibility of the National Congress to regulate, by legislative decree, the legal relations stemming from such measures.

§ 4°. The period referred to in § 3° shall start to run from the publication of the provisional measure. This period shall be interrupted while the National Congress is in recess.

§ 5°. The deliberation of each of the Houses of the National Congress on the merits of provisional measures shall depend upon a prior judgment as to their compliance with constitutional requirements.

§ 6°. If it has not been considered within forty-five days, counting from the date of its publication, the provisional measure shall be deemed in need of urgent consideration. Subsequently, in each of the Houses of the National Congress, all other legislative deliberations of the House to which it was presented should be suspended until it is finally voted upon.

§ 7°. The effectiveness of a provisional measure may be extended once for sixty days if during the sixty-day period counting from the date of its publication, it has not been submitted to a final vote in the two Houses of the National Congress.

§ 8°. Provisional measures shall be voted on first in the Chamber of Deputies.

§ 9°. A mixed commission of Deputies and Senators shall have the duty to examine provisional measures and to issue an opinion about them, prior to their being considered, in separate sessions, by the full membership of each of the Houses of National Congress.

§ 10°. It is forbidden to reissue, in the same legislative session, a provisional measure that has been rejected or that has lost its efficacy by the lapse of time.

§ 11°. If the legislative decree referred to in § 3° is not issued within sixty days after rejection or loss of efficacy of a provisional measure, the legal relations constituted under it or stemming from acts practiced during the time it was in effect shall remain in effect and shall be governed by these measures.

§ 12°. If a bill to convert or modify the original text of a provisional measure has been approved, the provisional measure shall be maintained integrally in force until the bill is signed or vetoed.

Notes

CHAPTER 1

1. I thank Dr. David Darmofal for this analogy.

2. For more on the agent-structure debate, see Friedman and Starr (1997), Carlsnaes (1992), and Wight (1999).

3. For instance, Will (1994) argues that the power of the US presidency has significantly grown in the post–World War II era due to the effects of television and the Cold War. For more on the growth of presidential power in the United States, see classics such as Schlesinger (1973) and Goldsmith (1974), as well as Eagleton (1974) and DeConde (2000). For ultrapresidentialism in Latin America, see O'Donnell's (1994) argument on delegative democracy and Nino's (1996) discussion of Argentina.

4. O'Connell (2008) makes a convincing argument to this effect: "In 2001, Congress passed 24 major statutes and 112 other public laws. By contrast, in that year, cabinet departments, the Executive Office of the President, and other independent agencies promulgated 70 significant rules and 3,383 other rules" (892).The congressional information data are drawn from Jill Barshay's *2001 Legislative Summary*, published in the *CQ Weekly* on Dec. 22, 2001, 3018–55, and from the *Congressional Record* of 149-D456 (daily ed., May 6, 2003), *Final Résumé of Congressional Activity: First Session of the One Hundred Seventh Congress.* Data on the federal administrative state are drawn from the GOA Federal Rules Database Research, available at http:/www.gao.gov/fedrules/. Barshay notes that "'significant' or 'major' rules are those that have at least an annual $100 million, or otherwise 'materially adverse' effect on the economy."

5. See Richard Cohen, *Washington Post*, "Too Quick to Fall for a Smile," Jan. 26, 2010.

6. See Arthur Schlesinger Jr.'s *Imperial Presidency* (New York: Houghton Mifflin, 1973); Richard Neustadt's *Presidential Power: The Politics of Leadership from FDR to Carter* (New York: Wiley and Sons, 1980); Theodore Lowi's *Personal President: Power Invested, Promise Unfulfilled* (Ithaca, NY: Cornell University Press, 1985); and Stephen Skowronek's *The Politics Presidents Make: Leadership From John Adams to George Bush* (Cambridge, MA: Belknap Press of Harvard University Press, 1993).

7. For more on institutionalism, see Thelen and Steinmo (1992).

8. The "fast track" stands opposed to what Lowi (1991, 238–39) describes as the "slow track" or the "Separation of Powers Track, permitted by a longer time horizon, and desirable wherever time permits, yet highly unpredictable, uncontrollable, public, full of leaky holes and dominated not merely by the legislature but by a large and pluralistic process fueled by greed."

9. State governments may fall into an alternative category of government whose institutional design is a particular hybrid form of the two systems (mixed democracy). Presidential and parliamentary systems are the most discussed in the literature and are the two original types of democratic constitution (Shugart and Carey 1992). Authors have warned against the overly simplistic comparison made between presidential and parliamentary systems. See Carey and Shugart (ibid., particularly 1–2) on the false promise of the presidential-parliamentary dichotomy. For more on the debate of presidentialism versus parliamentarianism, see Linz and Valenzuela (1992, 1994); Lijphart (1992); Stepan and Skach (1993); Horowitz (1996); Przeworski et al. (2000); and Cheibub, Przeworski, and Saiegh (2004). For more on the differences between presidential,

parliamentary and semipresidential systems, see Mahler (2008) and Peixoto (1988). The term *semipresidential* denotes those regimes that maintain a divided executive that comprise both a president and a prime minister (see the government designs of France, Portugal, Finland, the Republic of Korea, the Republic of China [Taiwan], and Ukraine). Others have described these regimes as "mixed democracies" or "presidential-parliamentary systems." For a detailed analysis of the characteristics of semipresidential systems, see Duverger (1980).

10. From this point on the term *executive term limits* is used synonymously with *presidential term limits.*

11. Juan Linz (1978, 1988, 1990) was one of the first to call attention to the differences between parliamentarism and presidentialism in the mid-1980s, specifically the problematic nature of presidentialism in its institutional rigidity when compared to its parliamentary counterpart. See also Valenzuela (1985) and Lamounier and Nohlen (1993).

12. The two presidential democracies that have been "steadily democratic" since 1950, according to Dahl (2002), are the United States and Costa Rica.

13. See Blondel's (1987) data on 221–24.

14. To be sure, there are many variables to consider when evaluating the stability and efficiency of democratic systems aside from those that come from this parliamentary-presidential dichotomy. For instance, scholars of electoral systems argue that the level of multipartism or the relevant number of parties involved in Congress matters more than whether a country has presidents or prime ministers.

15. "Fixed term" here refers to any predetermined length of term. It does not refer to the number of terms the president is constitutionally permitted to serve. When presidential systems are juxtaposed with parliamentary ones, the definition of "fixed term" is clear. Cheibub (2007, 1) explains: "In presidential systems, the head of the government cannot be removed from office even if he or she favors policies opposed by the legislative majority" until that person has served out the predetermined term. In parliamentary systems either a new government is formed or new elections take place once the legislature passes a no-confidence vote. Parliament can force the executive to resign and either form a new cabinet or call for new elections at any point. Chief executives serve at the pleasure of parliament, whereas presidents serve out their predetermined term.

16. This trait was first described by Flaubert in *Correspondance,* vol. 5 (Paris: Conard, 1929), 111.

17. See O'Donnell (1994, 59–62) for a discussion of "delegative democracy." Regardless of whether a country fits the bill as a "delegative democracy," as O'Donnell describes, is beyond the scope of this discussion. What is pertinent is his description of presidents—their power, their mandate, and the conflict they face with regard to succeeding at both reelection and accomplishing long-term goals.

18. The presidents of the three countries in this analysis (the United States, Argentina, and Brazil) all serve as both head of government and head of state. This is always the case in *full* presidential systems, which can be distinguished from parliamentary and semipresidential systems. The former often has a head of state that is simply a ceremonial figurehead, a president or constitutional monarch. Examples of countries that maintain a ceremonial monarch as head of state and a prime minister as head of government are Australia, Belgium, Japan, Spain, and the United Kingdom. Ireland and Israel are two examples of countries that have a ceremonial president as head of state and a prime minister as head of government. In semipresidential systems the head of state shares executive power with the head of government. France is a prime example of this form of government. For more on various models of executive politics in parliamentary and semipresidential systems, see Elgie (1997) and Dunleavy and Rhodes (1995).

19. President Obama's open microphone moment occurred on Mar. 26, 2012, during a bilateral meeting at the Nuclear Security Summit in Seoul, South Korea.

20. The choice of using the term *decree* is discussed at length in section 4.3.

21. Of the 19 countries, 2 are in Africa, 4 in Asia, 3 in Europe, 3 in Oceania, and 7 in the Americas.

22. Of the 56 countries, 15 are in Africa, 11 in Asia, 23 in Europe, 3 in Oceania, and 4 in the Americas.

23. Mexico is the fourth country. Mexican presidents serve one six-year term.

24. See Heclo (1977) and Hart (1998).

25. For more on the problem of quantification with regard to presidential studies, see Bowles (1999).

26. The American Presidency Project was established in 1999 by John Woolley and Gerhard Peters at the University of California–Santa Barbara, www.presidency.ucsb.edu/.

27. Alexander Hamilton compares the executive office to that of the British king and state governors (Benjamin 1985).

28. Mayer finds that presidents double their average level of order issuance when they are faced with a successor from the opposition party. Yet of his ten cases, there are only two, FDR and Reagan, who did not have to hand over the presidency to a member of the opposition party, and FDR is a unique case since he is the only president in US history to have served three terms. Kennedy, of course, was killed and therefore could not anticipate his succession. Nixon resigned, leaving the presidency to his vice president. Because he was faced with almost certain impeachment and removal from office, his ability to issue executive orders was certainly compromised.

29. It is important to note, however, that Hedtke (2002) and Cunion (2005) find little difference in the behaviors of those two-term presidents serving before the Twenty-Second Amendment and those serving after it.

30. For the benefits of adopting and/or learning from foreign constitutional models, see Wiarda (1971) (focus on Latin America) and Miller (1997) (focus on Argentina). For the opposite view on the nontransferability of constitutions, see Seidman (1978, 34–36) and Selassie (1992, 4–5). Many scholars such as Atilio Borón, a leading Argentine sociologist, claim that constitution copying is doomed to failure. They recall Hegel's argument that "a constitution is not [just something] manufactured; it is the work of centuries . . . the consciousness of rationality so far that consciousness is developed in a particular motion" and his insistence that "the constitution of any given nation depends in general on the character and development of its self-consciousness. In its self-consciousness its subjective freedom is rooted and so, therefore, is the actuality of its constitution" (Miller 1997, citing Borón 1993, 339–40, and Hegel 1967, 286–87).

31. See note 11, this chapter.

32. Shugart and Carey (1992, 2) claim that "most of the scholarly literature on the subject comes out quite squarely behind parliamentarism as the preferred alternative." In contrast, Mainwaring and Shugart (1997) argue that presidentialism has its virtues. Among other things, in comparison to parliamentary systems, presidential democracies have more executive accountability and greater congressional independence and offer voters more choice.

33. Maltz (2007, 128–29) constructs a dataset of ninety-two countries. Each country has more than two million people, a modest degree of political openness, and a presidential or semipresidential system. He finds that out of those ninety-two countries, twenty-six presidents have contravened their term limits.

34. In December 2007 Argentina's Cristina Fernández succeeded her husband, Néstor Kirchner, as president, prompting accusations that the couple found a way to circumvent the

country's term limit rules (Hawley 2009). Similarly, in March 2011 Guatemalan president Álvaro Colom announced that he would divorce his wife, Sandra Torres, so that she could run for president. Guatemala's constitution bars relatives of the president from holding that same office. Colom claims that he and his wife are making "a real sacrifice" for their country. See the *Washington Post* article by Al Kamen, titled "Patriotism Conquers True Love," Mar. 24, 2011.

35. Ginsburg (2010, 3) calls attention to the African countries of Niger, Cameroon, Chad, Gabon, Guinea, Namibia, Togo, Tunisia, and Uganda and to countries of Eurasia such as Azerbaijan, Belarus, Kazakhstan, Tajikistan, and Uzbekistan, where executive term limits have all been "relax[ed]."

CHAPTER 2

1. For more on the history of institutionalism in the discipline of political science, see Peters (2005), Pierson (2004), and Rothstein (1996).

2. Ragsdale and Theis (1997, 1282) explain that "the term 'institution' has become something of a buzz word in the social sciences." They go on to say that "Many writers assume they know the meanings of these terms [institutionalization, to institutionalize, institution, and institutionalism], even when they do not define them."

3. See Aristotle's *Politics*, book 7, trans. Benjamin Jowett (2000).

4. Examples of microlevel institutions are religious/ethnic associations, trade unions, health clinic kinship networks, and epistemic communities. At the macrolevel, international regimes can be described as an institution. The norms and conventions of practice established by these regimes can also be described as institutions. For a nice overview and conceptualization of international institutions, see Simmons and Martin (2002).

5. This study focuses on presidents from the United States, Argentina, and Brazil. Presidents in this analysis have served their terms consecutively. Yet the constitutions of the United States, Argentina, and Brazil do not require them to do so. For instance, US president Grover Cleveland served two nonconsecutive terms (1885–1889 and 1893–1897). For this reason, I use the term *subsequent.*

6. See Bueno de Mesquita's (1983, 27–29) version of the "unitary actor" model. He assumes that individuals and/or groups who make key decisions operate as units and, therefore, should be conceived as unitary actors. I thank Dr. Harvey Starr for directing me to this point.

7. Allison (1971), in his seminal work, *Essence of Decision: Explaining the Cuban Missile Crisis,* suggests three models for the analysis of elite decision making. Model I, or the Rational Actor Model, perceives policy behavior as purposeful acts of a rational, unitary decision maker. The rational actor calculates the costs and benefits of every action and reaction. An action is simply a calculated response to a strategic problem. The actor sees one set of goals, one set of options, and then estimates the consequences that follow from each option. The primary actor is the national government, but the focus may be placed on the individual leader or leadership group most responsible for setting the utility function of perceived goals, options, and estimation of consequences. Model II (Organizational Process Model) and Model III (Governmental Politics Model) do not view acts and choices as an output of one unitary actor. According to the Organizational Process Model, state behavior is a result of the independent output of many organizations that are coordinated by the head of state. The Governmental Politics Model, on the other hand, views behavior as an outcome of a competitive bargaining game played by many individual players. Players range from the head of state to cabinet members to members of the press. In comparing the institutions of the US presidency to Congress, Moe (1993, 374) claims that "presidents are not hobbled by collective action problems and can simply make authoritative

decisions about what is best for the presidency"; furthermore, "[there is] substantial congruence between the president's individual interests and the interests of the institution [the presidency] far more so than within Congress." With this in mind, this study treats the presidencies of the United States, Argentina, and Brazil all as unitary institutions.

8. See Almond and Genco's (1977, 499) discussion of mixing choice with constraint and regularity with innovation.

9. King, Keohane, and Verba (1994) note Mill's ([1843] 2002) plurality of causes.

10. The highest ambition of interpretation (narrative analysis) is to move beyond subjectivity, where knowledge is anchored in certainty beyond subjective intuition (Taylor 1973, 7). Gould (1991) reminds us that our use of an unsystematic method of observation lets events of little value, as well as the true relationships that may underlie these events, go unnoticed and that humans, through the methods of common sense, often imagine many relations that actually *do not* exist. Humans are eager to impart meaning to patterns. Ordinary human inquiry is plagued by inaccurate observations, overgeneralization, selective observations, and illogical reasoning, and therefore the verifiable systematic method of scientific knowledge should supplement interpretive methods like narrative analysis (King, Keohane, and Verba 1994).

11. Keohane (1984, 58) declares that rules are more specific and more easily changed than norms, but still it is difficult to separate them. Also see discussions in Ruggie and Kratochwil (1986, 753–76) and Young (1986, 106).

12. Finnemore and Sikkink (1998, 891) call attention to the types of norms discussed in the literature "regulative" and "constitutive" norms. Regulative norms "order and constrain behavior," whereas constitutive norms "create new actors, interests, or categories of action." See also Katzenstein (1996, 5), Finnemore (1996, 22), and Klotz (1995).

13. The Twenty-Second Amendment, §1, states the following:

> No person shall be elected to the office of the President more than twice, and no person who has held the office of President, or acted as President, for more than two years of a term to which some other person was elected President shall be elected to the office of the President more than once. But this article shall not apply to any person holding the office of President when this article was proposed by the Congress, and shall not prevent any person who may be holding the office of President, or acting as President, during the term within which this article becomes operative from holding the office of President or acting as President during the remainder of such term.

14. Willis and Willis (1952, 469) claim that for a short stint (between Jackson and Lincoln) a one-term tradition prevailed, "candidly justified as an expression of the Whig philosophy of legislative supremacy."

15. For more on who introduced these resolutions, see 93 Cong. Rec. 847, 864 (1947).

16. See Peabody's (2001) analysis of Washington's remarks on term limits and presidential leadership. Also see Milkis and Nelson (1994, 90) and Smith (1969).

17. See note 11, this chapter.

18. See studies by Carey, Niemi, and Powell (2000); Farmer, Rausch, and Green (2002); Sarbaugh-Thompson et al. (2004); Kousser (2005); Carey et al. (2006); and Chen and Niou (2005).

19. See Moe (1985, 1993), Lowi (1985), Pika (1988), and Burke (1992).

20. See Balz (2007), Grossman et al. (2000), Peabody (2001), Shogan (2006), Skowronek (1993), Crockett (2008), Maltz (2007), and Howell and Mayer (2005).

21. Note the attempts at healthcare reform made by US presidents Clinton and Obama.

22. From this point on the term *Congress* is used to refer to a legislative assembly. See Bond and Fleisher (1990), Jones (1994), and Rudalevige (2002) on US presidents' inability to push legislation through Congress because of second-term politics.

23. This has been dubbed the "Thurmond rule," for the late senator Strom Thurmond, R-SC, who came up with the rule in 1968. The rule stands for action taken by the party seeking the White House to "shut down judicial confirmations some time before Election Day." See the *New Yorker* article by Jeffrey Toobin, titled, "Obama's Unfinished Judicial Legacy," July 31, 2012.

24. On the flipside of this coin, Finkel (2004) finds (also using the case of Argentina) that the likelihood of implementing judicial reform increases as the ruling party's probability of reelection declines.

25. O'Connell (2009), in her twenty-year analysis (1983–2003) of federal agencies' semi-annual reports in the *Unified Agenda of Federal Regulatory* and *Deregulatory Actions,* finds that cabinet departments often complete more regulatory action in an administration's final year than at any other time. She finds this to be true during both Ronald Reagan's and George H. W. Bush's administrations but not during the Clinton administration. Cabinet departments (as a group) finished more action during Clinton's honeymoon period in 1994 than in his last quarter as president. Federal Circuit Judge S. Jay Plager, a former Office of Information and Regulatory Affairs administrator under President George H. W. Bush argues that "the haste with which midnight regulations are pushed out the door results in a 'a certain amount of sloppiness' and 'makes control of the regulatory apparatus appear to be a Washington game'" (Morrow 2001, 3).

26. The Bush administration called for new regulations planned for the end of tenure to be proposed by June 1, 2008, and for all regulations to be promulgated by November 1, 2008. See Franks's opening statement at the hearing. The hearing, complete with witness testimony and other materials submitted for the hearing record, are available at http://www.gpo.gov/fdsys/pkg/CHRG-111hhrg47033/html/CHRG-111hhrg47033.htm.

27. A large body of evidence supports this claim. For instance, the Government Accountability Office (GAO) calculates that federal agencies submitted thirty "major rules" or rules with economic impact of at least $100 million each in October and November of 2008. During that same period in 2007 federal agencies submitted only thirteen "major rules." For more examples, see works mentioned earlier in the text.

28. See Combs's (2001) analysis of these events. In late December of 1980, Reagan described the Iranians as "nothing better than criminals and kidnappers." (See Steven R. Weisman, "Reagan Is Angered at Teheran's Stand in Hostage Release, *New York Times,* Dec. 25, 1980). Four days later the *New York Times* then reported that Edwin Meese III, the head of Reagan's transition team, warned Iran "that Mr. Reagan might take a tougher line in his dealings on the captives" and that "a delay in releasing the hostages would lead to the new president's "taking appropriate action when the time comes.'" (See "Reagan Aide Warns Iranians," *New York Times,* Dec. 29, 1980). The Iranian hostage crisis is discussed at length in the conclusion of chapter 5, given that it was "the most dramatic foreign policy controversy since the end of the Vietnam War" and that it occurred during a presidential transition (Combs 2001, 306).

29. In writing during the Cold War, Mosher, Clinton, and Lang (1987, 32) go so far as to claim that "there is a periodicity in international relations that synchronizes with American presidential elections."

30. The US aircraft made an emergency landing on Hainan Island, and the PRC detained twenty-four crew members for eleven days. A 2003 US Navy report has since acknowledged that "compromise by the People's Republic of China of undestroyed classified material . . . is highly

probable and cannot be ruled out" (Hersh 2010). Washington and Beijing disagree over the cause of the collision. This event is known as the Hainan Island Incident.

31. See Jonathan Soble and Katherine Hille's Feb. 6, 2013, *Financial Times* article, "Sensaku Row Raises Militarisation Fears." Other examples abound. According to Mosher, Clinton, and Lang (1987), the Soviet Union "test(ed) his [new US president's] will and the limits to which he can be pushed" during the Cold War. There is also the example of North Korean action during South Korean presidential transition. Victor Cha, a Korea expert at the Center for Strategic and International Studies, claims that North Korea has taken violent action in the first months after the inauguration of each South Korean president since 1992. See David Ignatius's Mar. 14, 2013, *Washington Post* article, "Preparing for the Worst with North Korea."

32. See Soble and Hille's piece noted in note 31, this chapter.

33. See a 2008 report by the Panel of the National Academy of Public Administration on presidential transitions at http://www.napawash.org/wp-content/uploads/2008/08–05.pdf.

34. See Korzi (2011, 145–51).

35. See Weissert and Halperin (2004, 2007) and Green, Marquette, and Farmer (2006) for survey evidence of US public support of legislative term limits. Most striking is Weissert and Halperin's (2007, 524) point that with regard to legislative term limits "the only place where term limits have been successfully overturned by voters is at the local level." Jacob (1994, 27) adds the following: "Polls have consistently put support for term limits on Congress at between 75 and 80 percent with some polls showing support as high as 86 percent." Currently, in the United States, fifteen state legislatures maintain term limit rules, eight of the ten largest US cities have term limits for their city councils and/or mayor, and thirty-seven states have term limits for their constitutional officers (US Term Limits 2009). Moreover, US Term Limits is a national group that encourages the public to vote for legislative term limits. Find this group on the web at http://termlimits.org/.

36. Becker (1990) lists incumbency advantages for congresspersons, and some of these may be applied to presidents: "name recognition, opportunities to go on television and radio, franking privileges (the right to send job-related mail without paying postage), power to do favors for constituents and other interest groups, and much easier access to campaign funds than challengers [have]."

37. Maltz (2007, 135), focusing on electoral authoritarian regimes that had term limits during the 1992–2006 time period, finds the following:

> In the twenty instances between 1992 and 2006 when the opposition won the presidency (in non-founding elections), Freedom House scores (the average of the scores for 'political rights' and 'civil liberties') improved by 0.9 points on a 7-point scale from one year before the turnover to two years after it. Further, where the opposition took the presidency after two or more terms of ruling-party incumbency, as happened on twelve occasions, the Freedom House scores improved by 1.3 points. This includes six instances of dramatic political liberalization. Significantly, the average Freedom House scores did not budge between three years prior and one year prior to the turnover, demonstrating that the shift in control over the presidency from one party to another party or set of parties was a crucial event.

38. Not surprisingly, electoral authoritarian regimes as opposed to democratic ones are much more likely to have presidents that violate term limits. In fact, Maltz (2007, 128) points

out that not a single democracy eliminated term limits altogether, whereas 23 percent of electoral authoritarian regimes did so. Democratic regimes, on the other hand, engage in what Maltz describes as *soft contravention,* "staying in office in excess of the tenure the constitution had initially mandated, but without entirely eliminating term-limit provisions."

39. Quite chilling are the words of Justice John Paul Stevens, which he read aloud in his dissent of the court's ruling in this case: "[The court's ruling] . . . threatens to undermine the integrity of elected institutions across the Nation. The path it has taken to reach its outcome will, I fear, do damage to this institution . . . A democracy cannot function effectively when its constituent members believe laws are being bought and sold." For more on this case, see the Supreme Court of the United States (SCOTUS) blog sponsored by Bloomberg Law at http://www.scotusblog.com/2010/01/citizens-united-v-fec-in-plain-english/.

40. Becker (1990, 18), in discussing congressional term limits, counters this argument. He suggests that congressional incumbents can avoid dependence on interest groups better than newcomers precisely because they know the ropes and can use "the various advantages of incumbency."

41. Carey (2003, 126) explains that it is assumed and "practically axiomatic by many political scientists" that presidents seeking reelection have an incentive to be more attentive to the citizenry than those who are constitutional lame ducks. See also Kamber (1995) and Peabody (2001).

42. Louis R. Cohen, in oral arguments before the Supreme Court in US Term Limits v. Thornton, no. 93–1456, argued that it was the public's place, not that of Congress or the states, to decide whether a candidate was worthy of another term in office: "My theory of the Constitution, which I think is also Madison's and Hamilton's theory of the Constitution on this point, is that the Constitution deals comprehensively with the filling of the office of the Congress that it created, that it prescribes fixed qualifications that may not be supplemented by either Congress or the States, and that it gives both the States and Congress the power to set time, place, and manner regulations so as to assure [*sic*] fair and orderly elections, but that that is an essentially procedural power, leaving the people at each election to choose whom they please to govern them." For more on this case (i.e., oral arguments, judicial conclusion and opinions), see the Oyez Project, a multimedia online archive of US Supreme Court cases at http://www.oyez.org/.

43. For more on the influence of the US Constitution on political systems, see Rapaczynski (1990), who pays particular attention to the influence of the US model on the political systems found in Canada, Australia, Israel, India, Scandinavia, Europe, Africa, and Latin America.

44. The *Federalist Papers* is a series of eighty-five essays by James Madison (authored twenty-eight), Alexander Hamilton (authored fifty-two) and John Jay (authored five) in 1787 and 1788. These essays are available at http://www.foundingfathers.info/federalistpapers/.

45. See Beard (1913), Buchanan and Tullock (1962), McGuire (1988), Jillson and Eubanks (1984), Heckelman and Dougherty (2007).

46. At the time, however, the delegates had to consider that short terms required the electors to travel a great distance to the nation's capital rather frequently (Jillson 1988, 107–109).

47. In 1776, governors served either one-, two- or three-year terms.

48. Nineteenth-century Argentinean constitutional texts and Alberdi's draft can be found in Arturo Enrique Sampay's (ed.) 1975 book, *Las constituciones de la Argentina.* Aside from Alberdi, Miller (1997) notes that the US Constitution captivated other important Argentinean figures during this period—figures such as Juan María Gutierrez and José Benjamín Gorostiaga, key draftsmen at the Constitutional Convention of 1853; Domingo Faustino Sarmiento, an intellectual visionary influential in the 1860 constitutional reforms and a later Argentinean presi-

dent; and even General Justo José de Urquiza, the president of the Argentinean Confederation from 1854 to 1860.

49. Article 66 incorporated the line item veto; Art. 83, §10, allowed for cabinet ministers to be named without subsequent Senate consent; Art. 83, §19, granted the president power to announce a state of siege, with the consent of the Senate required if in session; Art. 83, §20, authorized the detention of persons threatening public tranquility (Miller 1997, 1511).

CHAPTER 3

1. Taken from the *Washington Post* article by Ruth Marcus, titled "Obama Unleashed. Don't Bet on It," Apr. 26, 2012.

2. The Jerusalem syndrome is an actual psychiatric disorder characterized by "eccentric conduct and bizarre behavior" due to one's proximity to the holy places of Jerusalem. Psychiatrists claim the psychotic decompensation is caused by a visit to Jerusalem (mostly by those deemed previously psychotic) because it is the "geographical locus containing the *axis mundi* of [their] religious beliefs" (Kalian and Witztum 2000). For further information on the Jerusalem syndrome, see Bar-el et al. (2000).

3. I thank Dr. William Ascher for calling this point to my attention.

4. See work in psychology, specifically evolutionary theories of leadership. The work of Maner and Mead (2010) and Van Vugt, Hogan, and Kaiser (2008) is particularly applicable.

5. Simonton (1986, 278) explains that "historiometric research on the eminence of political leaders tends to endorse an eponymic position"—meaning that political leaders generally hold rank in history if they come to symbolize epochs or a distinctive event in history.

6. O'Loughlin and Grant (1990, 523) find, for instance, that US public opinion of the president on foreign policy has little relevance to the amount of time presidents devote to addressing the public on such matters. They add that "foreign-policy decisions rarely have the same impact on their popularity as domestic events."

7. In fact, Bunce (1981, 222–56) finds that, in both capitalist and socialist countries, great innovation occurs when leaders turn over—even within the same party.

8. Although President Johnson finished President John F. Kennedy's term and one of his own, he was entitled to run for another term since he had not served more than six years in office. Prior to the passing of the Twenty-Second Amendment, presidents James Polk (1845–1849), James Buchanan (1857–1861), and Rutherford B. Hayes (1877–1881) all declined to seek a second term. Hayes even proposed a single term in his inaugural address (Neale 2009, 6–7).

9. Each presidential case must meet this criterion in order to be appropriate for this analysis. For example, the current president of Brazil, Dilma Rousseff, may not be appropriate for a comparative analysis like the one presented here. According to a Brazilian government official, she has "often floated the idea of not running again in private conversations." See the *Buenos Aires Herald*'s Aug. 17, 2011, article titled "Brazil's President May Not Run Again in 2014." This must be considered in case selection.

10. The irony described by Light (1981) is that as presidents lose support, they also grow in effectiveness through experience, knowledge, and sensitivity to office politics.

11. From 1866 to 1994, the president's party lost House seats in all but one of the thirty-three midterm elections (Campbell 2003, 203). One could argue that in both the 1998 and 2002 midterm elections the president's party gained seats in Congress—posing a challenge to the presidents' midterm loss claim. Yet the losses incurred by the president's party in both the 2006 and 2010 midterm elections tell us that the midterm results of 1998 and 2002 may have been atypical.

12. See Brace and Hinckley's (1993) table 5, p. 395.

13. Joshua Bolton, President George W. Bush's White House chief of staff, said the president in 2007 directed him to "go all-out to make sure that the transition is as effective as it possibly can be, especially in the national security area" (Kumar 2010a).

14. Gaddis (1982) analyzes leadership changes and their effect on US strategies of containment during the post–World War II era.

15. *Public Papers of the President* (Woolley and Peters 2010).

16. Duties specified under the Presidential Transition Acts of 1963 and 2000. See also http://www.gsa.gov/portal/content/315449.

17. The Presidential Transition Act of 1963 (PTA) first authorized federal funding to incoming and outgoing administrations for the purpose of facilitating the transition process. See Public Law 88–277, Mar. 4, 1964; 78 Stat. 153; 3 USC. §102 note. Funds totaled $900,000 under the PTA of 1963 and were to be divided equally among outgoing and incoming administrations (Smith 2008, 3). Prior to the passing of this act, administrations relied on political party funds for transition needs. According to Smith (ibid., 12), President Kennedy made "unprecedented" preparations for office in 1960–1961 and is credited by historians for sparking the substantial preparatory activity, particularly on the part of the incoming administration, which is carried out before Inauguration Day. In 1976 the PTA was amended, increasing funds from $900,000 to $3 million, with $1 million available to the outgoing administration (Public Law 94–499, Oct. 14, 1976; 90 Stat. 2380). In 1988, the Presidential Transitions Effectiveness Act (Public Law 100–398, Aug. 17, 1988; 102 Stat. 985) increased federal funding for changes of administration to $5 million, where the outgoing administration received an addition $500,000 in transition funding. Of the $5 million, $3.5 million went to the incoming administration unless the outgoing vice president was subsequently elected president, in which case $250,000 of the $3.5 million had to be returned to the Treasury. This was the case for President George H. W. Bush. In 2000 Congress authorized additional support services for the president-elect's newly appointed senior staff. Then, in 2000, Congress passed Public Law 106–293, the Presidential Transition Act of 2000, which authorized additional support for the president-elect's newly appointed senior staff.

18. Under the Presidential Transition Foundation, Inc., a private corporation, President Reagan raised undisclosed funds to help with his pre- and postelection transition activities (Smith 2008, 6–7). A 1988 Senate report found the following:

> President-elect Reagan raised approximately $1.25 million for both his pre-election and post-election transition activities in 1980. None of the sources or expenditures associated with the private cash were ever disclosed to the public, creating the potential for hidden conflicts of interests. See US Congress, Senate, Presidential Transitions Effectiveness Act of 1988, April 20, 1988. S.Rept. 100–317, 100th Congress, 2nd Session.

19. Smith (2008) and Hogue (2012), in their respective research reports to Congress, provide the texts of presidential transition statutes as well as a short but detailed history of federal funding for presidential transitions.

20. Public Law 108–458.

21. Ibid., Subtitle F, Section 7601, subsection (a)(8)(A)(v).

22. See p. 78 of this National Academy of Public Administration report at http://www.politicalappointeeproject.org/sites/default/files/napadhhs.pdf.

23. See Al Kamen's July 20, 2012, *Washington Post* article "Transition Teams Must Put Cart before Donkey and Elephant."

24. Ibid. The GSA also lists the Federal Vacancies Reform Act of 1998 as federal legislation governing presidential transition. This act "sets requirements for reporting to Congress and the Comptroller General actions related to Presidential Appointment with Senate Confirmation (PAS) positions as well as the qualifications for and term limits on acting PAS officers." See the GSA's website for presidential transition, http://www.gsa.gov/portal/category/26427, which contains a host of resources, including information to help presidential appointees "familiarize themselves with Federal service and the agencies with which they will be working" and legal requirements for outgoing members of the prior administration. Stephen Hess of the Brookings Institute also has an interesting series, titled "A Workbook for the President-Elect," at http://www.brookings.edu/about/projects/presidential-transition/workbook-for-the-president-elect.

25. A reviewer pointed out that this could be an artifact of the financial crisis unfolding at the time.

26. Globalization and the age of transnational capital have transformed the very notion of *state* from what it entailed in centuries past, and this has surely blurred the line between domestic and foreign affairs. Labor regulation and particularly trade liberalization affect a country's foreign relations. Yet these areas' laws and regulations intimately affect the lives of its citizens—making them prominent domestic issues.

27. Authors often claim that many historical events in US history qualify as imperialistic. For instance, Williams (1980) describes the territorial expansion westward as the first imperialist-like effort. Throughout the nineteenth century, the United States involved itself in the Caribbean, Latin and Central America, Asia, Europe, and even parts of Africa. Moreover, US participation in World War I and II resulted in the establishment of US military bases around the world—in South Korea, Japan, Britain, Germany, Italy, the Middle East, and North Africa. By the late 1900s, Zevin (1972, 328) claims, "the business of promoting and defeating revolutions abroad had by now become a standard facet of American foreign policy." For more on US imperialism and empire see Ikenberry's (2006) *Liberal Order and Imperial Ambition* and Layne and Thayer's (2006) *American Empire: A Debate.*

CHAPTER 4

1. For discussions on the constitutionality of US executive order issuance see Fleishman and Aufses (1976), Jack (1986), Tauber (1982), Rosenberg (1981), Neighbors (1964), Cross (1988), and Cash (1963).

2. Of course, a leader may initiate action without having any authority to do so. This, however, moves leaders beyond the folds of democracy. Recall that all of the presidents in this study serve in countries that meet democratic criteria. See Gurr and Marshall's (2013) Polity IV Project at http://www.systemicpeace.org/polity/polity4.htm.

3. To this effect, Carey and Shugart (1998, 14) make note of what they call "paraconstitutional initiative," authority that is not clearly constitutionally delineated.

4. See Przeworski (1991), Conaghan and Malloy (1994), Huber (1992), Conaghan, Malloy, and Abugattas (1990), O'Donnell (1994), Cooper (2002), Deering and Maltzman (1999), and Kubicek (1994). For tests of US presidents' issuance of executive orders in relation to levels of congressional support, see Krause and Cohen (1997), Krause and Cohen (2000), Mayer (1999), and Deering and Maltzman (1999).

5. See Carey and Shugart (1998), Mayer (2001), and Krause and Cohen (1997).

6. There is substantial literature on the reasons legislators choose to delegate when they do. For instance, Huber and Shipan (2002) link delegation to politicians' level of professionaliza-

tion, while Epstein and O'Halloran (1999) link delegation to hypotheses of unified and divided government.

7. Negretto (2004, 535) points out that this remains true even when Congress delegates legislative powers on certain issues. Presidents are still issuing decrees that have the immediate force of law.

8. Others, like Gaziano (2001), place these tools under the heading "presidential directives."

9. Cooper (2002, 251n6) cites the cases of Menotti v. Dillon, 167 US 703 (1897) and United States v. Oregon and California Railroad, 176 US 28 (1900), where the court found the effect of the executive orders on citizen property and companies permissible.

10. See the Code of Federal Regulations at http://www.gpoaccess.gov/cfr/.

11. Similarly, I find that policy-based proclamations account for only 12 percent of the total proclamations issued. Some examples: Proclamation 4895 declares the week of Feb. 5, 1982, "National Scleroderma Week"; Proclamation 6421 declares Apr. 14, 1992, "Education and Sharing Day, USA."; Proclamation 7247 declares November 1999 "National American Indian Heritage Month." Proclamations that announce the death of public figures are also classified as hortatory.

12. See *Public Papers* of President Reagan, May 18, 1983, specifically the "Remarks on Signing a Resolution and a Proclamation Declaring National Andrei Sakharov Day."

13. For more on the proclamations issued under the Antiquities Act, see Tseng (2003), Lacey (2000), and Biasi (2002).

14. From the pool of documents gathered, only seventy-one memoranda are specifically titled "memorandum of disapproval" or "memorandum returning without approval" from presidents Jimmy Carter through George W. Bush—seventeen for Carter, thirty-six for Reagan, sixteen for George H. W. Bush, one for Clinton, and one for George W. Bush. I found on more than one occasion that a memorandum was a "memorandum of disapproval," but such a designation was not clear from the memorandum's title.

15. President Obama may be an exception to this case. According to the American Presidency Project, all memoranda authored by President Obama are titled with a number.

16. He uses the term *presidential directive.*

17. Most presidents have their own terminology for NSDs distinct from that of their predecessors. For instance, NSDs were called National Security Action Memoranda (NSAMs) under President Johnson, National Security Decision Memoranda (NSDMs) under President Nixon, Presidential Directives (PDs) under President Carter, National Security Decision Directives (NSDDs) under President Reagan, National Security Directives (NSDs) under President George H. W. Bush, Presidential Decision Directives (PDDs) under President Clinton, and National Security Presidential Directive (NSPDs) under President George W. Bush.

18. Adopted in 1935, the Federal Register Act mandates the publication of most official pronouncements by the executive branch. The US Government Printing Office defines the *Federal Register* as "the official daily publication for rules, proposed rules, and notices of Federal agencies and organizations, as well as executive orders and other presidential documents" (see http://www.gpo.gov/).

19. For more information on security classification of directives see Information Security Oversight Office (ISOO) at http://www.archives.gov/isoo/.

20. In Lower Brule Sioux Tribe v. Deer [911 F.Supp. 395, 401 (D.S.D. 1995)], a federal court implied that memoranda and executive orders were similar, if not identical.

21. See, for instance, President George W. Bush's Executive Order 13203, signed on Feb. 17, 2001, which revokes not only Clinton's Executive Orders 12871, 12983, and 13156 but also his presidential memorandum of Oct. 28, 1999, titled "Reaffirmation of Executive Order 12871—Labor-Management Partnerships."

22. See the example of President Kennedy's establishment of the National Communication System cited just before note number 26.

23. Available online at http://www.archives.gov/federal-register/laws/administrative-procedure/552.html (accessed June 3, 2010).

24. Contrubis (1999, 23) cites the following cases as proof of this claim: Armstrong v. US, 80 US 154 (1871); Farkas v. Texas Instrument Inc., 372 F. 2d 629 (5th Cir. 1967); Farmer v. Philadelphia Electric Co., 329 F. 2d 3 (3d Cir. 1964); and Jenkins v. Collard, 145 US 546, 560–61 (1893).

25. Memorandum on Privately Funded Abortions at Military Hospitals, *Federal Register* 58(17) (1993): 6439.

26. This memorandum has been amended and superseded over time by various executive orders. See President Reagan's Executive Order 12472, signed Apr. 3, 1984, and President George W. Bush's Executive Order 13286, signed Feb. 28, 2003.

27. 74 *Federal Register* 24693 (2009).

28. See Youngstown Sheet, Tube v. Sawyer, 343 US 579 [1952].

29. Michael Abramowitz and Jonathan Weisman, "To Implement Policy, Bush to Turn to Administrative Orders," *Washington Post*, Oct. 31, 2007.

30. See note 24, this chapter.

31. 49 Stat. 501. On June 19, 1962, President Kennedy issued EO 11030, which specifies "the preparation, presentation, filing and publication of executive orders and proclamations." This order instructs that these documents are to be routed through both the Office of Management and Budget and the attorney general and then published. Cooper (2002, 19) points out that under certain circumstances this publication requirement does not apply. For instance, the Register Act states the following: "This chapter does not apply to treaties, conventions, protocols, and other international agreements, or proclamations thereof by the President."

32. The memorandum is titled "Legal Effectiveness of a Presidential Directive, as Compared to an Executive Order," dated Jan. 29, 2000, and comes from Office of Legal Counsel, US Department of Justice. It is available at http://www.fas.org/irp/offdocs/predirective.html.

33. Art. II §1, 2, and 3.

34. More recently, the Supreme Court has examined presidents' claims of statutory validity. See, for instance, Hamdi v. Rumsfeld, 542 US 507 (2004) (the court allowed President George W. Bush to detain enemy combatants under Authorization for Use of Military Force [AUMF]); Hamdi v. Rumsfeld, 548 US 557 (2006) (the court found President Bush lacked statutory authority to try combatants for conspiracy before stated military commission); and Medellin v. Texas, 128 Ct. 1346 (2008) (the court found that President Bush lacked authority to order compliance with a non-self-executing treaty). For more on the history of the Supreme Court's review of presidential action under statute, see Stack (2009).

35. See Dames and Moore v. Regan, 453 US 654 (1981); Haig v. Agee, 453 US 280 (1981); AFL-CIO v. Kahn, 618 F. 2d 784 (1979).

36. For more on the Supreme Court's deference to presidents on statutory interpretation see Bradley and Goldsmith (2005), Goldsmith and Manning (2006), and Eskridge and Baer (2008).

37. Interestingly, Mayer (2001, 11n55) cites examples of the court's constitutional "sidestepping" on executive action. He explains that in these cases the court acted out of fear that its decision would be unenforceable and cause loss of its legitimacy.

38. Olson and Woll (1999, 10) maintain that this has happened to at least 239 executive orders.

39. P.L. 103–43, 107 Stat 133. § 121 (Contrubis 1999).

40. See Midwest Oil v. US, 236 US 459 (1915).

41. See Warber's (2006) discussion on p. 130.

42. For each proclamation, memorandum, and order, the project lists the president responsible for its issuance, its title, and the date of its issuance and provides a link to its full text.

43. The US Government Printing Office website, http://www.gpo.gov/, explains that "from 1977 onward, all material appearing in the *Weekly Compilation of Presidential Documents* is incorporated into the Public Papers of the Presidents of the United States."

44. Documents included are those noted or titled as presidential determinations, military orders, notices, and presidential orders. (Only one document filed during Carter's administration falls under the heading "presidential order," *September 26, 1977, for the nomination of commissioners for the copyright Royalty Tribunal.*) Permits are the only type excluded.

45. Two subcategories are excluded from the domestic policy count (see table 5.2).

CHAPTER 5

1. *Public Papers of the President* (Woolley and Peters 2010).

2. Warber (2006) distinguishes executive orders by their function. He names three types: policy orders, symbolic orders, and routine orders.

3. See Przeworski (1991), Conaghan and Malloy (1994), Huber (1992), Conaghan, Malloy, and Abugattas (1990), O'Donnell (1994), Cooper (2002), Mayer (2001), and Kubicek (1994). For tests of US presidents' issuance of executive orders in relation to levels of congressional support, see Krause and Cohen (1997),Krause and Cohen (2000), Mayer (1999, 2001), Deering and Maltzman (1999), Howell (2003) and Warber (2006).

4. His analysis covers executive orders issued from April 1936 to December 1999.

5. See Edwards, Barrett, and Peake (1997) for an opposing argument that divided government impedes legislative activity.

6. Cowling, Hutton, and Shaw (2006, 33) explain that a negative binomial distribution is used "where each individual experiences events according to a Poisson process with event rate $\lambda_i v_i$, where λ_i depends on the covariates and v_i is a random term, which follows a gamma distribution."

7. Presidents declare their authority to make such restoration of law and order decrees according to Chapter 15 of Title 10 of the US Code, the Emergency Natural Gas Act of 1977, or the Energy Policy and Conservation Act. There is one exception. President Clinton used the NEA as authority to declare a state of emergency because of a shortage in domestic grain due to "an extended drought and other natural disasters in feed grain–producing areas of the United States" (Proclamation 6907, July 1, 1996).

8. Terrorist attacks that are carried out by foreign nationals on US soil fall under this category.

9. Proclamation 7463, "Declaration of National Emergency by Reason of Certain Terrorist Attacks," for example, is not excluded. This decree, issued by President Bush in September of 2001, is not solely fixed on the restoration of law and order in New York City and Washington, DC, where the terrorist attacks occurred, but rather on measures to be taken outside the borders of the United States in response to terrorism carried out by foreign nationals.

10. According to Chapter 15 of Title 10 of the US Code, the United States includes the territories of Guam and the Virgin Islands.

11. President H. W. Bush issued Proclamation 6427 on May 1, 1992, in response to the widespread violence that occurred after a jury acquitted Los Angeles police officers of wrongdoing in the beating of black motorist Rodney King.

12. The included period for two-term presidents actually lasts 220 weeks since the period begins the day after they win reelection and continues until their last day in office.

13. 90 Stat. 1255; 50 USC. 1601–1651. The NEA did a number of things to limit and monitor presidents in their exercise of emergency powers. The statute consists of five titles. Title I states that any declaration of national emergency or "any declaration of general emergency" in effect on September 14, 1976, had a mandatory termination in two years. In Title II, the act stipulates that emergency declarations terminate after one year unless the president issues a formal continuance extending the emergency a year longer. Either the president or Congress can terminate an emergency early. In order for Congress to rescind a national emergency declaration, a joint resolution by both houses of Congress is required. Title III states that the president must detail exactly what powers and authorities are being activated in response to an emergency. Title IV further specifies accountability and reporting provisions. Title V outlines the circumstances and requirements for the repeal and continuation of statutes delegating emergency powers.

14. Taken from the document archive of the American Presidency Project under the Public Papers of President Richard Nixon (Woolley and Peters 2010).

15. The Special Senate Committee notes that finding these provisions was no easy task: "Nowhere in the Government, in either the Executive or Legislative branches, did there exist a complete catalog of all emergency statutes. Many were aware that there had been a delegation of an enormous amount of power but, of how much power, no one knew."

16. US Congress, Senate Special Committee on the Termination of the National Emergency, Emergency Powers Statutes, 93rd Congress, 1st Session, S. Rept. 93–549 (1973).

17. See the *Washington Post,* "Up All Night—President Obama's Nighthawks," July 4, 2010.

18. Relyea (2001, 4) quotes a political scientist's testimony of what constitutes a national emergency during 1973 congressional committee hearings on emergency powers. For more on the concept of emergency with regard to US constitutional law and tradition, see Corwin (1948).

19. US Congress, Senate Special Committee on the Termination of the National Emergency (1973).

20. EO 12865, Sept. 16, 1993.

21. EO 12934, Oct. 25, 1994.

22. EO 12947, Jan. 23, 1995.

23. EO 12978, Oct. 21, 1995.

24. Proclamation 6867, Mar. 1, 1996.

25. EO 13047, May 22, 1997.

26. EO 13067, Nov. 3, 1997.

27. EO 12722, Aug. 2, 1990.

28. EO 12775, Oct. 4, 1991.

29. EO 12808, May 30, 1992.

30. Cochran uses quarterly data drawn from the *Federal Register* between 1975 and 1999. He uses the log of its pages as a proxy for regulatory activity. In contrast, de Rugy and Davies's data extend to 2006 (from 1975,) and these authors use the number of pages in the *Federal Reg-*

ister as a percentage of the total pages published during the calendar year as a proxy for regulatory activity.

31. He exempts purely administrative orders.

32. Mayer and Price (2002) find that presidents (1949–1999) issue "significant" executive orders at a much higher rate when their successor is from the opposing party (from 1.03 to 2.34). These authors read the content of executive orders and use secondary sources to determine whether an executive order is significant.

33. President George H. W. Bush's pardoning of Reagan administration officials involved in the Iran-Contra scandal, President Clinton's prohibition on rough-cut diamonds from Sierra Leone, and his establishment of the Northwestern Hawaiian Islands Coral Reef Ecosystem Reserve are a few examples.

34. Also known as the Algiers Declarations. For more on the signing of the accords during presidential transitions, see Combs (2001).

35. See the full document of Algiers Accords at http://www.parstimes.com/history/algiers_accords.pdf.

36. See *Frontline*'s timeline of UN/US involvement in Somalia from 1991 to 1995 at http://www.pbs.org/wgbh/pages/frontline/shows/ambush/etc/cron.html.

37. All of President Reagan's physicians argue to the contrary, that they saw no evidence of Alzheimer's disease while he was president. His doctors claim that overt signs of the disease were not detected until late 1992 (Altman 1997).

38. See the *Washington Post*, "Son Suggests Reagan Had Alzheimer's as President," Jan. 15, 2011.

CHAPTER 6

1. See Busey (1967) and Rosenn (1990). For this observation on Argentina, see Calvert and Calvert (1989).

2. For instance, Martínez and Santiso (2003) link politics to the financial crises those countries experienced. They find that significant financial crises took place (Brazil in 1999 and Argentina in 2001) during a corresponding presidential election year.

3. There are two opposing approaches to the management of macroeconomic policy. First is the "economic populist" approach, defined as the "political use of economic policy in which the emphases on growth and income redistribution are given preference over concerns with inflationary trends and external constraint" because they induce "plebiscitarian legitimation of the power of the president." This contrasts with the "economic pragmatist" approach, which emphasizes "monetary stability and external constraints, even at the expense of growth, increased employment, and the redistribution of income" (Faro de Castro and de Carvalho 2003, 469–81). Economic populism can be more clearly associated with accepting short-term benefits for long-term costs, whereas those who advocate economic pragmatist policies are more likely to support alternative reforms—those requiring short-term costs for long-term benefits. For more on economic populism in Latin America, see Dornbusch and Edwards (1991) and Cardoso and Helwege (1991).

4. Kaufman (1985, 479–80), citing Olson's (1965) *Logic of Collective Action,* explains the collective action problem in Argentina, Brazil, and Mexico with regard to the stabilization measures:

> [I]f we assume that many of the benefits to be derived from stabilization efforts are collective in nature (e.g., reduced inflation), appeals for coopera-

> tion based on the enlightened self-interest of competing groups can be expected to founder on the "free-rider" issue. It simply does not make sense for most labor unions or business firms to pay the costs of stabilization if they cannot be excluded from its benefits. If all groups attempt to evade the costs, of course, the program fails—which is what typically happens in Latin America. But because most labor and business organizations are too small to have a direct influence on this outcome, they are still better off if they evade the "short-term" sacrifices asked by governmental elites. In any event, Olson argues, for all but very large peak associations the advantages of defending or enlarging distributive shares of wages will almost always outweigh the costs that the groups incur from consequent contractions of the national economy.

5. Faro de Castro and de Carvalho (2003, 475) claim that it is exactly this "lack of an appropriate internal-external link" or "the lack of a coherent and proactive foreign policy that would negotiate and craft international arrangements suitable to ongoing internal political and economic changes" that has plagued the government of Brazil.

6. The text of the Aug. 22, 1994, change does not state whether it is indeed a new constitution or simply an amendment to the constitution of 1853/1860. For the purposes of this book, I refer to this constitutional change as the Constitutional Reform of 1994.

7. For more on the curtailment of presidential power due to the 1994 constitutional reform, see Sagüës (1996).

8. Constitutional Amendment 16 modified arts. 14 § 5° and 82 of Brazil's 1988 constitution.

9. Brazilian Constitution 1988, translated and revised by Istvan Vajda, Patricia de Queiroz Carvalho Zimbres, and Vanira Tavares de Souza. Brasília: Senado Federal, Subsecretaria de Edições Técnicas. Published by the *Brazzil Magazine* at http://www.brazzil.com/carta88.htm, accessed Nov. 22, 2010.

10. Note the exception of the Peronist constitution, which was in force from 1949 to 1956.

11. See Power (1998), Pereira, Power, and Rennó (2005), Reich (2002), Negretto (2004), and Rennó (2010).

12. For more on the Argentine Supreme Court's response to the review of DNUs, see Negretto (2004).

13. See Article 86.2 of the 1853/1860 Constitution and Article 99.2 of the 1994 Constitution.

14. See Article 31 of the Argentine Constitution.

15. Recall that US emergency power decrees, by my definition, are issued pursuant to acts passed by Congress, the NEA, or the IEEPA.

16. Posner and Vermeule (2007, 892) point out that, in the United States, the public would likely be more inclined to believe the president in a declaration of an emergency rather than a judge's or a legislator's denial of one. For more on the dangers of normalizing emergency rhetoric, see Ackerman (2004).

17. Ackerman (2004) explores what an ideal emergency constitution in the United States would look like. His proposal is built on extensive research of emergency law from nations current and past. Particularly thought provoking is his research on Canadian law. In Canada, legal differentiation is made between types of emergencies (natural disasters, threats to public order,

international emergencies, and states of war), and, as a consequence, each receives separate treatment in the eyes of the law. See pp. 1061–62, especially notes 75–78.

18. There are also other reasons for decree reissuance. A legal mistake made in the original may require an issuance of a corrected version, or two or more original decrees may be combined into one new reissued decree. Moreover, a decree may not be reissued if such a reissuance is unnecessary, for instance, when the decree sets up a regulation of policy for a fixed time period and this time period expires.

19. EC32 was approved with 427 "yes" votes in the Chamber of Deputies, with only one "no" vote. Similarly, there was only one "no" vote in the Senate, with 65 "yes" votes. EC32 is now article 62 in Brazil's Constitution.

20. The Board of Directors (*mesa directora*) presides over the Chamber of Deputies. The board includes the Chamber of Deputies' president, two vice presidents, four secretaries, and their substitutes. The chamber president's role is analogous to the Speaker of the House in the US House of Representatives (see Pachón-Buitrago 2008, 35n6).

21. If there happen to be differences in the Senate's and the Chamber's approved versions of the decree, the Chamber holds a second vote to determine whether to keep its version or adopt the Senate's.

22. Except as provided for in art. 167, § 3°.

23. Constitutional Amendment no. 7 (CA 7), adopted in 1995, was another attempt to restrict the use of MPVs. In exchange for lifting state monopolies on transportation, the amendment prohibited the regulation of any constitutional amendments by MPV. This applied to all amendments promulgated from 1995 on. Article 246 of the amendment states the following: "The adoption of any provisional measure for the regulation of any article of the Constitution the wording of which has been altered by means of an amendment enacted as of 1995 is forbidden." Since then, more than fifty amendments have been promulgated (Pachón-Buitrago 2008, 79). Discussion here is limited to EC32 since it changes the fundamental procedural requirements of MPVs in general. Since CA 7 does not change the procedural requirements of MPVs and since the amendment was adopted at the start of President Cardoso's term, this study does not incorporate a discussion of its likely effects. For more on Brazil's constitutional amendments see Georgetown University's *Political Database of the Americas* at http://pdba.georgetown.edu/.

24. "Decree laws" are laws promulgated by de facto governments. They are distinct from DNUs.

25. Although the Argentine Constitution made no mention of DNUs or the presidential authority to issue legislative decrees until 1994, Negretto (2004, 551) counts President Alfonsín's 1985 decree, initiating the Austral Plan, as the first "de facto" DNU. Alfonsín took office in 1983 in the midst of Argentina's democratic transition and instituted the Austral Plan with the intent to rein in inflation.

26. See Article 99(3).

27. In Brazil, for instance, the president can introduce bills, and the Supreme Federal Tribunal, individual legislators, and even ordinary citizens can do so as well. See Brazil's Constitution, Article 61.

28. This is the case if the point of democratic consolidation is marked by the presidential election of 1985.

29. Power (1997, 202) links weak parties and accountability problems to Brazil's open-list, proportional representation (PR) system. Nicolau (1993, 108) adds that because coalitions of parties can run more candidates than there are seats available, voters often have a hard time

choosing a candidate. As of 2007 Brazil's Supreme Court has prohibited members of Congress from party switching. This may create stronger party ties over time.

30. This has been the case for Chile. Mainwaring (1990, 168) notes that "Chile is the only case in the world of a multi-party presidential democracy that [has] endured for twenty-five years or more." Yet despite the longevity of the Chilean system, presidents have found it difficult to govern effectively in its multiparty system (Valenzuela 1985). Every Chilean president has tried to broaden executive power by either bypassing Congress or trying to reform the constitution (Mainwaring 1990, 169).

31. *Economist,* Sept. 30, 2010, "Lula's Legacy," http://www.economist.com/node/17147828, accessed July 27, 2013.

32. See Arthur Ituassu's article "Brazil's Prospect: Consensus versus Division," published on Oct. 19, 2010, on openDemocracy.net.

33. See Palanza (2009) and Alston and Mueller (2006).

34. Prior to the passing of EC32, MPVs were not required to go through Congress. Legislators were essentially cut out of the process, and as a result their institutional power suffered. For this reason, they had a stake in obstructing presidents' decree issuance. Now that EC32 requires that MPVs go through Congress, legislators always have input. This, therefore, neutralizes the cost felt by legislators in the enactment of a decree over a statute. Palanza (2009, 130–49) explains further: "After Amendment 32, the effective enforcement of hurdle factors led legislators to be indifferent between decrees and statutes, as their payoffs do not vary with the choice of instrument," and therefore legislators are "less inclined to go out of their way to maintain a strong grip on high-stakes policies." She finds some empirical support for this claim. It is worth noting that her sample size is quite small. Her calculations are based on MPVs and legislation from 1988 to 2005, leaving only four years of data for the post-EC32 period.

35. This calculation is based on data collected from Sept. 20, 2001, through July 2006.

36. Rennó (2010, 216–17) estimates that in 2008 MPVS blocked approximately 55 percent of the deliberative sessions in the Chamber of Deputies (both ordinary and extraordinary sessions).

37. Observations are limited since Temer's clarification occurred in March of 2009. Rennó (2010) runs three models to determine whether the positive count of MPVs differs statistically from the period before the reform (January 2008 to February 2009) to the period after the reform (March 2009 to December 2009). The first model shows the difference in periods to be statistically significant at the 0.11 level in a one-tailed test. Rennó then excludes outlier months in Model 2. In Model 3 he excludes extraordinary credit requirement MPVs. Both the second and third models confirm the results of Model 1.

38. Not a single MPV was rejected from the launching of the Real Plan to the year 2000 (Figueiredo and Limongi 2000, 156).

39. Note that if a decree is rejected, its effects are still valid for a period of time. This has the potential to create a legal quagmire, which requires further regulation. See Negretto (2004), note 18. Presidents approved an overwhelming majority (87 percent) of the congress-amended MPVs largely because they dealt with politically sensitive issues (Reich 2002, 20–22).

40. Pereira, Power, and Rennó (2008, 7) add that "routine bills almost never reach the top of the parliamentary agenda."

41. See ibid., table 2, p. 9.

42. As of 2010 the 2005 proposal for PEC 72 had yet to be approved.

43. Here "the court" refers to the Supreme Federal Tribunal, or STF. The Brazilian judicial system also includes the Supreme Justice Tribunal (STJ), five federal regional tribunals

(TRFs), 560 *varas federales,* and forty-eight "*juizados especiais federais autônomos,* which are separate labor, military, and electoral courts. For an explanation of Brazil's judicial structure, see Rios-Figueroa and Taylor (2006).

44. As in the United States, state and federal courts can adjudicate on the constitutionality of primary legislation. Yet in Brazil's case the court's decision (even the STF's) is binding only for the parties involved in the lawsuit. Other courts do not have to adhere to decision standards.

45. Brazil fell behind Costa Rica, Honduras, and Uruguay. See Galindo (2003, 32–33). The public's trust in the judiciary contrasts with its lack of trust in the other two branches of government. In 2008 Brazil scored a −0.03 on the World Bank's Control of Corruption Index, where the scale ranges from −2.5 for the worst to +2.5 for the best.

46. In 1994, of the thirty-three hundred candidates registered to take the judiciary's examination, only forty-one received approval (Ballard 1999, 246n72).

47. See Article 103 of Brazil's Constitution. Despite the broad grant of group standing, Taylor (2006) argues that standing is still limited to specific groups. Therefore, the ability to bypass lower courts to challenge the constitutionality of federal or state law and address Brazil's High Court directly privileges access to the courts and ensures a faster route to resolution for these groups.

48. See the *Economist*'s May 21, 2009, article titled "Brazil's Supreme Court: When Less Is More, Reforms Improve the Judicial System."

49. One of the reforms created the National Court of Justice, which hears complaints on the conduct of judges; another bestowed on the Supreme Court the power to issue a binding summary, which requires all courts and public administration agencies to adhere to its rulings. For more on these 2004 reforms, see Taylor (2006).

50. Refer to the *Economist* reference in note 48, this chapter.

51. Four types of law can be used to implement federal policy—constitutional amendment, complementary law, ordinary law, and provisional measure, or MPVs. Constitutional amendments are the most difficult to get approved, requiring committee votes in addition to the majority of votes (60 percent) in both houses tallied four times—votes taken twice from each house. Complementary laws require one absolute majority vote, and ordinary laws require one simple majority vote. Of course, MPVs can be issued at any time by the president and temporarily have the effect of law without a vote from Congress, making them the easiest way to implement federal policy.

52. Kapiszewski's sample here includes the twenty-six most important cases on economic policy (according to data collected from experts) that have come before the Supreme Federal Tribunal in the two decades following the postauthoritarian period (1985–2004).

53. Taylor (2006) draws his cases from the 1988 to 2002 time period. In addition, ADIns are more widely used than any other instrument to challenge the constitutionality of a federal or state law; it is the tool that allows parties direct access to the STF. Taylor runs a binary logistic regression model to test his data.

54. See ibid., notes 2 and 4.

55. See Justice Celso de Mello's response in *Medida cautelar em mandato de segurança* 27.931–1.

56. See Rennó (2010), 217.

57. For more discussion on this, see Alston and Mueller (2006).

58. Even though Menem's party controlled both chambers for most of his term, there is evidence that his party was less than cohesive when it came to support on economic reform issues. For more on the PJ's intraparty conflict during Menem's tenure, see Mustapic (2002).

59. Alianza won majorities in thirteen of the twenty-three provinces and in the city of Buenos Aires (Finkel 2004).

60. Argentine Constitution (1994), Article 112. For more details on the tremendous level of questioning by academics and the Argentine press concerning the court's motives and loyalties, see Miller (2000, 374n19).

61. See Graciela Römer y Asociados, "Confianza en la Policía y la Justicia 8" (April 1997), unpublished report on file with Graciela Römer y Asociados, Buenos Aires.

62. See Bumin, Randazzo, and Walker (2009, 131) on the connection between term length of judges and judicial durability, specifically the hypothesis that shorter terms likely make judges more susceptible to political influences.

63. For more on Menem's packing of the court, see Larkins (1998).

64. *Luis A. Peralta y otros, c/Estado Nacional, Ministerio de Economía, BCRA.* [Dec. 27, 1990].

65. *Cocchia y otros, c/Poder Ejecutivo Nacional* [Dec. 2, 1993].

66. *Alejandro Nieva y otros, c/Poder Ejecutivo Nacional* [Dec.17, 1997]. An important point to remember is that the Argentine courts lack *stare decisis* in civil law systems. Courts do not have to respect precedent established by prior decisions (Bowen and Rose-Ackerman 2003, 176).

67. See Rios-Figueroa and Taylor (2006, 743) on the potential pitfalls of using judicial decisions against the government as a proxy for judicial independence.

68. Helmke (2002) finds a significant increase in antigovernment decisions clustered at the end of Menem's tenure.

69. Note that the practice of using funds in exchange for support is not endemic to Argentine presidents or even to President Menem. Both presidents Cardoso and Lula used pork in exchange for votes on policy reform and amendments to the constitution. See Alston and Mueller (2006). The difference is that Menem did so on a grand scale and perhaps by less than fully legal measures.

70. See Anthony Faiola, "When Politics Gets Personal—Frustrated Argentines Make Daily Life Difficult for Public Officials," *Washington Post,* Feb. 27, 2002. By Manzetti's (2003, 358) estimates, "had Menem refrained from political patronage, he could have cut interest payments by almost half and most likely averted the economic meltdown of 2001."

71. Bowen and Rose-Ackerman use data from Jones (1997, 259). This count includes both "recognized" and "unrecognized" decrees. This method of counting is explained in further detail in chapter 7.

72. Quote cited in Kapiszewski (2007, 280).

73. See Bowen and Rose-Ackerman's (2003, 175–76) discussion of the Auditoría general (external organ for executive oversight) and the Sindicatura general (internal organ for executive oversight).

74. According to Bowen and Rose-Ackerman (2003, 177), Article 43, which states that "Any person shall file a prompt and summary proceeding regarding constitutional guarantees, provided there is no other legal remedy, against any act or omission of the public authorities or individuals which currently or imminently may damage, limit, modify, or threaten rights and guarantees recognized by this Constitution, treaties, or laws, with open arbitrariness or illegality. In such case, the judge may declare that the act or omission is based on an unconstitutional rule . . . Any person shall file this action to obtain information on the data about himself and their purpose, registered in public records or data bases, or in private ones intended to supply information," is generally interpreted very narrowly.

75. Faiola, "When Politics Gets Personal" (note 70, this chapter).

76. Ibid.

77. Among other things, the electoral college would no longer be in play. The president and vice president would be directly elected if the president captured 45 percent of the votes cast or even only 40 percent so long as at least a 10 percent gap in votes existed from the next candidate with the most votes. Otherwise, a second round of voting would occur between the two candidates who received the highest votes (Article 98). A third senator for each province and for the city of Buenos Aires was added, and the ordinary session for Congress was extended (Article 63). Congress could not delegate legislative powers to the president outside of matters of administration or public emergency for a set period (Article 76). The legislative process changed (see Articles 79 and 81). A new process was devised for selecting judges below the Supreme Court. For other significant changes, see Sagüës (1996).

78. See Article 100(13).

79. Under the 1994 constitutional reform, the council could select lower-level federal judges, exercise disciplinary powers over judges, issue regulations with regard to judicial organization, remove subordinate federal judges of the court, control the judicial budget, and determine the judiciary's internal regulations (see Articles 114 and 115).

80. As chapter 7 explains in more detail, a variable for *unified government* in the context of these two countries is difficult to ascertain. Neither country operates under a two-party system. The number of seats attained by the president's party is not necessarily a valid indication of legislative support.

81. For example, see Nino (1996) and Llanos (2001).

CHAPTER 7

1. Although Ferreira Rubio and Goretti's (1998) analysis covers only the years from 1989 to 1994, it is fair to assume that DNUs issued during Menem's second term do not take on issues entirely different from the ones found here. Of the 270 DNUs issued by Néstor Kirchner, president of Argentina from May 2003 to December 2007, 219 addressed salaries, allowances, budget, public works, tax benefits, and the financial system (Capriata 2008). Ferreira Rubio and Goretti's (1998) count includes both "recognized" and "unrecognized" decrees. Of the 336 DNUs issued from 1989 to 1994, only 166, or 49 percent, are recognized by the executive as DNUs. The other 170 are nonrecognized decrees but are as such according to Ferreira Rubio and Goretti's analysis. Their classification is discussed in depth later.

2. See Amorim Neto and Tafner's (2002) table 3.

3. Cardoso and Lula are the only two presidents who have completed full terms since the promulgation of the Brazilian Constitution. President José Sarney's term (April 1985–March 1990) carried through the promulgation of the 1988 constitution. Fernando Collor de Mello (March 1990–September 1992) resigned following his impeachment by Congress, and Itamar Franco, his vice president, finished out his term as acting president (October 1992–December 1994). Similarly, Menem and Kirchner are the only presidents who have completed full terms since the promulgation of the Argentine Constitution. Fernando de la Rúa resigned in December 2001, after only two years in office. Adolfo Rodríguez Saá Páez Montero resigned just seven days into his term as interim president (December 23–30, 2001). Eduardo Alberto Duhalde finished de la Rúa's term (January 2002–May 2003).

4. I draw data from fourteen years of this seventeen-year period since, between 2000 and 2003, three presidents served but failed to complete their terms.

5. Mexico is the third country.

6. Others like Palanza (2009) use only a three-month period rather than a full year in their analysis to account for the transition period.

7. See ibid., table 4.4, p. 148.

8. Rennó demonstrates that "there are no relevant changes between 2008 and 2009 in the political and economic settings," thereby warranting a t-test.

9. A visual inspection of the recognized DNU counts reveals that the trends found in the total count (recognized and unrecognized DNUs combined) apply here as well. See Ferreira Rubio and Goretti (2000), figure 2, p. 7.

10. Presidency of the Republic website, https://www.planalto.gov.br/ccivil_03/MPV/Quadro/_Quadro%20Geral.htm#posterioremc, accessed Jan. 10, 2011.

11. Polling data on Brazilian presidents were collected by Datafolha Research Institute, available at http://datafolha.folha.uol.com.br/. Polling data for Argentinean presidents are from Angus Reid Public Opinion, available at http://www.angus-reid.com.

12. See Amorim Neto and Taftner (2002), Palanza (2009), and Pereira, Power, and Rennó (2005, 2008).

13. Pereira, Power, and Rennó (2008, 31n11) find that by "discount[ing] the final six months of Cardoso's presidency," the means of decree rejection pre- and post-EC32 reform are approximately the same.

14. Amorim Neto's (2000) analysis covers only the 1985 to 1999 period.

15. One must also consider the issues of corruption and congressional vote buying in Argentina and Brazil. Note the congressional vote-buying scandal known as the *mensalão* during Lula's first term in 2005.

16. See Cardoso's 2001 publication titled *Charting a New Course: The Politics of Globalization and Social Transformation,* which provides a collection of Cardoso's works. Also, Ted Goertzel, retired sociology professor at Rutgers University in Camden, New Jersey, maintains a website of Cardoso's scholarly works by year of publication. As Goertzel explains, "Cardoso's bibliography is very extensive and confusing because he often published essentially the same paper in several different versions and translations, sometimes with different titles." On his website, http://crab.rutgers.edu/~goertzel/fhcbib.htm, Goertzel carefully catalogues what he believes to be "Cardoso's most important works, speeches, and interviews."

17. See Lally Weymouth's *Newsweek* article titled "I have Changed: An Interview with Lula, Brazil's President-Elect," published on Nov. 11, 2002.

CHAPTER 8

1. Tocqueville and Marx both acknowledge the high rate of social mobility or class turnover in the United States. Marx ([1852] 2010, III) states that, in "the United States of North America, . . . though classes exist, they have not yet become fixed, but continually change and interchange their elements in constant flux." Likewise, Tocqueville ([1835] 2010, 57) writes, "Not that there are no wealthy people in the United States, just as there are everywhere. Indeed, I know of no other country where the love of money occupies as great a place in the hearts of men or where people are more deeply contemptuous of the theory of permanent equality of wealth. But wealth circulates there with incredible rapidity, and experience teaches that it is rare for two successive generations to garner its favors."

2. In a sense, the Puritan, Quaker, and Virginia settlements were utopian experiments in the laboratory of a new land, disinfected of the formal institutional barriers present in England. The Puritans could divide religious and political power as they saw fit. Their community could be reinforced and consensus built through sermons of their choosing and through town meet-

ings. The Quakers were able to align their religious beliefs with "inventive civic projects" and to practice consensus and cooperation in places that were commonly rife with conflict (treatment of criminals and those with mental illness) (Abbott 1991, 32). In Virginia, slavery and venture capital could feed the creation of an all-new aristocracy in which "members of the ruling class saw themselves as purer judges of society than their English counterparts" (ibid., 36). Different community experiments sprang up all over North America, and as a result people came to have a unique understanding of community as something that could be invented or generated from scratch as long as religious, political, or economic similarities existed.

3. See William Casey King's *Washington Post* article titled "In Obama's White House, Ambition Looks a Little Different," Jan. 18, 2013.

4. For instance, in 2008 Facebook had 50 million users—and Google+ did not exist. Four years later Facebook had 845 million users, and Google+ was on its way to having 400 million users. Obama had only 100,000 followers on Twitter in 2008. Four years later he had garnered more than 12.5 million followers (Kessler 2012).

5. It is difficult to quantify the number of staffers and volunteers involved over time since, to the best of my knowledge, no formal count has been made. Drawing from various sources, the *Congressional Quarterly Press Guide to the Presidency* (2008, online edition) gives rough estimates of the size of transition teams: 100 for Eisenhower (1952/1953), 50 for Kennedy (1960/1961), 125–150 for Nixon (1968/1969), 300 for Carter (1976/1977), 1,550 for Reagan (1980/1981), 250–300 for G. Bush (1988/1989), 450 for Clinton (1992/1993), and 800 for G. W. Bush (2000/2001). See the *CQ Press Guide*, table 5–11 at http://transition.cqpress.com/GetPage.aspx?id=22.

6. The Bush administration also produced a host of regulations at the end of 2008 to promote his antiregulation philosophy. Many of the regulations are perceived as antienvironmental, such as the new rules relaxing pollution-control standards for power plants or the new directives allowing mining companies to continue dumping excess rock and soil into valleys and streams. See witness testimony and other materials submitted to the Hearing Record of the Subcommittee on Commercial and Administrative Law of the Committee on the Judiciary House of Representatives at http://judiciary.house.gov/hearings/printers/111th/111-2_47033.PDF.

7. In September 2002 Cardoso issued decrees setting aside nearly fifty million hectares of the most sensitive rain forest ecosystems—3.6 percent of the planet's remaining tropical forests. This is said to be equivalent to the entire US parks system. See Alanna Mitchell, "Brazil Unveils Project to Save Rainforest," *Globe and Mail*, Sept. 7, 2002, International News Section.

8. Although taken from a report by the US Congress, Senate Special Committee on the Termination of the National Emergency (1973), these acts can also be applied to emergency power use in the Argentine and Brazilian cases.

9. For more on the history of how and when leaders have used emergencies, see Ackerman (2004).

10. For this point on Brazil, see Amorim Neto, Cox, and McCubbins (2003, 560).

11. Recall research by Linz and Valenzuela (1994), Blondel (1987), and Przeworski et al. (2000) that shows that presidential systems are more vulnerable than parliamentary ones. Refer to section 1.1 in chapter 1 of this book.

12. Of course, the personalization of leadership is not exclusive to presidential systems. Yet as Linz (1990) explains, in contrast to presidential systems, where the public identifies with *one* person in executive leadership, most of the time the public identifies with a pool of people and often a number of well-known subleaders in parliamentary systems.

13. Thomas Eagleton was a US Senator from Missouri who served from 1968 to 1987.

14. Sabato (2008) argues that the US Constitution should be revised so that presidents can serve only one six-year term. Specifically, he argues that the Constitution should be revised to "establish a new six-year, one-time presidential term with the option for the president to seek two additional years in an up/down referendum of the American people." He argues that one six-year term will remove executive decisions from reelection concerns and the problematic nature of election cycles. Moreover, he asserts that a national referendum (coincidentally, similar to those in Mexico) would allow the people to decide whether the president should serve an additional one or three years. This is only one of Sabato's twenty-three proposals for US constitutional change cited in his book *A More Perfect Constitution.*

15. O'Connell (2008, 901) explains that executive agencies first publish "notices of intent to promulgate a rule" in the *Federal Register.* The agency considers comments from the public to decide whether to promulgate a final rule or withdraw its proposed rule. This distinguishes notice-and-comment rules from other rule types.

16. See *Frontline*'s interviews for the series titled "The Choice 2012," http://www.pbs.org/wgbh/pages/frontline/oral-history/choice-2012/obama-s-ambition/.

17. See note 16.

18. See their Jan. 21, 2013, story on Politico.com titled "President Obama Goes on the Offense for Liberalism," http://www.politico.com/story/2013/01/obama-on-offense-for-liberalism-86526.html, accessed July 11, 2013.

19. See his *Chicago Tribune* article titled "Obama: The Sequel," Jan. 23, 2013.

20. See the *Washington Post* article by Philip Rucker titled "Obama Remolds Federal Bench," Mar. 4, 2013.

21. Howard Schneider quotes Stokes in the *Washington Post* article titled "From a Skeptical Beginning, Obama Has Set a Global Round of Trade Talks in Motion," Mar. 8, 2013.

22. See Meredith Dake's Jan. 21, 2013, piece, "Where Are the 23 Executive Orders?" at http://www.breitbart.com/Big-Government/2013/01/20/Where-Are-The-23-Executive-Orders.

23. President Obama's comment during an open microphone moment, Mar. 26, 2012, at a bilateral meeting at the Nuclear Security Summit in Seoul, South Korea.

Bibliography

Abbott, Alden F. 1987. "The Case against Federal Statutory and Judicial Deadlines: A Cost-Benefit Analysis." *Administrative Law Review* 39: 171.

Abbott, Philip. 1991. *Political Thought in America.* Itasca, IL: Peacock.

Abramowitz, Alan I., Albert D. Cover, and Helmut Norpoth. 1986. "The President's Party in Midterm Elections: Going from Bad to Worse." *American Journal of Political Science* 30: 562–76.

Achen, Christopher, and Duncan Snidal. 1989. "Rational Deterrence Theory and Comparative Case Studies." *World Politics* 41: 143–69.

Ackerman, Bruce. 2004. "The Emergency Constitution." *Yale Law Journal* 113(5): 1029–91.

Alesina, Alberto, and Howard Rosenthal. 1989. "Partisan Cycles in Congressional Elections and the Macroeconomy." *American Political Science Review* 83: 373–98.

Allison, Graham. 1971. *Essence of Decision: Explaining the Cuban Missile Crisis.* Boston: Little, Brown.

Almond, Gabriel A., and Stephen J. Genco. 1977. "Clocks, Clouds, and the Study of Politics." *World Politics* 29(4): 489–522.

Alston, Lee J., and Bernardo Mueller. 2006. "Pork for Policy: Executive and Legislation Exchange in Brazil." *Journal of Law, Economics, and Organization* 22(1): 87–114.

Altman, Lawrence. 1997. "Reagan's Twilight—A Special Report: A President Fades into a World Apart." *New York Times,* October 5. http://query.nytimes.com/gst/fullpage.html?res=9F02E1DE133DF936A35753C1A961958260, accessed February 5, 2009.

Amorim Neto, Octavio. 2000. "Gabinetes presidenciais, ciclos eleitorais e disciplina legislativa no Brasil." *Dados—Revista de Ciências Sociais* 43(3): 479–519.

———, Gary W. Cox, and Matthew D. McCubbins. 2003. "Agenda Power in Brazil's Camara dos Deputados, 1989–1998." *World Politics* 55(4): 550–78.

Amorim Neto, Octavio, and Paulo Tafner. 2002. "Governos de coalizao e mecanismos de alarme e incendio no controle legislativo das medidas provisorias." *Dados—Revista de Ciências Sociais* 45(1): 5–38.

Aristotle. (1885). 2000. *Politics,* trans. Benjamin Jowett. New York: Dover.

Ascher, William. 2009. *Bringing in the Future: Strategies for Farsightedness and Sustainability in Developing Countries.* Chicago: University of Chicago Press.

Ballard, Megan J. 1999. "The Clash between Local Courts and Global Economics: The Politics of Judicial Reform in Brazil." *Berkeley Journal of International Law* 17: 230–76.

Balz, Dan. 2007. "Bush's Ambitious Second-Term Agenda Hits Reality." In *Second-Term Blues: How George W. Bush Has Governed,* ed. John C. Fortier and Norman Ornstein, 17–38. Washington, DC: Brookings/American Enterprise Institute.

Barber, James David. 1992. *The Presidential Character: Predicting Performance in the White House,* 4th ed. Upper Saddle River, NJ: Prentice-Hall.

Bar-el, Yair, Rimona Durst, Gregory Kutz, Josef Zislin, Ziva Strauss, and Haim Y. Knobler. 2000. "Jerusalem Syndrome." *British Journal of Psychiatry* 176: 86–90.

Beard, Charles. 1913. *An Economic Interpretation of the Constitution of the United States.* New York: Macmillan.

Becker, Gary S. 1990. "Reforming Congress: Why Limiting Terms Won't Work." *Business Week* (August 6): 18.

Beckman, Matthew, and Joseph Godfrey. 2007. "The Policy Opportunities in Presidential Honeymoons." *Political Research Quarterly* 60(2): 250–62.

Beerman, Jack. 2003. "Presidential Power in Transitions." *Boston University Law Review* 83: 947–1016.

Benjamin, Gerald. 1985. "The Diffusion of Executive Power in American State Constitutions: Tenure and Tenure Limitations." *Publius* 15(4): 71–84.

Bender, Thomas. 2006. *A Nation among Nations: America's Place in World History.* New York: Hill and Wang.

Bennett, Andrew. 2007. "Case Study Methods: Design, Use, and Comparative Advantages." In *Models, Numbers, and Cases: Methods for Studying International Relations,* ed. Detlef F. Sprinz and Yael Wolinsky-Nahmias, 19–55. Ann Arbor: University of Michigan Press.

Biasi, Heidi M. 2002. "The Antiquities Act of 1906 and Presidential Proclamations: A Retrospective and Prospective Analysis of President William J. Clinton's Quest to 'Win the West.'" *Buffalo Environmental Law Journal* 9: 189–244.

Blondel, Jean. 1987. *Political Leadership: Towards a General Analysis.* London: Sage.

Böhmer, Martin. 2000. "La corte de los '80 y la corte de los '90: Un diálogo sobre el *Rule of Law Argentina.*" Trabajo preparado para el SELA 2000.

Bond, Jon R., and Richard Fleisher. 1990. *The President in the Legislative Arena.* Chicago: University of Chicago Press.

Borón, Atilio. 1993. "Latin America: Constitutionalism and the Political Traditions of Liberalism and Socialism." In *Constitutionalism and Democracy: Transitions to the Contemporary World,* ed. Douglas Greenberg, Stanley N. Katz, Steven C. Wheatley, and Melanie Beth Oliviero, 339. New York: Oxford University Press.

Bowen, Jeff, and Susan Rose-Ackerman. 2003. "Partisan Politics and Executive Accountability: Argentina in Comparative Perspective." *Supreme Court Economic Review* 10: 157–210.

Bowles, Nigel. 1999. "Studying the Presidency." *Annual Review of Political Science* 2: 1–23.

Brace, Paul, and Barbara Hinckley. 1993. "Presidential Activities from Truman through Reagan: Timing and Impact." *Journal of Politics* 55(2): 382–98.

Bradley, C. A., and Jack Goldsmith. 2005. "Congressional Authorization and the War on Terrorism." *Harvard Law Review* 118(7): 2047–2133.

Brito, Jerry, and Veronique de Rugy. 2009. "Midnight Regulations and Regulatory Review." *Administrative Law Review* 61: 163–96.

Bruyneel, Kevin. 2006. "Should the 22nd Amendment Be Repealed?" *New York Times Upfront* (April 24, 2006), http://teacher.scholastic.com/scholasticnews/indepth/upfront/debate/index.asp?article=d0424, accessed July 18, 2013.

Buchanan, James M., and Gordon Tullock. 1962. *The Calculus of Consent.* Ann Arbor: University of Michigan Press.

Bueno de Mesquita, Bruce. 1983. *The War Trap.* New Haven, CT: Yale University Press.

———, Alastair Smith, Randolph Siverson, and James Morrow. 2003. *The Logic of Political Survival.* Cambridge, MA: MIT Press.

Bumin, Kirill M., Kirk A. Randazzo, and Lee D. Walker. 2009. "Institutional Viability and High Courts: A Comparative Analysis of Post-Communist States." *Australian Journal of Political Science* 44(1): 127–53.

Bunce, Valerie J. 1980. "Changing Leaders and Changing Policies: The Impact of Elite Succession on Budgetary Priorities in the United States with Some Cross-National Comparisons." *American Journal of Political Science* (August): 373–96.

———. 1981. *Do New Leaders Make a Difference? Executive Succession and Public Policy under Capitalism and Socialism.* Princeton, NJ: Princeton University Press.

Burke, John. 1992. *The Institutional Presidency.* Baltimore: Johns Hopkins University Press.

Busey, James L. 1967. "Observations on Latin American Constitutionalism." *The Americas* 24(1) (July): 46–66.

Calvert, Susan, and Peter Calvert. 1989. *Argentina: Political Culture and Instability.* Pittsburgh: University of Pittsburgh Press.

Campbell, James C. 1991. "The Presidential Surge and Its Midterm Decline in Congressional Elections: 1868–1988." *Journal of Politics* 53(2): 477–87.

———. 2003. "The 2002 Midterm Election: A Typical or an Atypical Midterm?" *PS: Political Science and Politics* 36(2): 203–207.

Canes-Wrone, Brandice, and Kenneth W. Shotts. 2004. "The Conditional Nature of Presidential Responsiveness to Public Opinion." *American Journal of Political Science* 48(4): 690–706.

Cannon, Carl. 2001. "The Long Goodbye." *National Journal* (January 27): 274.

Capriata, Laura. 2008. "Kirchner firmó cada seis días un decreto de necesidad y urgencia: Superó a Menem y no hay presidente que haya dictado más normas de ese tipo." *La Nacion* (April 13, 2008), http://www.lanacion.com.ar/1003971-kirchner-firmo-cada-seis-dias-un-decreto-de-necesidad-y-urgencia, accessed July 2, 2013.

Cardoso, Eliana, and Ann Helwege. 1991. "Populism, Profligacy and Redistribution." In *The Macroeconomics of Populism in Latin America,* ed. Rudiger Dornbush and Sebastian Edwards, 47–70. Chicago: University of Chicago Press.

Cardoso, Fernando Henrique. 2001. *Charting a New Course: The Politics of Globalization and Social Transformation,* ed. Mauricio A. Font. New York: Rowman and Littlefield.

Carey, John M. 2003. "The Reelection Debate in Latin America." *Latin American Politics and Society* 45(1): 119–33.

———, Richard G. Niemi, and Lynda W. Powell. 2000. *Term Limits in the State Legislatures.* Ann Arbor: University of Michigan Press.

———, and Gary F. Moncrief. 2006. "A New Survey of the 50 States." *Legislative Studies Quarterly* 21: 105–34.

Carey, John M., and Matthew Soberg Shugart. 1998. *Executive Decree Authority.* New York: Cambridge University Press.

Carlsnaes, Walter. 1992. "The Agent-Structure Problem in Foreign Policy Analysis." *International Studies Quarterly* 36(3): 432–48.

Carter, Jimmy. 1984. *Negotiation: The Alternative to Hostility.* Macon, GA: Mercer University Press.

Cash, Robert B. 1963. "Presidential Power: Use and Enforcement of Executive Orders." *Notre Dame Lawyer* 39: 44–55.

Cheibub, José Antonio. 2007. Presidentialism, Parliamentarism, and Democracy. New York: Cambridge University Press.

———. 2009. "Reforming Presidential and Semi-Presidential Democracies." In *Making Presidentialism Work,* ed. Andrew Ellis, J. Jesús Orozco Henríquez, and Daniel Zovatto, 3–31. Stockholm: International Institute for Democracy and Electoral Assistance (IDEA).

———, Adam Przeworski, and Sebastian M. Saiegh. 2004. "Government Coalition and Legislative Success under Presidentialism and Parliamentarism." *British Journal of Political Science* 34(4): 565–87.

Chen, Kong-Pin, and Emerson M. S. Niou. 2005. "Term Limits as a Response to Incumbency Advantage." *Journal of Politics* 67(2): 390–406.

Cochran, J. 2001. "The Cinderella Constraint: Why Regulations Increase Significantly during Post-Election Quarters." Working paper, George Mason University.

Coleman, James S. 1971. "The Development Syndrome: Differentiation—Equality—Capacity." In (*Crises and Sequences in Political Development,* ed. Leonard Binder, James S. Coleman, Joseph LaPalombara, Lucian W. Pye, Sidney Verba, and Myron Weiner, 73–100. Princeton, NJ: Princeton University Press.

Combs, Nancy Amoury. 2001. "Carter, Reagan, and Khomeini: Presidential Transitions and International Law." *Hastings Law Journal* 52: 303–439.

Conaghan, Catherine M., and James M. Malloy. 1994. *Unsettling Statecraft: Democracy and Neoliberalism in the Central Andes.* Pittsburgh: University of Pittsburgh Press.

———, and Luis A. Abugattas. 1990. "Business and the Boys: The Politics of Neoliberalism in the Central Andes." *Latin American Research Review* 25(1): 3–29.

Contrubis, John. 1999. "Executive Orders and Proclamations." *CRS Report 95–772.* Washington, DC: Congressional Research Service, Library of Congress.

Cooper, Phillip J. 2001. "The Law: Presidential Memoranda and Executive Orders: Of Patchwork Quilts, Trump Cards, and Shell Games." *Presidential Studies Quarterly* 31(1): 126–41.

———. 2002. *By Order of the President: The Use and Abuse of Executive Direct Action.* Lawrence: University of Kansas Press.

Corwin, Edward S. 1948. *The President: Office and Powers, 1787–1948.* New York: New York University Press.

Cowling, B. J., J. L. Hutton, and J. E. H. Shaw. 2006. "Joint Modeling of Event Counts and Survival Times." *Journal of the Royal Statistical Society,* ser. C (Applied Statistics), 55(1): 31–39.

Crockett, David A. 2008. "The Contemporary Presidency, 'An Excess of Refinement': Lame Duck Presidents in Constitutional and Historical Context." *Presidential Studies Quarterly* 38(4): 707–21.

Cropsey, Joseph. 1955. "What Is Welfare Economics?" *Ethics* 65(2): 116–25.

Cross, Frank B. 1988. "Executive Orders 12,291 and 12,498: A Test Case in Presidential Control of Executive Agencies." *Journal of Law and Politics* 4: 483–542.

Crowther, Edward R. 2000. "Emancipation Proclamation." In *Encyclopedia of the American Civil War,* ed. David S. Heidler and Jeanne T. Heidler, 650–52. New York: Norton.

Cunion, William. 2005. "Second-Term Presidents: Free Birds or Lame Ducks?" In *In the Public Domain,* ed. Lori Han and Diane Heith, 113–33. Albany: State University of New York.

Dahl, Robert A. 2002. *How Democratic Is the American Constitution?* New Haven, CT: Yale University Press.

De Cremer, D., and E. Van Dijk. 2005. "When and Why Leaders Put Themselves First: Leader Behaviour in Resource Allocations as a Function of Feeling Entitled." *European Journal of Social Psychology* 35: 553–63.

DeConde, Alexander. 2000. *Presidential Machismo: Executive Authority, Military Intervention, and Foreign Relations.* Boston: Northeastern University Press.

Deering, Christopher J., and Forrest Maltzman. 1999. "The Politics of Executive Orders: Legislative Constraints on Presidential Power." *Political Research Quarterly* 52(4): 767–83.

De Rugy, Veronique, and Antony Davies. 2009. "Midnight Regulations and the Cinderella Effect." *Journal of Socio-Economics* 38(6): 886–90.

Diamond, Larry. 2000. "The Global State of Democracy." *Current History* 99(641): 413–18.

Dornbush, Rudiger, and Sebastian Edwards, eds. 1991. *The Macroeconomics of Populism in Latin America.* Chicago: University of Chicago Press.

Dunleavy, Patrick, and R. A. W. Rhodes. 1995. *Prime Minister, Cabinet, and Core Executive.* New York: St. Martin's.

Duverger, Maurice. 1980. "A New Political System Model: Semi-Presidential Government." *European Journal of Political Research* (8)2: 165–87.

Eagleton, Thomas F. 1974. *War and Presidential Power: A Chronicle of Congressional Surrender.* New York: Norton.

Eaton, Kent. 2000. "Parliamentarism versus Presidentialism in the Policy Arena." *Comparative Politics* 32(3): 355–76. Review of some important works on the influence of executive format on policy making.

Edwards, George C., III, Andrew Barrett, and Jeffrey Peake. 1997. "The Legislative Impact of Divided Government." *American Journal of Political Science* 41: 545–64.

Edwards, George C., III, John H. Kessel, and Bert A. Rockman, eds. 1993. *Researching the Presidency: Vital Questions, New Approaches.* Pittsburgh: University of Pittsburgh Press.

Elgie, Robert. 1997. "Models of Executive Politics: A Framework for the Study of Executive Power Relations in Parliamentary and Semi-Presidential Regimes." *Political Studies* 45: 217–31.

Elster, Jon. 2009. *Alexis de Tocqueville: The First Social Scientist.* Cambridge: Cambridge University Press.

Epstein, David, and Sharyn O'Halloran. 1999. *Delegating Powers: A Transaction Cost Politics Approach to Policy Making under Separate Powers.* Cambridge: Cambridge University Press.

Eskridge, William N., and Lauren E. Baer. 2008. "The Continuum of Deference: Supreme Court Treatment of Agency Statutory Interpretations from Chevron to Hamdan." *Georgetown Law Journal* 96: 1083–1226.

Fahrenthold, David A., and Peter Wallsten. 2012. "Obama Allies, Foes Speculate on a Big—and Hypothetical—Second-Term Agenda." *Washington Post* (March 5), A1.

Farmer, Rick, John David Rausch, and John C. Green. 2002. *The Test of Time: Coping with Legislative Term Limits.* Lexington, MA: Lexington.

Farnham, Barbara. 2004. "Impact of the Political Context on Foreign Policy Decision-Making." *Political Psychology* 25(3): 441–63.

Faro de Castro, Marcus, and Maria Izabel Valladão de Carvalho. 2003. "Globalization and Recent Political Transitions in Brazil." *International Political Science Review* 24(4): 465–90.

Ferreira Rubio, Delia, and Matteo Goretti. 1998. "When the President Governs Alone: The Decretazo in Argentina." In *Executive Decree Authority,* ed. John M. Carey and Matthew Soberg Shugart, 33–61. Cambridge: Cambridge University Press.

———. 2000. "Executive-Legislative Relationship in Argentina: From Menem's *Decretazo* to a New Style?" Lecture at seminar, "Argentina 2000: Politics, Economy, Society and International Relations," St. Antony's College, Oxford University, May 15–17, 2000. http://www.deliaferreira.com.ar/pdf/at-gobierno/GobiernoporDecreto-Oxford2000.pdf, accessed July 3, 2013.

Figueiredo, Argelina Cheibub, and Fernando Limongi. 1997. "O Congresso e as medidas provisórias: Abdicação ou delegação." *Novos Estudos Cebrap* 47: 127–54.

———. 2000. "Presidential Power, Legislative Organization, and Party Behavior in Brazil." *Comparative Politics* 32(3): 151–70.

Finkel, Jodi. 2004. "Judicial Reform in Argentina in the 1990s: How Electoral Incentives Shape Institutional Change." *Latin American Research Review* 39(3): 56–80.

Finnemore, Martha. 1996. *National Interests in International Society.* Ithaca, NY: Cornell University Press.

———, and Kathryn Sikkink. 1998. "International Norm Dynamics and Political Change." *International Organization* 52: 887–917.

Fleishman, Joel L., and Arthur H. Aufses. 1976. "Law and Orders: The Problem of Presidential Legislation." *Law and Contemporary Problems* 40: 1–45.

Friedman, Gil, and Harvey Starr. 1997. *Agency, Structure, and International Politics: From Ontology to Empirical Inquiry.* London: Routledge.

Gaddis, John Lewis. 1982. *Strategies of Containment: A Critical Appraisal of Postwar American National Security Policy.* New York: Oxford University Press.

Galindo, Pedro. 2003. "Report on the State of Justice in the Americas, 2002–2003." Santiago: Centro de Estudias de Justicia de las Américas (CEJA).

Gargarella, Roberto. 1998. "Después del diluvio: El perfeccionismo conservador en la nueva jurisprudencia de la Corte Suprema (1990–1997)." *Desarrollo Económico Revista de Ciencias Sociales.* Instituto de Desarrollo Económico y Social 38(149): 439–56.

Gaziano, Todd F. 2001. "Legal Memorandum: The Use and Abuse of Executive Orders and Other Presidential Directives." Heritage Foundation. http://www.heritage.org/research/reports/2001/02/the-use-and-abuse-of-executive-orders-and-other-presidential-directives, accessed July 2, 2013.

Gersen, Jacob E., and Anne Joseph O'Connell. 2008. "Deadline in Administrative Law." *University of Pennsylvania Law Review* 156: 923–78.

Ginsburg, Tom. 2010. "On the Evasion of Term Limits." Unpublished paper http://works.bepress.com/tom_ginsburg/31, accessed July 2, 2013.

Goldsmith, Jack, and John F. Manning. 2006. "The President's Completion Power." *Yale Law Journal* 115: 2280–2312.

Goldsmith, William M. 1974. *The Growth of Presidential Power: A Documented History.* New York: Chelsea House.

Gould, Stephen Jay. 1991. "The Streak of Streaks." In *Bully for Brontosaurus: Reflections in Natural History,* ed. Stephen Jay Gould, 463–72. New York: Norton.

Green, John C., Jesse Marquette, and Rick Farmer. 2006. "Assessing Legislative Term Limits in Ohio." Akron, OH: Ray C. Bliss Institute of Applied Politics, University of Akron. http://www.uakron.edu/bliss/research/archives/2002/AssessingLegislativeTermLimitsinOhioV.pdf, accessed July 27, 2013.

Grier, Robin M., and Kevin B. Grier. 2000. "Political Cycles in Nontraditional Settings: Theory and Evidence from the Case of Mexico." *Journal of Law and Economics* 43(1): 239–64.

Grossman, Michael Baruch, and Martha Joynt Kumar. 1981. *Portraying the President: The White House and the News Media.* Baltimore: Johns Hopkins University Press.

———, and Francis E. Rourke. 2000. "Second-Term Presidencies: The Aging of Administration." In *The Presidency and the Political System,* ed. Michael Nelson. 224–36. Washington, DC: Congressional Quarterly Press.

Guinote, Ana. 2007. "Power and Goal Pursuit." *Personality and Social Psychology Bulletin* 33: 1076–87.

Hagopian, Frances. 2000. Political Development, Revisited. *Comparative Political Studies* 33(6/7): 880–912.

Hart, John. 1998. "Neglected Aspects of the Study of the Presidency." *Annual Review of Political Science* 1: 379–99.

Hartz, Louis. 1955. *The Liberal Tradition in America.* New York: Harcourt, Brace.

Hawley, Chris. 2009. "Latin America Leaders Extend Terms." *USA Today* (January 27, 2009), 6A.

Heckelman, Jac C., and Keith C. Dougherty. 2007. "An Economic Interpretation of the Constitutional Convention of 1787 Revisited." *Journal of Economic History* 67(4): 829–48.

Heclo, H. 1977. *Studying the Presidency.* New York: Ford Foundation.

Hedtke, James. 2002. *Lame Duck Presidents: Myth or Reality.* Lewiston, NY: Edwin Mellen Press.

Hegel, Georg Wilhelm Friedrich. 1967. *The Philosophy of Right,* trans. T. M. Knox. Oxford: Oxford University Press.

Helmke, Gretchen. 2002. "The Logic of Strategic Defection: Court-Executive Relations in Argentina under Dictatorship and Democracy." *American Political Science Review* 96(2): 291–303.

Hersh, Seymour M. 2010. "The Online Threat: Should We Be Worried about a Cyber War?" *New Yorker* (November 1, 2010), http://www.newyorker.com/reporting/2010/11/01/101101fa_fact_hersh, accessed July 18, 2013.

Hirschman, Charles. 1963. *Journeys toward Progress: Studies of Economic Policy-Making in Latin America.* New York: Twentieth Century Fund.

Hoddie, Matthew, and Stephen Routh. 2004. "Predicting the Presidential Presence: Explaining Presidential Midterm Elections Campaign Behavior. *Political Research Quarterly* 57(2): 257–65.

Hofstadter, Richard. 1958. "American Ethics and Public Policy." In *The American Style,* ed. Elting E. Morison, 369. New York: Harper.

Hogue, Henry B. 2012. "Presidential Transition Act: Provisions and Funding." *CRS Report 7–5700.* Washington, DC: Congressional Research Service, Library of Congress.

Holt, Robert T., and John M. Richardson Jr. 1970. "Competing Paradigms in Comparative Politics." In *The Methodology for Comparative Research,* ed. Robert T. Holt and John E. Turner, 21–71. New York: Free Press.

Horowitz, Donald. 1996. "Comparing Democratic Systems." In *A Global Resurgence of Democracy,* ed. Larry Diamond and Marc F. Plattner, 143–49. Baltimore: Johns Hopkins University Press.

Howell, William G. 2003. *Power without Persuasion: The Politics of Direct Presidential Action.* Princeton, NJ: Princeton University Press.

———, and Kenneth Mayer. 2005. "The Last One Hundred Days of Presidential Campaigns." *Presidential Studies Quarterly* 35(3): 533–54.

Huber, John D. 1992. "Restrictive Legislative Procedures in France and the United States." *American Political Science Review* 86: 675–87.

———, and Charles R. Shipan. 2002. *Deliberate Discretion? The Institutional Foundations of Bureaucratic Autonomy.* Cambridge: Cambridge University Press.

Hudelson, Robert. 1999. *Modern Political Philosophy: Explorations in Philosophy.* New York: Sharpe.

Hughes, William J. 1995. "The 'Not-So-Genial' Conspiracy: The *New York Times* and Six Presidential 'Honeymoons,' 1953–1993." *Journalism and Mass Communication Quarterly* 72(4): 841–50.

Huntington, Samuel P., and Jorge I. Domínguez. 1975. "Political Development." In *Handbook of Political Science.* Vol. 3, *Macropolitical Theory,* ed. Fred I. Greenstein and Nelson W. Polsky, 1–114. Reading, MA: Addison-Wesley.

Hurrell, Andrew. 2002. "Norms and Ethics in International Relations." In *Handbook of International Relations,* ed. Walter E. Carlsnaes, Thomas Risse, and Beth A. Simmons, 137–54. London: Sage.

Ikenberry, John. 2006. *Liberal Order and Imperial Ambition: Essays on American Power and International Order.* Malden, MA: Polity.

Indyk, Martin, and Harvey Sicherman. 2008. "The Final Year: End-of-Term Presidents and the Middle East." Washington Institute for Near East Policy. PolicyWatch #1339: Special Forum Report. http://www.ciaonet.org/pbei/winep/0002106/index.html, accessed December 5, 2008.

Jack, W. Andrew. 1986. "Executive Orders 12,291 and 12,498: Usurpation of Legislative Power or Blueprint for Legislative Reform?" *George Washington Law Review* 54: 512–40.

Jacob, Paul. 1994. "From the Voters with Care." In *The Politics and the Law of Term Limits,* ed. Edward H. Crane and Roger Pilon, 27–44. Washington, DC: Cato Institute.

Jacobson, Gary C., Samuel Kernell, and Jeffrey Lazarus. 2004. "Assessing the President's Role as Party Agent in Congressional Elections: The Case of Bill Clinton in 2000." *Legislative Studies Quarterly* 29 (2): 159–84.

Gurr, Ted Robert, and Monti Marshall (founder and principal investigator). 2013. "Polity IV Project Data Set: Political Regime Characteristics and Transition, 1800–2012." Vienna, VA: Center for Systemic Peace.

Jillson, Calvin C. 1988. *Constitution Making: Conflict and Consensus in the Federal Convention of 1787.* Boulder, CO: Agathon Press.

———, and Cecil L. Eubanks. 1984. "The Political Structure of Constitution Making: The Federal Convention of 1787." *American Journal of Political Science* 28(3): 435–58.

Johnson, Toni. 2008. "Presidential Transitions and Foreign Policy." Working paper, Council on Foreign Relations.

Jones, Charles. 1994. *The Presidency in a Separated System.* Washington, DC: Brookings Institution Press.

Jones, Mark. 1997. "Evaluating Argentina's Presidential Democracy, 1983–1995." In *Presidentialism and Democracy in Latin America,* ed. Scott Mainwaring and Matthew Shugart, 259. Cambridge: Cambridge University Press.

Kalian, Moshe, and Eliezer Witztum. 2000. "Correspondence: Comments on Jerusalem Syndrome." *British Journal of Psychiatry* 176: 492–98.

Kamber, Victor. 1995. *Giving Up on Democracy: Why Term Limits Are Bad for America.* Washington, DC: Regnery.

Kapiszewski, Diana. 2007. "Challenging Decisions: High Courts and Economic Governance in Argentina and Brazil." PhD diss., Department of Political Science, University of California at Berkeley.

Katzenstein, Peter. 1996. *The Culture of National Security: Norms and Identity in World Politics.* New York: Columbia University Press.

Kaufman, Robert. 1985. "Democratic and Authoritarian Responses to the Debt Issue: Argentina, Brazil, Mexico." *International Organization* 39(3): 473–503.

Kemeny, John. 1959. "Mathematics without Numbers." *Daedalus* 88: 577–91.

Keohane, Robert. 1984. *After Hegemony: Cooperation and Discord in the World Political Economy.* Princeton, NJ: Princeton University Press.

Kessler, Andy. 2012. "When Will Social Media Elect a President?" *Wall Street Journal,* (February 29), http://online.wsj.com/article/SB10001424052970203960804577244961842322348.html, accessed July 2, 2013.

King, Gary, Robert O. Keohane, and Sidney Verba. 1994. *Designing Social Inquiry: Scientific Inference in Qualitative Research.* Princeton, NJ: Princeton University Press.

Klotz, Audie. 1995. *Norms in International Relations: The Struggle against Apartheid.* Ithaca, NY: Cornell University Press.

Korzi, Michael J. 2011. *Presidential Term Limits in American History: Power, Principles, and Politics.* College Station: Texas A&M University Press.

Kousser, Thad. 2005. *Term Limits and the Dismantling of State Legislative Professionalism.* New York: Cambridge University Press.

Krause, George A., and David B. Cohen. 1997. "Presidential Use of Executive Orders, 1953–1994." *American Politics Quarterly* 25: 458–71.

Krause, George A., and Jeffrey Cohen. 2000. "Opportunity, Constraints, and the Development of the Institutional Presidency: The Case of Executive Order Issuance, 1939–1996." *Journal of Politics* 62: 88–114.

Krehbeil, Keith. 1992. *Information and Legislative Organization.* Ann Arbor: University of Michigan Press.

Krutz, Glen, Richard Fleisher, and Jon Bond. 1998. "From Abe Fortas to Zoe Baird: Why Some Presidential Nominations Fail in the Senate." *American Political Science Review* 92(4): 871–81.

Kubicek, Paul. 1994. "Delegative Democracy in Russia and Ukraine." *Communist and Post-Communist Studies* 27(4): 423–311.

Kumar, Martha Joynt. 2010a. "The 2008–2009 Presidential Transition: Successful Cooperation." Bureau of International Information Programs, U.S. Department of State, http://iipdigital.usembassy.gov/st/english/publication/2010/01/20100126112707mlenuhret0.8004201.html#axzz2Xv5mvOha, accessed July 2, 2013.

Kumar, Martha Joynt. 2010b. *Managing the President's Message: The White House Communications Operation.* Baltimore: Johns Hopkins University Press.

———, George C. Edward III, James Pfiffner, and Terry Sullivan. 2000. "Meeting the Freight Train Head On: Planning for the Transition to Power." The White House 2001 Project, White House Interview Program, Report 2.

Kyvig, David E. 1996. *Explicit and Authentic Acts: Amending the U.S. Constitution, 1776–1995.* Lawrence: University Press of Kansas.

Lacey, Marc. 2000. "Blocked by Congress, Clinton Wields a Pen." *New York Times* (July 5).

Lamounier, Bolivar, and Dieter Nohlen. 1993. *Presidencialismo ou parlamentarismo: Perspectivas sobre a reorganização institucional brasileira.* São Paulo, Brazil: Edições Loyola, IDESP.

Lane, Jan-Erik. 1996. *Constitutions and Political Theory.* Manchester, UK: Manchester University Press.

Larkins, Christopher. 1998. "The Judiciary and Delegative Democracy in Argentina." *Comparative Politics* 30: 423–43.

Layne, Christopher, and Bradley Thayer. 2006. *American Empire: A Debate.* New York: Routledge.

Levitsky, Steven, and Maria Victoria Murillo. 2008. "Argentina: From Kirchner to Kirchner." *Journal of Democracy* 19(2): 16–30.

Light, Paul C. 1981. *The President's Agenda.* Baltimore: Johns Hopkins University Press.

Lijphart, Arend, ed. 1992. *Parliamentary versus Presidential Government.* New York: Oxford University Press.

Linz, Juan J. 1978. *The Breakdown of Democratic Regimes: Crisis, Breakdown, and Reequilibrium.* Baltimore: Johns Hopkins University Press.

———. 1988. "Democracia presidencialista o parlamentarista: Hay alguna diferencia?" In *Presidencialismo versus parlamentarismo: Materiales para el estudio de la reforma constitucional,* ed. Consejo para la Consolidación de la democracia, 19–43. Buenos Aires, Eudeba.

———. 1990. "The Perils of Presidentialism." *Journal of Democracy* 1(1): 51–69.

———. 1994. "Presidential or Parliamentary Democracy: Does It Make a Difference?" in *The Failure of Presidential Democracy: Comparative Perspectives,* ed. Juan J. Linz and Arturo Valenzuela, 3. Baltimore: Johns Hopkins University Press.

———, and Arturo Valenzuela, eds. 1992. *Presidential or Parliamentary Democracy: Does It Make a Difference?* Baltimore: Johns Hopkins University Press.

———. 1994. *The Failure of Presidential Democracy: Comparative Perspectives.* Baltimore: Johns Hopkins University Press.

Lizza, Ryan. 2012. "The Second Term: What Will Obama Do Now That He's Reelected?" *New Yorker* (June 18, 2012), http://www.newyorker.com/reporting/2012/06/18/120618fa_fact_lizza, accessed July 18, 2013.

Llanos, Mariana. 2001. "Understanding Presidential Power in Argentina: A Study of the Policy of Privatisation in the 1990s." *Journal of Latin American Studies* 33(1): 67–99.

Loewenstein, George, and Jon Elster, eds. 1992. *Choice over Time.* New York: Russell Sage Foundation.

Loewenstein, George, and Richard H. Thaler. 1989. "Anomalies: Intertemporal Choice." *Journal of Economic Perspectives* 3(4): 181–93.

Lowi, Theodore J. 1985. "The State in Politics: The Relation between Policy and Administration." In *Regulatory Policy and the Social Sciences,* ed. R. G. Noll, 67–105. Berkeley: University of California Press.

———. 1991. "Afterword: Presidential Power and the Ideological Struggle over Its Interpretation." In *The Constitution and the American Presidency,* ed. Martin L. Fausold and Alan Shank, 227–44. New York: State University of New York Press.

Madison, James. (1787) 1920a. "Notes of Thursday, May 31, 1787." In *Notes of Debates in the Federal Constitution of 1787,* ed. Gallard Hund and James Brown Scott. New York: Oxford University Press. http://avalon.law.yale.edu/18th_century/debates_531.asp, accessed July 19, 2013.

———. (1787) 1920b. "Notes of Thursday, July 19, 1787." In *Notes of Debates in the Federal Constitution of 1787,* ed. Gallard Hund and James Brown Scott. New York: Oxford University Press. http://avalon.law.yale.edu/18th_century/debates_719.asp, accessed July 19, 2013.

Mahler, Gregory. 2008. *Comparative Politics: An Institutional and Cross-National Approach.* Upper Saddle River, NJ: Pearson Prentice-Hall.

Mahoney, J. 1999. "Nominal, Ordinal, and Narrative Appraisal in Macrocausal Analysis." *American Journal of Sociology* 104(4): 1154–96.

Mainwaring, Scott. 1990. "Presidentialism in Latin America." *Latin American Research Review* 25(1): 157–79.

———, and Matthew Soberg Shugart. 1997. *Presidentialism and Democracy in Latin America.* Cambridge: Cambridge University Press.

Maltz, Gideon. 2007. "The Case for Presidential Term Limits." *Journal of Democracy* 18(1): 128–42.

Maltzman, Forrest, James H. Lebovic, Elizabeth Saunders, and Emma Furth. 2012. "Unleashing Presidential Power: The Politics of Pets in the White House." *PS: Political Science and Politics* 45(3): 395–400.

Maner, Jon K., and Nicole Mead. 2010. "The Essential Tension between Leadership and Power: When Leaders Sacrifice Group Goals for the Sake of Self-Interest." *Journal of Personality and Social Psychology* 99(3): 482–97.

Mann, Thomas. 1994. "Congressional Term Limits: A Bad Idea Whose Time Should Never Come." In *The Politics and the Law of Term Limits,* ed. Edward H. Crane and Roger Pilon, 83–98. Washington, DC: Cato Institute.

Manzetti, Luigi. 2003. "Political Manipulations and Market Reforms Fiascoes." *World Politics* 55: 315–60.

Martínez, Juan, and Javier Santiso. 2003. "Financial Markets and Politics: The Confidence Game in Latin American Emerging Economies." *International Political Science Review* 24(3): 363–95.

Marx, Karl. (1852) 2010. *Eighteenth Brumaire of Louis Bonaparte,* trans. Daniel de Leon. New York: Mondial.

Maslow, Abraham. 1943. "A Theory of Human Motivation." *Psychological Review* 50(4): 370–96.

———. 1954/1987. *Motivation and Personality.* New York: HarperCollins.

Mayer, Kenneth. 1999. "Executive Orders and Presidential Power." *Journal of Politics* 61(2): 445–66.

———. 2001. *With the Stroke of a Pen: Executive Orders and Presidential Power.* Princeton, NJ: Princeton University Press.

———, and Kevin Price. 2002. "Unilateral Presidential Powers: Significant Executive Orders, 1949–99." *Presidential Studies Quarterly* 32: 367–86.

Mayhew, David. 1991. *Divided We Govern: Party Control, Lawmaking, and Investigations, 1946–1990.* New Haven, CT: Yale University Press.

McGuire, R. A. 1988. "Constitution Making: A Rational Choice Model of the Federal Convention of 1787." *American Journal of Political Science* 32: 483–522.

McLaughlin, Patrick A. 2011. "The Consequences of Midnight Regulations and Other Surges in Regulatory Activity." *Public Choice* 147(3) (April): 395–412.

———, and Jerry Ellig. 2011. "Does OIRA Review Improve the Quality of Regulatory Impact Analysis? Evidence from the Final Year of the Bush II Administration." Special edition, *Administrative Law Review* 63: 179.

Mendelson, Nina. 2003. "Agency Burrowing: Entrenching Policies and Personnel before a New President Arrives." *New York Law Review* 78: 557–78.

Milkis, S. M., and M. Nelson. 1994. *The American Presidency: Origins and Development, 1776–1993.* Washington, DC: Congressional Quarterly Press.

Mill, John Stuart. (1843) 2002. *A System of Logic: Ratiocinative and Inductive.* Honolulu: University Press of the Pacific.

Miller, Jonathan M. 1997. "The Authority of a Foreign Talisman: A Study of U.S. Constitutional Practice as Authority in Nineteenth-Century Argentina and the Argentine Elite's Leap of Faith." *American University Law Review* 46(5): 1483–1572.

———. 2000. "Evaluating the Argentine Supreme Court under Presidents Alfonsín and Menem (1983–1999)." *Southwestern Journal of Law and Trade in the Americas* 7: 369.

Moe, Terry. 1985. "The Politicized Presidency." In *The New Direction in American Politics,* ed. John Chubb and Paul Peterson, 235–71. Washington, DC: Brookings.

———. 1993. "Presidents, Institutions and Theory." In *Researching the Presidency: Vital Questions, New Approaches,* ed. George Edwards, John Kessel, and Bert Rockman, 289–337. Pittsburgh: University of Pittsburgh Press.

Moniz Bandeira, Luiz Alberto. 2006. "Brazil as a Regional Power and Its Relation with the United States." *Latin American Perspectives* 33(3): 12–27.

Morrow, William S., Jr. 2001. "Midnight Regulations: Natural Order or Disorderly Governance?" *Administrative and Regulatory Law News* (Spring): 3, 18.

Mosher, Frederick C., W. David Clinton, and Daniel G. Lang. 1987. *Presidential Transitions and Foreign Affairs.* Baton Rouge: Louisiana University Press.

Moteff, John. 2004. "Computer Security: A Summary of Selected Federal Laws, Executive Orders, and Presidential Directives." *CRS Report RL32357.* Washington, DC: Resources, Science, and Industry Division, Congressional Research Service, Library of Congress.

"Moves to Limit the Term, 1787–1946." 1947. *Congressional Digest* 26: 14–16.

Mueller, John. 1973. *War, Presidents, and Public Opinion.* New York: Wiley.

Mustapic, Ana Maria. 2002. "Oscillating Relations: President and Congress in Argentina." In *Politics in Latin America,* ed. Scott Morgenstern and Benito Nacif, 23–47. New York: Cambridge University Press.

Neale, Thomas H. 2009. "Presidential Terms and Tenure: Perspectives and Proposals for Change." *CRS Report 7–5700.* Washington, DC: Congressional Research Service, Library of Congress.

Negretto, Gabriel L. 2004. "Government Capacities and Policy Making by Decree in Latin America: The Cases of Brazil and Argentina." *Comparative Political Studies* 37(5): 531–62.

Neighbors, William D. 1964. "Presidential Legislation by Executive Order." *University of Colorado Law Review* 37: 105–18.

Neustadt, Richard E. (1960) 1990. *Presidential Power and Modern Presidents.* New York: Free Press. Citations refer to the 1990 edition.

Nicolau, Jairo Marconi. 1993. *Sistema eleitoral e reforma política.* Rio de Janeiro: Foglio Editora.

Nietzsche, F. (1878) 1986. *Human, All Too Human,* trans. R. J. Hollingdale. Cambridge: Cambridge University Press.

Nino, Carlos Santiago. 1996. "Hyperpresidentialism and Constitutional Reform in Argentina." In *Institutional Design in New Democracies: Eastern Europe and Latin America,* ed. Arend Lijphart and Carlos Waisman, 165. Boulder, CO: Westview.

O'Connell, Anne Joseph. 2008. "Political Cycles of Rulemaking: An Empirical Portrait of the Modern Administrative State." *Virginia Law Review* 94(4): 889–986.

———. 2009. "Cleaning Up and Launching Ahead: What President Obama Can Learn from Previous Administrations in Establishing His Regulatory Agenda." Center for American Progress working paper.

O'Donnell, Guillermo. 1994. "Delegative Democracy?" *Journal of Democracy* 5(1): 55–69.

O'Loughlin, John, and Richard Grant. 1990. "The Political Geography of Presidential Speeches, 1946–87." *Annals of the Association of American Geographers* 80(4): 504–30.

Olson, Mancur. 1965. *The Logic of Collective Action: Public Goods and the Theory of Groups.* Cambridge, MA: Harvard University Press.

Olson, William, and Alan Woll. 1999. "Executive Orders and National Emergencies: How Presidents Have Come to 'Run the Country' by Usurping Legislative Power." *Cato Policy Analysis* 358: 1–79.

Pachón-Buitrago, Monica. 2008. "Cross-Avenue Politics: The Case of Colombia and Brazil." PhD diss., Political Science and International Affairs Department, University of California at San Diego.

Palanza, Valeria. 2009. "Lawmaking in Separation of Powers Systems: On the Choice of Decrees vs. Statutes." PhD diss., Department of Politics, Princeton University.

Pallitto, Robert M., and William G. Weaver. 2007. *Presidential Secrecy and the Law.* Baltimore: Johns Hopkins University Press.

Park, Jack J., Jr. 2009. "Executive Order on Preemption." *Federalist Society for Law and Public Policy,* http://www.fed-soc.org/publications/detail/executive-order-on-preemption, accessed July 2, 2013.

Peabody, Bruce G. 2001. "George Washington, Presidential Term Limits, and the Problem of Reluctant Political Leadership." *Presidential Studies Quarterly* 31: 439–53.

Peixoto, Martin. 1988. "Parlamentarismo y presidencialismo: Dónde están las diferencias?" *Cuadernos del CLAEH* 47: 5–17.

Pellet Lastra, Arturo. 2001. *Historia Política de la Corte 1930–1990.* Buenos Aires: Editorial Ad-Hoc S.R.L. Villela Editora.

Pereira, Carlos, Timothy J. Power, and Lucio Rennó. 2005. "Under What Conditions Do Presidents Resort to Decree Power? Theory and Evidence from the Brazilian Case." *Journal of Politics* 67(1): 178–200.

———. 2008. "Agenda Power, Executive Decree Authority, and the Mixed Results in the Brazilian Congress" *Legislative Studies Quarterly* 33(1): 5–33.

Peters, Guy. 2005. *Institutional Theory in Political Science: The New Institutionalism.* New York: Continuum.

Petracca, Marc. 1992. "Commentary: Predisposed to Oppose: Political Scientists and Term Limitations." *Polity* 24(4): 657–72.

———, and Darci Jump. 1992. "From Coast to Coast: The Term Limitation Express." *National Civic Review* 81: 352–65.

Pfiffner, James P. 1996. *The Strategic Presidency: Hitting the Ground Running.* Lawrence: University Press of Kansas.

Pierson, Paul. 2004. *Politics in Time: History, Institutions, and Social Analysis.* Princeton, NJ: Princeton University Press.

Pika, Joseph. 1988. "Management Style and the Organizational Matrix." *Administration and Society* 20: 3–29.

Posner, Eric, and Adrian Vermeuli. 2007. "The Credible Executive." *University of Chicago Law Review* 74(3): 865–913.

Power, Timothy J. 1997. "Parties, Puppets, and Paradoxes: Changing Attitudes Toward Party Institutionalization in Postauthoritarian Brazil." *Party Politics* 3(2): 189.

———. 1998. "The Pen Is Mightier than the Congress: Presidential Decree Authority in Brazil." In *Executive Decree Authority,* ed. John Carey and Matthew Soberg Shugart, 197–230. New York: Cambridge University Press.

Prillaman, William C. 2000. *The Judiciary and Democratic Decay in Latin America: Declining Confidence in the Rule of Law.* Westport, CT: Praeger.

Przeworski, Adam. 1991. *Democracy and the Market: Political and Economic Reforms in Eastern Europe and Latin America.* New York: Cambridge University Press.

———, Michael E. Alvarez, Jose Antonio Cheibub, and Fernando Limongi. 2000. *Democracy and Development: Political Institutions and Well-Being in the World, 1950–1990.* New York: Cambridge University Press.

Pye, Lucian W. 1965. "Introduction: Political Culture and Political Development." In *Political Culture and Political Development,* ed. Lucian W. Pye and Sidney Verba, 3–26. Princeton, NJ: Princeton University Press.

Ragsdale, Lyn, and John J. Theis. 1997. "The Institutionalization of the American Presidency, 1924–1992." *American Journal of Political Science* 41: 1280–1318.

Ramos, Raphaël. 2008. "United States: Presidential Transition and Implications for National Security in 2008–2009." European Strategic Intelligence and Security Center Report. Posted September 29, 2008, http://intelligence-summit.blogspot.com/2008/10/united-states-presidential-transition.html, accessed July 3, 2013.

Rapaczynski, Andrzej. 1990. "Bibliographical Essay: The Influence of U.S. Constitutionalism Abroad." In *Constitutionalism and Rights: The Influence of the United States Constitution Abroad,* ed. Louis Henkin and Albert J. Rosenthal, 405–62. New York: Columbia University Press.

Reich, Gary. 2002. "Executive Decree Authority in Brazil: How Reactive Legislators Influence Policy." *Legislative Studies Quarterly* 27: 5–31.

Relyea, Harold. 2001. "National Emergency Powers." *CRS Report 98–505.* Washington, DC: Congressional Research Service, Library of Congress.

———. 2007. "Presidential Directives: Background and Overview." *CRS Report 98–611.* Washington, DC: Congressional Research Service, Library of Congress.

Rennó, Lúcio. 2010. "Executive-Legislative Relations in Brazil: Is 2009 the First Year of the Rest of Our Lives?" *Revista de ciencia política* 30(2): 213–30.

Riker, William H. 1984. "The Heresthetics of Constitution-Making: The Presidency in 1787, with Comments on Determinism and Rational Choice." *American Political Science Review* 78(1): 1–16.

Rimmerman, Craig A. 1993. *Presidency by Plebiscite: The Reagan-Bush Era in Institutional Perspective.* Boulder, CO: Westview.

Rios-Figueroa, Julio, and Matthew M. Taylor. 2006. "Institutional Determinants of the Judicialisation of Policy in Brazil and Mexico." *Journal of Latin American Studies* 38: 739–66.

Robertson, David Brian. 2005. "Madison's Opponents and Constitutional Design." *American Political Science Review* 99(2): 225–43.

Rockman, Bert A. 1984. *The Leadership Question: The Presidency and the American System.* New York: Praeger.

Romero, José Luis. 1963. *A History of Argentine Political Thought,* trans. Thomas F. McGann. Stanford, CA: Stanford University Press.

Rosenberg, Morton. 1981. "Beyond the Limits of Executive Power: Presidential Control of Agency Rulemaking under Executive Order 12291." *Michigan Law Review* 80: 193–247.

Rosenn, Keith S. 1990. "The Success of Constitutionalism in the United States and Its Failure in Latin America: An Explanation." *University of Miami Inter-America Law Review* 22(1) (Fall): 1–39.

———. 2008. "Introductory Notes and Summaries of Amendments to the Constitution of the Federative Republic of Brazil, 1992–2007." In *Constitutions of the Countries of the*

World, ed. Albert P. Blaustein, Gisbert H. Flanz, Rainer Grote, and Rüdiger Wolfrum. New York: Oxford University Press.

Rothstein, Bo. 1996. "Political Institutions: An Overview." In *A New Handbook of Political Science,* ed. Robert E. Goodin and Hans-Dieter Klingemann, 133–66. Oxford University Press.

Rottinghaus, Brandon, and Jason Maier. 2007. "The Power of Decree: Presidential Use of Executive Proclamations, 1977–2005." *Political Research Quarterly* 60(2): 338–43.

Rouse, Robert. 2006. "Happy Anniversary to the First Scheduled Presidential Press Conference—93 Years Young." *American Chronicle* (March 15), http://amchron.soundenterprises.net/articles/view/6883, accessed July 3, 2013.

Rudalevige, Andrew. 2002. *Managing the President's Program: Presidential Leadership and Legislative Policy Formation.* Princeton, NJ: Princeton University Press.

Ruggie, John, and Friedrich Kratochwil. 1986. "International Organization: A State of the Art on the Art of the State." *International Organization* 40: 753–80.

Sabato, Larry. 2008. *A More Perfect Constitution: Why the Constitution Must Be Revised: Ideas to Inspire a New Generation.* New York: Walker.

Sagüës, Néstor Pedro. 1996. "An Introduction and Commentary to the Reform of the Argentine National Constitution." *University of Miami Inter-American Law Review* 28(41): 41–59.

Sampay, Arturo Enrique. 1975. *Las constituciones de la Argentina entre 1810 y 1972 con introducción.* Buenos Aires: Editorial Universitaria de Buenos Aires.

Samuels, David. 2003. *Ambition, Federalism, and Legislative Politics in Brazil.* Cambridge: Cambridge University Press.

Sarbaugh-Thompson, Marjorie, Lyke Thompson, Charles D. Elder, John Strate, and Richard C. Elling. 2004. *The Political and Institutional Effects of Term Limits.* New York: Palgrave.

Schlesinger, Arthur, Jr. 1973. *The Imperial Presidency.* New York: Houghton Mifflin.

———. 1991. "A Bad Idea Whose Time Has Come." *New York Times* (October 29), A-22.

Schmidt, Manfred G. 1999. "On the Political Productivity of Democracies." *Scandinavian Political Studies* 22(4): 281–94.

Schubert, Glendon A., Jr. 1953. "The Steel Case: Presidential Responsibility and Judicial Irresponsibility." *Western Political Quarterly* 6(1): 61–77.

Scribner, Druscilla. 2004. "Limiting Presidential Power: Supreme Court-Executive Relations in Argentina and Chile." PhD diss., University of California at San Diego.

Seidman, Robert B. 1978. *The State, Law, and Development.* New York: Palgrave.

Selassie, Alemante G. 1992. "Ethnic Identity and Constitutional Design for Africa." *Stanford Journal of International Law* 29(1) (Fall): 1–56.

Serrafero, Mario D. 1997. *Reelección y sucesión presidencial: Poder y continuidad Argentina, América latina y ee.uu.* Buenos Aires: Editorial de Belgrano.

Shogan, Colleen J. 2006. "The Contemporary Presidency: The 6th Year Curse." *Presidential Studies Quarterly* 36: 89–101.

Shugart, Matthew, and John Carey. 1992. *Presidents and Assemblies: Constitutional Design and Electoral Dynamics.* New York: Cambridge University Press.

Simmons, Beth A., and Lisa Martin. 2002. "International Organizations and Institutions." In *Handbook of International Relations,* ed. Walter E. Carlsnaes, Thomas Risse, and Beth A. Simmons, 192–211. London: Sage.

Simon, Herbert A. 1957. *Models of Man, Social and Rational: Mathematical Essays on Rational Human Behavior in a Social Setting.* New York: Wiley.

Simonton, D. K. 1984. "Leaders as Eponyms: Individual and Situational Determinants of Monarchal Eminence." *Journal of Personality* 52: 1–21.

———. 1986. "Presidential Greatness: The Historical Consensus and Its Psychological Significance." *Political Psychology* 7(2): 259–83.

Skocpol, Theda, and Margaret Somers. 1980. "The Uses of Comparative History in Macrosocial Inquiry." *Comparative Studies in Society and History* 22: 174–97.

Skowronek, Stephen. 1993. *The Politics Presidents Make: Leadership from John Adams to George Bush.* Cambridge, MA: Belknap Press of Harvard University Press.

Smith, James Morton. 1969. *George Washington: A Profile.* New York: Hill and Wang.

Smith, Pamela K., and Yaacov Trope. 2006. "You Focus on the Forest When You're in Charge of the Trees: Power Priming and Abstract Information Processing." *Journal of Personality and Social Psychology* 90: 578–96.

Smith, Rogers. 1993. "Beyond Tocqueville, Myrdal, and Hartz: The Multiple Traditions in America." *American Political Science Review* 87(3): 549–66.

Smith, Stephanie. 2008. "Presidential Transitions." *CRS Report RL30736.* Washington, DC: Congressional Research Service, Library of Congress.

Stack, Kevin. 2009. "The Reviewability of the President's Statutory Powers." *Vanderbilt Law Review* 62(4): 1171–1213.

Stepan, Alfred, and Cindy Skach. 1993. "Constitutional Frameworks and Democratic Consolidation: Parliamentarianism versus Presidentialism." *World Politics* 46(1): 1–22.

Stimson, James. 1976. "Public Support for American Presidents: A Cyclical Model." *Public Opinion Quarterly* 40(1): 1–21.

Stokes, Doug. 2005. "The Heart of Empire? Theorising U.S. Empire in an Era of Transnational Capital." *Third World Quarterly* 26(2): 217–36.

Stokes, Susan. 2001. *Mandates and Democracy: Neoliberalism by Surprise in Latin America.* New York: Cambridge University Press.

Tauber, Joseph. 1982. "Dames & Moore v. Regan: The Constitutionality of the Executive Orders Implementing the Agreement with Iran." *Ohio Northern University Law Review* 9: 519–27.

Taylor, Charles. 1973. "Interpretation and the Science of Man." In *Understanding and Social Inquiry,* ed. Fred Dallmayr and Thomas McCarthy, 3–30. New York: Basic Books.

Taylor, Matthew M. 2006. "Veto and Voice in the Courts: Policy Implications of Institutional Design in the Brazilian Judiciary." *Comparative Politics* 38(3): 337–55.

Thach, Charles C. 1923. *The Creation of the Presidency: 1775–1789.* Baltimore: Johns Hopkins University Press.

Thelen, Kathleen, and Sven Steinmo. 1992. "Historical Institutionalism in Comparative Politics." In *Structuring Politics: Historical Institutionalism in Comparative Analysis,* ed. Sven Steinmo, Kathleen Thelen, and Frank Longstreth, 1–32. New York: Cambridge University Press.

Tocqueville, Alexis de. (1835) 2010. *Democracy in America.* Teddington, UK: Echo Library.

Treisman, Daniel. 2004. "Stabilization Tactics in Latin America: Menem, Cardoso, and the Politics of Low Inflation." *Comparative Politics* 36(4): 399–420.

Tseng, Margaret. 2003. The Unilateral Presidency: The Lame Duck Effect. PhD diss., Georgetown University.

Turner, Charles William. 1945. *Ruy Barbosa, Brazilian Crusader for the Essential Freedoms.* New York: Abington-Cokesbury Press.

Tushnet, Mark. 2003. "Defending Korematsu?: Reflections on Civil Liberties in Wartime." *Wisconsin Law Review* 2: 283–98.

U.S. Term Limits. 2009. "About U.S. Term Limits." http:// termlimits.org/, accessed July 27, 2013.

Valenzuela, Arturo. 1985. "Origins and Characteristics of the Chilean Party System: A Proposal for a Parliamentary Form of Government." Wilson Center Working Paper no. 164. Washington, DC: Latin American Program, Woodrow Wilson Center.

Van Vugt, Mark, Robert Hogan, and Robert B. Kaiser. 2008. "Leadership, Followership, and Evolution: Some Lessons from the Past." *American Psychologist* 63: 182–96.

Walt, Stephen. 2005. "The Blame Game." *Foreign Policy* 151: 44–46.

Waltz, Kenneth. 1954. *Man, the State, and War: A Theoretical Analysis.* New York: Columbia University Press.

Warber, Adam. 2006. *Executive Orders and the Modern Presidency: Legislating from the Oval Office.* Boulder, CO: Lynne Rienner.

Ward, Peter, Victoria E. Rodriguez, and Enrique Cabrero Mendoza. 1999. *New Federalism and State Government in Mexico: Bringing the States Back In.* Austin: Lyndon B. Johnson School of Public Affairs, University of Texas at Austin.

Warren, Charles. 1928. *The Making of the Constitution.* Boston: Little, Brown.

Watts, Ronald L. 2008. *Comparing Federal Systems.* London: McGill-Queen's University Press.

Weissert, Carol S., and Karen Halperin. 2004. "Term Limits and the Public: Knowledge, Attentiveness, and Voter Dissatisfaction." Paper presented at Life with Term Limits Conference, April 29–30, Akron, OH.

———. 2007. "The Paradox of Term Limit Support." *Political Research Quarterly* 60(3): 516–30.

Wiarda, Howard J. 1971. "Law and Political Development in Latin America: Toward a Framework for Analysis." *American Journal of Comparative Law* 19(3): 434–63.

Wight, Colin. 1999. "They Shoot Dead Horses, Don't They? Locating Agency in the Agent-Structure Problematique." *European Journal of International Relations* 5(1): 109–42.

Will, George F. 1994. "Term Limits." In *The Politics and the Law of Term Limits,* ed. Edward H. Crane and Roger Pilon, 15–26. Washington, DC: Cato Institute.

Williams, Walter. 1980. "United States Indian Policy and the Debate over Philippine Annexation: Implications for the Origins of American Imperialism." *Journal of American History* 66(4): 810–31.

Willis, Paul G., and George L. Willis. 1952. "The Politics of the Twenty-Second Amendment." *Western Political Quarterly* 5(3): 469–82.

Wilson, Woodrow. 1885. *Congressional Government.* Boston: Houghton Mifflin.

Winkelmann, Rainer. 2008. *Econometric Analysis of Count Data.* Berlin: Springer.

Wood, Gordon. (1969) 1998. *The Creation of the American Republic, 1776–1787.* Chapel Hill: University of North Carolina Press. Citations refer to the 1969 edition.

Woolley, John T., and Gerhard Peters. 2010. *The American Presidency Project.* Santa Barbara, CA. http://www.presidency.ucsb.edu/ws/, accessed July 27, 2013.

Young, James P. 1996. *Reconsidering American Liberalism.* Boulder, CO: Westview.

Young, Oran. 1986. "International Regimes: Toward a New Theory of Institutions." *World Politics* 39: 106–31.

Zevin, Robert. 1972. "An Interpretation of American Imperialism." *Journal of Economic History* 32(1): 316–60.

Index

Other Books in the Joseph V. Hughes Jr. and Holly O. Hughes Series on the Presidency and Leadership

The Politics of Shared Power: Congress and the Executive, Louis Fisher
Shaping and Signaling Presidential Policy: The National Security Decision Making of Eisenhower and Kennedy, Meena Bose
Games Advisors Play: Foreign Policy in the Nixon and Carter Administrations, Jean A. Garrison
The Managerial Presidency, James P. Pfiffner
Good Advice: Information and Policy Making in the White House, Daniel E. Ponder
Congressional Abdication on War and Spending, Louis Fisher
Vicious Cycle: Presidential Decision Making in the American Political Economy, Constantine J. Spiliotes
Presidents and the People: The Partisan Story of Going Public, Mel Laracey
The Opposition Presidency: Leadership and the Constraints of History, David A. Crockett
The Presidency, Congress, and Divided Government: A Postwar Assessment, R. S. Conley
The White House World: Transitions, Organization, and Office Operations, Martha Joynt Kumar and Terry Sullivan, eds.
Between Law and Politics: The Solicitor General and the Structuring of Race, Gender, and Reproductive Rights Litigation, Richard Pacelle Jr.
The Presidency and Women: Promise, Performance, and Illusion, Janet M. Martin
Out of Touch: The Presidency and Public Opinion, Michael J. Towle
Power and Prudence: The Presidency of George H. W. Bush, Ryan J. Barilleaux and Mark J. Rozell
The Character Factor: How We Judge America's Presidents, James P. Pfiffner
The Nerve Center: Lessons in Governing from the White House Chiefs of Staff, edited by Terry Sullivan; foreword by James A. Baker III
Nixon's Business: Authority and Power in Presidential Politics, Nigel Bowles
Saving the Reagan Presidency: Trust Is the Coin of the Realm, David M. Abshire
Policy by Other Means: Alternative Adoption by Presidents, Steven A. Shull
Institutionalizing Congress and the Presidency: The U.S. Bureau of Efficiency, 1916–1933, Mordecai Lee
Scripted for Change: The Institutionalization of the American Presidency, Victoria A. Farrar-Myers
The American Campaign: U.S. Presidential Campaigns and the National Vote, Second Edition, James E. Campbell
Running against the Grain: How Opposition Presidents Win the White House, David A. Crockett
Intelligence and National Security Policymaking on Iraq, James P. Pfiffner and Mark Phythian
Honest Broker? The National Security Advisor and Presidential Decision Making, John P. Burke
The Leadership of George Bush: An Insider's View of the Forty-first President, Roman Popadiuk
Bridging the Constitutional Divide: Inside the White House Office of Legislative Affairs, Russell L. Riley
The Unitary Executive and the Modern Presidency, Ryan J. Barilleaux and Christopher S. Kelley

Other Books in the Joseph V. Hughes Jr. and Holly O. Hughes Series on the Presidency and Leadership (*continued*)

The Provisional Pulpit: Modern Conditional Presidential Leadership of Public Opinion, Brandon Rottinghaus

White House Politics and the Environment: Franklin D. Roosevelt to George W. Bush, Byron W. Daynes and Glen Sussman

Nixon's Super-Secretaries: The Last Grand Presidential Reorganization Effort, Mordecai Lee

A Presidency Upstaged: The Public Leadership of George H. W. Bush, Lori Cox Han

Presidential Term Limits in American History: Power, Principles, and Politics, Michael J. Korzi

The Politics of the President's Wife, MaryAnne Borrelli

The Clinton Presidency and the Constitutional System, Rosanna Perotti

Prosecution among Friends: Presidents, Attorneys General, and Executive Branch Wrongdoing, David A. Yalof

Taking the Measure: The Presidency of George W. Bush, Kelley and Shields